VOLUNTARY ACTION AND SOCIAL POLICY IN NORTHERN IRELAND

This book has received support from the Cultural Traditions programme of the Community Relations Council, which aims to encourage acceptance and understanding of cultural diversity.

Voluntary Action and Social Policy in Northern Ireland

Edited by

NICHOLAS ACHESON
ARTHUR WILLIAMSON

*Published in conjunction with the Centre for Voluntary Action Studies,
University of Ulster*

Avebury

Aldershot • Brookfield USA • Hong Kong • Singapore • Sydney

Published by
Avebury
Ashgate Publishing Limited
Gower House
Croft Road
Aldershot
Hants GU11 3HR
England

Ashgate Publishing Company
Old Post Road
Brookfield
Vermont 05036
USA

British Library Cataloguing in Publication Data

Voluntary Action and Social Policy in Northern Ireland
    I. Acheson, Nicholas II. Williamson, Arthur P.
    361.709416
ISBN 1 85628 669 X

Library of Congress Catalog Card Number: 95-76709

Printed and bound by Athenaeum Press, Ltd.,
Gateshead, Tyne & Wear.

Contents

Foreword

Voluntary action has deep roots within Northern Ireland and has played a significant part in shaping, and sustaining, the development of civil society during thirty years of community conflict. The themes of this book have as their main focus a key issue: the nature of the relationship between the state and the voluntary sector in a society whose deepest divisions surround national identity and the existence of the state itself.

Its twelve chapters present, for the first time, an overview of voluntary action in relation to social policy in Northern Ireland. The contributors reflect on the complex relationships which have developed between government and the region's voluntary and community associations. Bringing the broad perspective of the practitioner, the academic and the civil servant, they consider a wide spectrum of issues. These range from the developing importance of the European Union's social policies and programmes at the end of the twentieth century to the radical origins of voluntary action in Belfast in the late eighteenth century.

The editors wish to thank the contributors for writing the chapters which make up this volume. We would also like to express our warm thanks to Mrs Irene Simpson of the University of Ulster and to Mrs Joan Erskine for their cheerful, patient and professional secretarial and editorial support. Finally, we gratefully thank the Community Relations Council for its financial support.

We hope that this book will stimulate discussion and debate about the nature of voluntary action and citizenship in the late twentieth century and that it will be followed by many other studies of the voluntary contribution to social welfare, and to social reconstruction.

Nicholas Acheson
Arthur Williamson

List of abbreviations

ACE	Action for Community Employment
BBC	British Broadcasting Corporation
CCCCW	Churches' Central Council for Community Work
CCRU	Central Community Relations Unit
CCSP	Co-ordinating Committee on Social Problems (of the Department of Health and Social Services)
CDRG	Community Development Review Group
COI	Church of Ireland
CONI	Community Organisations Northern Ireland
CPSSAC	Central Personal Social Services Advisory Committee (of the Department of Health and Social Services)
CRC	Community Relations Council
CSF	Community Support Framework (of the European Union)
DENI	Department of Education for Northern Ireland
DFP	Department of Finance and Personnel
DH	Department of Health (England, Scotland and Wales)
DHSS	Department of Health and Social Services (Northern Ireland)
DSS	Department of Social Security (England, Scotland and Wales)
EC	European Community
EU	European Union
FOLD	Free the Old from Loneliness with Dignity
GDP	gross domestic product
HAA	Housing Action Area
HMSO	Her Majesty's Stationery Office
IDCRD	Inter-Departmental Committee on Rural Development
IFI	International Fund for Ireland
IRA	Irish Republican Army

NGO	non-governmental organisation
NIACRO	Northern Ireland Association for the Care and Resettlement of Offenders
NICHA	Northern Ireland Co-Ownership Housing Association
NICSFMC	Northern Ireland Community Support Framework Monitoring Committee
NICVA	Northern Ireland Council for Voluntary Action
NIFHA	Northern Ireland Federation of Housing Associations
NIHE	Northern Ireland Housing Executive
NILP	Northern Ireland Labour Party
NIRA	Northern Ireland Rural Association
NIVT	Northern Ireland Voluntary Trust
PCI	Presbyterian Church in Ireland
PPRU	Policy and Planning Research Unit (Department of Finance and Personnel)
RAP	Rural Action Programme
RDC	Rural Development Council
SACHR	Standing Advisory Committee on Human Rights
SDLP	Social Democratic and Labour Party
WEA	Workers Educational Association

The contributors

Nicholas Acheson is Assistant Director of Disability Action and was formerly Information Officer at the Northern Ireland Council for Voluntary Action and editor of *Scope*. He was educated at The New University of Ulster and Oxford University and is interested in the political aspects of voluntary action.

Jimmy Armstrong was born in County Fermanagh and educated at The Queen's University of Belfast and at The University of Reading. He has lectured at Exeter University and, in economic geography, at The Queen's University, Belfast. He was the Co-ordinator of the Rural Action Project and is currently Chief Executive of the Rural Development Council for Northern Ireland.

Professor Derek Birrell is Head of the School of Social and Community Sciences at The University of Ulster. The school's sixty-two academic staff embrace the areas of social policy and administration, sociology, social work, adult education and community development. Professor Birrell has carried out research and published widely in the areas of housing, public policy in Northern Ireland, local government and aspects of social policy and comparative study between Northern Ireland and the Republic of Ireland.

Dr Mari Fitzduff is Director of the Northern Ireland Community Relations Council which was established in 1990 and is funded by the British Government and the European Community. She is a Fellow of the Peace Studies Institute of Bradford University. She has worked extensively in the community relations field and was Co-ordinator of the Community Conflict Skills project. Her latest book, *Beyond Violence*, was published as part of the United Nations' series on Conflict and Governance.

Stevie Johnston is employed by the Workers Educational Association. He has been active in community development since 1987 and has worked for a number of organizations including Falls Community Council and the Brownlow Trust, part of the Fourth European Poverty Programme. He has an M Sc in Social Administration and Policy from the University of Ulster.

Jimmy Kearney is an Assistant Secretary in the Department of Health and Social Services where he heads the Social and Community Division and the Voluntary Activity Unit. He chairs the Interdepartmental Group on Voluntary Activity and Community Development, is Northern Ireland Liaison Officer to the Home Office's Voluntary Service Unit and represents Northern Ireland departments on the Government/Voluntary Sector Forum on Europe.

Ms Avila Kilmurray is director of the Northern Ireland Voluntary Trust. She worked as Co-ordinator of the Rural Action Project from 1987-1990. She was educated at University College, Dublin and at the Australian National University where she earned an MA in International Relations. She is a member of the Rural Development Council and of the Community Relations Council.

Dr Duncan Morrow is Lecturer in Politics at the University of Ulster. He has written widely on the churches in Northern Ireland and is a member of the Corrymeela Community. He read Politics, Philosophy and Economics at Oxford University and has a PhD in Politics from Edinburgh University. He has been active as a member of the Understanding Conflict Team at the University of Ulster.

Dr John Offer is Senior Lecturer in Social Administration and Policy at the University of Ulster where he is responsible for the Diploma and Masters course in Social Administration and Policy. His research interests include informal care and social work policy. His previous publications include *Informal Welfare* (1987) and *Herbert Spencer: Political Writings* (1994).

John Simpson is an economic commentator, broadcaster and journalist. Until 1989 he was Senior Lecturer in Economics at The Queen's University of Belfast. He is a member of the National Lottery Charities Board, of the Probation Board for Northern Ireland and of the European Economic and Social Committee.

Ms Marie Smyth is on the academic staff of the University of Ulster and of Smith College, Massachusetts. She is currently working on a community based action research project on sectarian segregation and intimidation in Derry. Her involvement in the women's movement dates back to the mid 1970s. She is also an individual, couples and family therapist and was founder member of Derry Wellwoman.

Dr Arthur Williamson is Senior Lecturer at the University of Ulster and director of the University's Centre for Voluntary Action Studies. Educated at Trinity College, Dublin his doctorate was a study of The New University of Ulster, 1964-1984. He is a member of the International Society for Third Sector Research, the Association for Research in the Voluntary and Community Sector, and of the Association for Research on Nonprofit Organizations and Voluntary Action. He has given papers on aspects of voluntary action in Northern Ireland at conferences in Jerusalem, Barcelona and London.

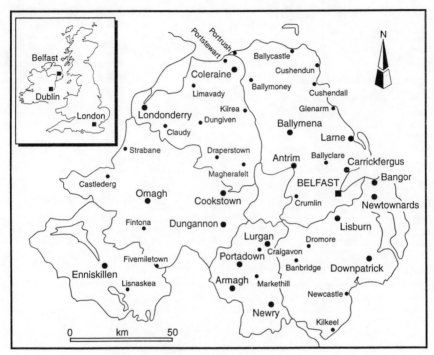

Northern Ireland

1 Introduction: voluntary action in Northern Ireland: some contemporary themes and issues

Nicholas Acheson and Arthur Williamson

This book considers the voluntary and community sector in Northern Ireland, analyses its relations with government and explores its role in implementing and in shaping, if not yet in formulating, social policy. Although the voluntary sector is notoriously difficult to define and to delineate, the importance of its contribution to the delivery of social services, and in the implementation of social policy, is increasingly being recognized in many countries and there is a rapidly growing international body of scholarly research dealing with this topic (Defourny & Monzon Campos, 1994; Gidron et al. 1992; Ruddle & O'Connor, 1992; Salamon & Anheier, 1994). To date little attention has been given to this field by researchers in Northern Ireland. Detailed studies of the many important elements of voluntarism and of voluntary action are long overdue, and are eagerly awaited.

Voluntary organizations have developed a highly significant role in Northern Ireland society having survived the days when the dominance of the welfare state might have marginalized them to the point of exclusion. Since the inception of the welfare state in the late 1940s Northern Ireland has shared in the social policies implemented in the countries of the United Kingdom. Social policies in Northern Ireland have been governed by the principle of parity with the rest of the United Kingdom and have been subject to most of the same ideological and economic influences. And the form that these changes has taken has been modified by the conflict which, since the late 1960s, has cost more than 3,100 lives.

People with an interest in the developing relationships between the various sections of society in advanced industrial countries will find it rewarding to consider the experience of Northern Ireland during the last twenty-five years. During the 1980s in Britain and in the United States market solutions were sought to remedy the perceived failures of welfarism. In the mid 1990s a new

1

consensus is emerging that the market alone cannot solve social and economic problems. New relations are being sought between government and voluntary organizations. A new kind of contract may be emerging between the state and its citizens. In Northern Ireland where, for a significant section of the population, the legitimacy of the government is in dispute, those relationships exhibit particularly interesting features.

Throughout the 1980s the Conservative Government sought to redraw the boundaries between the responsibilities of the state and those of individual citizens in regard to welfare. Now, in the less certain political climate of the 1990s, the limitations of market driven approaches to welfare are becoming increasingly apparent. A modified consensus is emerging concerning the respective roles of the state and of voluntary associations in which the two sides would work in partnership to promote social welfare and social cohesion. This change underscores the potential of the voluntary sector as a potent instrument of social policy.

The key themes which this book explores are, firstly, the manner and extent to which conflict in Northern Ireland has influenced relationships between government and the voluntary sector and, secondly, the contribution of the voluntary sector to social welfare, to community life and community relations and to the course of the conflict.

Some of the themes which are considered are, in no particular order: the role of the churches; the role of women; the contribution of voluntary associations to rural development; the potential of voluntary bodies to support informal carers; the impact of European Union legislation and funding; the role of the voluntary and community sector in managing violence and in promoting community relations; the origins of voluntary action in Belfast in the nineteenth century; the contribution of housing associations and the growth of the community development movement. In several chapters there is discussion of the issues which arise between government and voluntary organizations when the legitimacy of the government is rejected by the communities in which the organizations work and from which their membership is drawn. Always at the heart of the relationship between government and significant elements of the voluntary sector in Northern Ireland lies the question of national identity.

Several noteworthy factors set Northern Ireland apart from much of the rest of the United Kingdom. The first is the much stronger attachment to denominational religion than elsewhere. This is accompanied by a strong and radical egalitarianism, evidence for which has emerged from a series of three annual social attitude surveys carried out since 1990 (Stringer & Robinson, 1991, 1992, 1993). Although commentators have differed in their interpretations of the results of the evidence, it shows a shared belief in egalitarian values among members of Catholic and Protestant communities.

The third survey, conducted in 1992, included questions about charitable giving and about attitudes concerning the division of responsibility between charities and the state.

Charitable giving appeared to be ubiquitous with fewer than one per cent of respondents stating that they had not given to charity within the previous year (though how useful this information is may be open to doubt because no evidence was obtained concerning the amount contributed). Macaulay (1993, p. 28) notes a close correspondence between Catholic and Protestant views and reports consistent support from a majority of respondents for the view that the state should have sole, or main, responsibility for health and housing issues. The survey reveals similarly high levels of support in each community for redistributive taxation. Although some small differences in emphasis were noted as between Catholic and Protestant respondents, a high general level of correspondence on these social attitudes, at least among people aged 35-55 years, suggests that views on economic and social matters may be independent of religious background. Macaulay, however, cautions that the available evidence 'is not yet refined enough to allow a great imaginative leap forward to the notion that, after all, Protestants and Catholics possess, at root, identical social values and priorities'. Younger people, he notes, seem to possess the more secular and individualistic values of the 1980s and among them the notion of redistribution and egalitarianism is less in evidence.

Shared attitudes, at least among those in middle age, support what is sometimes referred to as a 'non-sectarian space' within which voluntary organizations can operate. But this is constrained by a second set of considerations. Voluntary organizations, like other aspects of Northern Irish society, are often structured along sectarian lines. This is manifested most obviously by the levels of voluntary activity associated with the formally organized churches and is supported by high, though falling, levels of church attendance.

Furthermore, locally based voluntary organizations reflect the social characteristics of their local area. During the past two decades there has been a dramatic increase in the degree of spatial segregation between Protestant and Catholic communities. The 1991 census revealed that only 7 per cent of the population were living in areas where there were similar numbers of Protestants and Catholics and about half lived in areas which were at least 90 per cent homogenous. In the twenty years since the 1971 census the number of segregated housing areas had doubled. It is widely recognized that concepts of social solidarity, the way people organize themselves and their reasons for doing so, differ between the two communities. The opportunities for inter-communal activity are often quite limited.

The actual extent and nature of these inter-communal divisions remains a matter of debate. It is simplistic to think of Northern Ireland as a society

3

divided into two clearly delineated, and antagonistic, communities. Not only are there divisions between the two main communities; there are deep divisions within them. On the Catholic side, some accept and some reject the legitimacy of violence to achieve political objectives. On the Protestant side the members of different religious denominations, perhaps reflecting latent differences in social class as well as of theology, exhibit, to a greater or lesser extent, differences in relation to political and social attitudes.

At what point do voluntary organizations, pursuing a social welfare agenda, encounter divisions which are beyond their capacity to surmount? The various contributors to this book make clear that the answer often depends on the particular issue being considered. Some, but not all organizations, supported by a strong consensus about social and economic issues, have developed a vigorous shared agenda on matters such as housing, health, rural development, women's issues and disability.

In many respects this development has parallelled developments elsewhere. In the last ten years or so, many voluntary organizations have given increasing attention to the extension of social rights and to campaigning for social and political change and have moved away somewhat from their long-standing commitment to providing services. This has been happening at the same time as government has been looking increasingly to the voluntary sector to ameliorate social problems and hence to enlarge their service roles. Northern Ireland has participated in this trend while, simultaneously, it has been experiencing high levels of violent conflict.

As the chapter on community relations demonstrates, voluntary associations have been active in reconciliation work since the end of the 1960s. Indeed some influential voluntary organizations were established as a response to communal violence and conflict. Now some are apprehensive that their potential, and their widespread support and acceptance, might be exploited by government as it seeks to involve them in working to mitigate the causes and effects of the conflict. Seeing the potential for voluntary bodies and community organizations to contribute to the process of reconciliation and to community relations work, government has provided considerable sums of money, some of which has come from the European Union, to support these activities. The relationship between government and the voluntary sector and that between the sector and community conflict is ambiguous and contains tensions which are always implicit.

For more than twenty years since the local parliament was prorogued in 1972, and since the emasculation of local government at about the same time, there has not been a legislative forum in Northern Ireland. The 'democratic deficit' which has resulted, with its lack of opportunity for political debate, has often been remarked upon. Voluntary organizations have tended to move into this vacuum and have provided a kind of proto-representative forum for

4

many of their members and for their communities. In some cases they have provided, for the people of the areas in which they work, the only forum for discussion of social and economic issues. To that extent they have provided a valuable quasi political service for their communities. Furthermore, in the virtual absence of any effective local form of representation, the leaders of these organizations have acquired a salience and informal legitimacy which could disturb conventional politicians.

The chapter by Kearney discusses the long-standing relationship between government and the voluntary sector and sees recent developments as a further logical step in the evolution of this process. He draws attention to two important recent events, the publication of the government's *Strategy for the Support of the Voluntary Sector and for Community Development in Northern Ireland* (1993) and the subsequent establishment of the Voluntary Activity Unit within the Department of Health and Social Services. These important initiatives break new ground. For the first time government policy toward the voluntary sector and for community development has been made explicit. The Voluntary Activity Unit has a specific role in facilitating and encouraging the development of voluntary action. The fact that the Charities Branch (formerly of the Department of Finance and Personnel) has been merged with the Voluntary Activity Unit should enable a more co-ordinated approach by government to voluntary action. Furthermore, government is now committed to seeking to involve voluntary organizations in policy formulation across the full range of public policy.

Little is known about the economics of the voluntary sector in Northern Ireland. John Simpson identifies the scale of government assistance as being in excess of £150 million per annum and considers the value of the services provided by the sector as in excess of £200 million, the equivalent of nearly 2 per cent of the gross domestic product and involving over 10,000 people in various roles. His chapter draws attention to the various ways in which the sector receives assistance from government and to recent trends in financial assistance including the influence of contracting. He comments on the degree of variation from year to year in the level of funding allocated to voluntary organizations and points to the need to ensure that the principles, methods and amounts of grant aid are applied consistently.

Writing from a different perspective about some of the same issues, Acheson draws attention to a dilemma facing government. In advanced industrial societies welfare has an important role in promoting social cohesion and in securing the assent of citizens to the legitimacy of the political system. Acheson argues that, as voluntary organizations become increasingly important providers of welfare services, so their role in legitimatizing the political system will increase in importance. He refers to the controversy which has surrounded decisions by government in relation to support for organizations which have as members paramilitary personnel who are dedicated to the overthrow of the state. Experience since 1985 demonstrates that, when welfare goals and less tangible political or security priorities conflict, welfare goals may be abandoned. In the interests of security and of conflict reduction government has decided to withdraw funding from some organizations with the result that their welfare work has been restricted.

Fitzduff explores the potential for voluntary organizations to contribute to reconciliation and to improving community relations. She observes that much voluntary action and community development takes place in, and among, the most deprived and marginalized communities. This has been one of the most positive aspects of voluntary action during the past twenty-five years. Some of this issue-focused work has crossed the community divide. Commenting on the fact that community work has tended to marginalize politicians she suggests that voluntary organizations must find creative ways to involve politicians in dealing with social problems. She draws attention to the fact that leaders of many voluntary organizations have developed close working relationships with civil servants, an arrangement which has been welcomed by both sides. Drawing from experience gained in an earlier phase of the conflict, she warns that to ignore, or to by-pass, political representatives may eventually limit the potential of the sector to improve community relations and lead to a negative reaction from politicians.

The divisions in Northern Ireland reflect ethnicity and religious affiliation. Accordingly the role of the churches in voluntary action is of profound importance. Since the early 1980s there has been a growing relationship between government and the Protestant and Catholic churches as they have become increasingly important contributors to government-sponsored temporary employment schemes for long-term unemployed people. Furthermore, some churches have recently become involved on a congregational basis in government-funded initiatives to improve community relations. Morrow reflects on how deep-seated differences in theology, tradition and organization between the Catholic and Protestant churches have influenced the shape of the voluntary sector with regard both to church-based and non-denominational organizations. In his analysis of the Protestant churches he draws attention to the large voluntary economy which they represent. This is true particularly in terms of the wide variety of church activities and the ability of the churches to raise money, not only for specifically religious purposes, but also, as in the case of the Ethiopian Famine, for overseas relief. In a society which has a high level of church attendance much voluntary activity is absorbed by the churches. Morrow suggests that the ethos of voluntarism and the propensity of individuals to associate for voluntary purposes is closely related to the intrinsic spirit of Protestantism.

6

The theme of the interaction of religion and voluntary action is again explored in Williamson's chapter which examines the origins of voluntary action in Belfast. At the beginning of the nineteenth century religious dissent, political radicalism and social concern motivated a number of Belfast's voluntary activists among whom the most notable were Mary Ann McCracken and Dr James Macdonnell. As the city grew and industrialised, particularly during the later part of the century, sectarian tensions and rivalries increased until voluntary action became almost completely segregated along religious lines. Successive Catholic bishops invited orders of nuns to come to Belfast as nursing sisters and teachers, and to set up orphanages to meet the spiritual and social needs of the Catholic urban poor who had migrated from rural areas to work in the city's new factories and mills. At parish level lay members of the St Vincent de Paul Society provided welfare under the guidance of the parish priest. An increasingly affluent Protestant middle-class produced some remarkable activists and philanthropists like Forster Green and the celebrated Miss Isabella Tod who established and endowed the city's hospitals and administered relief in times of destitution and campaigned for women's suffrage, for temperance and for the education of girls. The difference in outlook as between the Catholic and Protestant communities in relation to voluntary social action is remarkable.

The increased involvement of women in voluntary action is considered by Smyth who examines the growth of the women's movement and points out that voluntary action by women underpins every aspect of the voluntary movement. She explores the role of women in relation to the search for better community relations and peace and refers to research which suggests that women were more pessimistic about the state of community relations and its future, than were men. While women form the backbone of much community organizing, Smyth notes that they only occasionally assume leadership positions and their roles tend to be restricted to those associated with caring. She warns that a likely consequence of the increasing involvement of women with the government's Care in the Community policy is that it may become more difficult for women who are preoccupied with caring roles to move into leadership.

The growth of the housing association movement and of community development is reviewed by Birrell who draws attention to the fact that several major voluntary organizations and the Northern Ireland Council for Voluntary Action have made a community development approach central to their aims and methods. Community development continues to play an important role in many communities. Its growth has been assisted by a number of government initiatives including, most notably, the inauguration of the Northern Ireland Voluntary Trust in 1979 and of the Action for Community Employment scheme in 1981. Birrell also discusses the emergence of the housing association movement which resulted from legislation introduced in 1976 and is largely sustained by government finance. The movement tries to bridge the gap between local people and the remoteness of the statutory housing authority and of central government. Despite the fact that it is so heavily dependent on government for its finance, the movement has pioneered innovative approaches to housing matters, particularly in relation to the needs of older people and of people living in rural areas.

Offer draws attention to the fact that some of the earliest policy statements in relation to the introduction of the welfare state ensured a continuing role for the voluntary sector at least in the field of personal social services. He traces the origins of the present emphasis on the importance of informal care and care in the community and draws attention to recent research into informal care in both urban and rural settings. Women provide, and receive, most of the care. There is in Northern Ireland a comparative deficit in relation to respite for carers. Offer's review of research leads him to conclude that '... at least until recently, the voluntary sector in Northern Ireland was of little significance for informal carers'. Recent developments, however, suggest that in the future the voluntary and community sector may play a much more important part in the support both of carers and the people they care for.

Readiness on the part of government to involve the voluntary sector in policy formulation is partly a response to a growing sophistication within voluntary organizations in relation to the policy dimensions of its work. Armstrong and Kilmurray, in their discussion of the contribution of the voluntary sector to the formulation of policies for rural development, provide a striking example of the potential strengths of current opportunities for partnerships with government. As a result of the lead taken by voluntary organizations, with the aid of finance from government and from European Union sources, the rural development agenda has widened from the narrow ground of farm income subsidy to a recognition of the need to sustain rural communities as viable places to live and of the vital contribution of community development to that process.

A theme underlying developments in the voluntary sector in Northern Ireland during the last twenty years is the search for issues and structures which would enable voluntary organizations to transcend the deep divisions in society and to articulate a social vision grounded on a higher degree of consensus between the two main communities. The influence of European Union policy and the availability of funding from that source has contributed to this process. Johnston draws attention to the crucial role played by the European Union particularly in the light of the British Government's hostility to the direction and content of much European social policy. It is true that the complexity of these relationships and the difficulties experienced by many groups in gaining access to European funding have tended to limit the impact of these developments. Yet, as Armstrong and Kilmurray's chapter indicates, European initiatives have the potential to influence profoundly the development of the voluntary sector and the effectiveness of its contribution to social policy at a local level. The language of European social policy and, in particular, its emphasis on the concept of 'social exclusion' have proved attractive to many people who work in voluntary organizations. Johnston ends by suggesting that voluntary groups interested in this issue should be co-operating with other social partners, particularly with local authorities and trades unions, to look to European support programmes to remedy the negative impact of restrictive national policies.

It is a common, but false, assumption that the immense diversity of organizations which make up modern society may be divided under two broad headings, or into two sectors, the *market* and the *state*. The inadequacy of this categorization is increasingly being recognized. There is a third sector. In the 1990s due to the crisis of socialism, the world-wide reappraisal of the welfare state, and increasing burdens on public finances, governments are calling increasingly on voluntary organizations to play a much larger part in public policy. Throughout the world voluntary action makes a major, perhaps *the* major, contribution to the alleviation of human problems. As this book demonstrates, this is not a new phenomenon. Voluntary action in Northern Ireland is vigorous and all-pervasive. During the long years of conflict it has done much to sustain hope and to bring services to places and groups whose needs neither the state nor the market could meet. The editors hope that this collection of papers will draw attention to the important role of voluntary action in the social and economic life of Northern Ireland and that a strengthened voluntary and community sector, working in partnership with government and its Voluntary Activity Unit, will continue to play a central role in the reconstruction of the province.

References

Defourny, Jacques & Monzon Campos, Jose L. (1994), *Economie Sociale: Entre Economie Capitaliste et Economie Publique*, De Boeck-Wesmael S.A., Brussels.

Gidron, B., Kramer, R. & Salamon, L.M. (1992), *Government and the Third Sector: Emerging Relationships in Welfare States*, Jossey-Bass, San Francisco.

Macaulay, Iain (1993), 'The Gift of Charity', pp. 21-32 in Stringer, P. & Robinson, G. (1993).

Ruddle, Helen & O'Connor, Joyce (1992), *Reaching Out: Charitable Giving and Volunteering in the Republic of Ireland*, Policy Research Centre, National College of Industrial Relations, Dublin.

Salamon, Lester M. & Anheier, Helmut K. (1994), 'The Non-profit Sector Cross Nationally: Patterns and Types' in Saxon-Harrold, Susan & Kendall, Jeremy (eds), *Researching the Voluntary Sector,* second edition, Charities Aid Foundation, London, pp. 147-63. See also, by the same authors (1994), *The Emerging Sector: the Nonprofit Sector in Comparative Perspective - an Overview*, The Johns Hopkins Comparative Nonprofit Sector Project, Institute for Policy Studies, Baltimore.

Stringer, P. and Robinson, G. (1991,1992,1993), *Social Attitudes in Northern Ireland, 1990-91; 1991-92; 1992-93,* Blackstaff Press, Belfast.

2 The development of government policy and its strategy toward the voluntary and community sectors

Jimmy Kearney

The publication in February 1993 of the *Strategy for the Support of the Voluntary Sector and for Community Development in Northern Ireland* (DHSS, 1993b) was a major landmark in the development of policy in this field. Government's commitment to working in partnership with the voluntary and community sector is clearly stated. So also is government's support for the process of community development. There is now a clear, strategic framework for government's support for the voluntary sector and a coherent policy framework which both recognizes and endorses the value of community development and the role of community groups in Northern Ireland.

What were the origins of the *Strategy*? What new ground did it break? If the *Strategy* is to be regarded as 'a building block, now firmly in place' and as 'the foundation ... for the development of an even closer partnership with the voluntary sector and for a new focus, dynamism and framework for the process of community development' (to quote from the address of the Secretary of State for Northern Ireland, Sir Patrick Mayhew, when he launched the *Strategy*[1]) what further action needs to be taken?

This chapter provides answers to some of these questions and offers some thoughts on future action. It traces the development of the concept of partnership between government and the voluntary sector, by reference to some of the reports and circulars which have helped to shape policy in this field.

The views expressed in this chapter are those of the author. They are not necessarily those of government or of the Department of Health and Social Services.

The origins of partnership

A common theme running through the major policy documents emanating from government from the 1970s to date is the need for and value of partnership based on commonality of purpose and interest, and the translation of this concept into action. Why is such a partnership needed? The answer lies in the belief that the statutory sector alone cannot and, in principle, should not, meet the increasing demand for services. Nor can the voluntary sector alone meet all social problems. This concept is not, of course, new. In his *Voluntary Action: a Report on Methods of Social Advance*, Lord Beveridge (1948) concluded that in a social welfare state, some social needs would remain. His eight point plan of action included the need for increased co-operation between state and voluntary agencies and for an extension of the programme of grants to voluntary bodies.

Another early example of policy underpinned by partnership was contained in the Welfare Services Act (Northern Ireland) 1949. The Ministry of Health and Local Government's circular letter W.28 on the implementation of the act on 1 February 1949 called for initial proposals, and contained a section on voluntary organizations. This referred to one of the outstanding features of the act as being the prominence given to voluntary bodies and the flexible provisions under which the statutory authorities could employ, aid and co-operate with them. This 'represented the declared policy of the Government, endorsed by Parliament'. While the act placed the primary legal responsibility on welfare committees, this policy was to be pursued 'on the strict understanding that welfare committees give to voluntary bodies the recognition which they deserve, consult closely with them and generally assist them not only to continue in being but to develop and expand'. This was described as partly a matter of expediency, but much more a matter of principle. The principle of voluntary action was strongly supported, and it was made plain that 'the Ministry wishes to see welfare committees enter now into close partnership with voluntary effort in every phase of their work'. The responsibility of voluntary organizations in this partnership was also mentioned. 'They must realise, for instance, that they are now being invited to share in the provision of statutory, public services and that this carries with it certain responsibilities. They will also realise that where public money is accepted, premises, books and accounts must be open to inspection, reports must be submitted and possibly a representative of the local authority added to the committee of management.'

12

The 1970s

In 1974, following the reorganization of the Health and Personal Social Services, the Department of Health and Social Services issued its first circular to health and social services boards on support for voluntary organizations (DHSS, 1974). This outlined the principles which would apply to all voluntary bodies in the health and social work field, including community groups. The circular identified substantial scope for the development of voluntary services in Northern Ireland in partnership with the statutory health and social work services. Unavoidable financial and other constraints on the development of statutory services meant that the objectives of those services could not be attained without the help of voluntary workers and voluntary organizations. It was, therefore, in the interest of the Department and boards to encourage voluntary effort to the full. But the involvement of voluntary bodies with statutory agencies in the pursuit of common objectives was seen as a desirable end in itself, since it helped to promote the active participation of individuals, groups and communities in the process of social development. The circular recognized, however, that voluntary bodies must not be regarded simply as an adjunct of the statutory services. Rather, they were seen as having an independent status and an independent part to play in their own right.

Health and social services boards were asked in the circular to adopt a positive policy for the encouragement and mobilization of voluntary effort in their areas. Such a policy should entail well-defined administrative arrangements for liaison between boards and voluntary bodies; appropriate financial and other forms of support for such bodies; and a clear understanding of the respective roles of the Department and boards in this field. General guidance was given on these matters.

1974 also saw the appointment by the Joseph Rowntree Memorial Trust and the Carnegie United Kingdom Trust of a Committee of Enquiry chaired by Lord Wolfenden to review the role and functions of voluntary organizations in the United Kingdom over the next twenty-five years. The committee's report *The Future of Voluntary Organisations* was published in 1978 (Wolfenden, 1978). It raised a number of important issues and made a number of specific recommendations both for the voluntary sector itself and for government at central and local level. The government of the day decided that its relationships with the voluntary sector should be reviewed in parallel with the process of self-examination to which the Wolfenden Report called the voluntary sector, and a consultative document *The Government and the Voluntary Sector* was published by the Home Office's Voluntary Services Unit in 1978 (Home Office, 1978).

The consultative document contained a separate chapter on Northern Ireland. In this, the vital importance of the voluntary sector in Northern Ireland was recognized, and the government's commitment to helping and encouraging voluntary and community organizations to expand and innovate, and to seeing new groups form as new problems needed to be addressed, was clearly stated. Views were sought on a number of specific questions from voluntary and community organizations in the Province.

The chapter noted the absence of major grant-making trusts in Northern Ireland and referred to an earlier announcement that government was considering the possibility of setting up an independent grant-making charitable trust. This would initially be financed by government and, again initially, would concentrate its resources on the areas of greatest social need in Belfast. In backing voluntary effort, the trust would complement the activities of government and statutory bodies with the added advantage of being able to respond to need with greater speed and flexibility. The Northern Ireland Voluntary Trust was subsequently established in March 1979, with an initial capital donation from government of £500,000 and an undertaking to match on a £ for £ basis any donations which the Trust might receive from private sources up to a maximum of a further £250,000.

Into the 1980s

Two further separate, but related, reviews were carried out in Northern Ireland between 1978 and 1980, one on an interdepartmental basis, the other focusing on policy towards support of voluntary organizations in the health and personal social services field.

Firstly, government had asked the Co-ordinating Committee on Social Problems[2] to undertake a wide-ranging review of government policy towards the voluntary sector in the social welfare field. This was to include consideration of whether there was a need in Northern Ireland for a local equivalent of the Voluntary Services Unit in the Home Office to ensure broad consistency of approach (including policy on grant aid) by government departments towards the voluntary sector, to deal with organizations operating across departmental boundaries, and to keep relevant developments under review.

Secondly, the Central Personal Social Services Advisory Committee[3] appointed a sub-committee to review the policy contained in the Department of Health and Social Services' 1974 circular to health and social services boards on *Support for Voluntary Organisations*. Its findings and recommendations were to feed into the wider Interdepartmental Review. The sub-committee's report in March 1979 (CPSSAC, 1979) placed emphasis on the need for attitudinal change, improvement in communication and the development of a meaningful partnership between statutory and voluntary agencies.

The Co-ordinating Committee's review also took into account the responses by voluntary organizations in Northern Ireland to the consultative document *The Government and the Voluntary Sector* and the questions of future policy raised in the New University of Ulster's report on voluntary organizations in Northern Ireland, entitled *Yesterday's Heritage or Tomorrow's Resource?* (Griffiths et al., 1978).

In its report *Tomorrow's Resource* published in November 1980 (CCSP, 1980) the committee considered that there needed to be a clearer picture of what the voluntary contribution was, and could and should be, if the potential of voluntary effort were to be fully developed and effectively deployed. This would require a willingness by statutory agencies to identify areas where voluntary organizations could complement statutory services or themselves undertake the provision of services; to consider which needs might be best met by encouraging community self-help, and to be prepared to provide financial assistance to unlock the reservoir of resources in the community. Such an approach would have three underlying principles. These were that:

a. voluntary effort is worthwhile for a variety of reasons and should be supported by appropriate statutory agencies;
b. there are times when voluntary activity is preferable and statutory bodies should be prepared to accept this;
c. voluntary bodies can usually contribute enthusiasm and manpower, and statutory agencies should be prepared to provide the resources to enable these to function effectively.

The report firmly restated the principle of partnership. While accepting that departments had already embraced the general policy of supporting voluntary effort on the basis of partnership, the report saw considerable scope for ensuring that at field level statutory bodies accept the voluntary sector as a partner in a meaningful relationship based on an open approach and mutual trust. The main elements of a partnership approach were also stated:

a. The common purpose should be to meet the needs of the community and the partnership should, therefore, be flexible and capable of meeting changing circumstances.
b. There must be a clear understanding of the respective roles of both partners in any given set of circumstances and that these roles can change with changing circumstances.
c. The statutory sector must accept the basic independence of the voluntary sector and must give voluntary bodies reasonable freedom to operate as

15

they see best within broadly agreed guidelines. In turn, these guidelines must be designed to ensure that the approach of the voluntary body supported from public funds is consistent with the broad drift of government policy within its field of operation.

d.   In the partnership situation, voluntary bodies must be prepared to accept the need for accountability to the agency making a grant, to their members and clients, and to the wider community. This will require voluntary bodies to be properly constituted with clearly defined procedures. It will include an assessment of the work which they are doing as well as an evaluation of their leadership and the efficiency of their organization. There must also be an acceptance that there are limitations on the overall availability of public finance.

e.   There is a need for overall co-ordination of effort and while this is primarily a matter for the statutory authorities, they should do everything possible to involve voluntary organizations in the planning of services, particularly at local level.

The report recommended that greater uniformity in general policy and approach towards the voluntary sector was not required, nor was a uniform policy for funding voluntary organizations. However, it enunciated a set of general guidelines and recommended that each department should have regard to them in the application of its funding policy. The establishment in Northern Ireland of a local equivalent of the Voluntary Services Unit was not recommended. The committee argued that the lines of communication were reasonably well established among departments, with co-operation and co-ordination being increasingly encouraged and developed through the committee itself.

In his foreword to the report, the then Secretary of State for Northern Ireland, Humphrey Atkins, endorsed the recommendations as indicating the general direction which government policy should take towards the voluntary sector in Northern Ireland and as providing the context within which departments and statutory agencies should frame their individual policies for working with voluntary bodies.

In the health and personal social services field, the Department of Health and Social Services issued a discussion paper to concentrate attention on, and elicit suggestions for, practical measures to realise further the principles in *Tomorrow's Resource* at field level. The outcome of this consultation process was the issue to health and social services boards in March 1985 of a circular *Co-operation Between the Statutory and Voluntary Sectors in the Health and Personal Social Services* (DHSS, 1985). This confirmed and augmented the guidance contained in the 1974 circular. It set out a programme for action for the Department, for health and social services boards and for the Northern

Ireland Council for Voluntary Action. The circular broke new ground in a number of areas. At departmental level, a commitment was given to set up interdepartmental co-ordinating machinery, subsequently the Interdepartmental Voluntary Action Group.[4] Health and social services boards were asked to draw up draft policy statements on their relations with voluntary organizations as a basis for further discussion with the Department and voluntary sector interests. Action to be taken by the Northern Ireland Council for Voluntary Action and by the Northern Ireland Branch of the National Council of Voluntary Child Care Organisations was also specified.

1989: Government support for the voluntary sector under the microscope

The extent of government funding of the voluntary sector (amounting in 1988/89 to £2.1 billion, of which £119 million was paid by Northern Ireland departments) was such that government needed to be satisfied that the assistance was being used efficiently and effectively and directed to the right purposes. In May 1989 the government announced an Efficiency Scrutiny of Government Funding of the Voluntary Sector, with the following terms of reference:

1. to examine:
   a. the full range of programmes for government funding of the voluntary sector;
   b. the purpose for which financial provision is made under those programmes;
   c. the different types of funding employed;
   d. arrangements for the identification and selection of suitable voluntary organizations for particular tasks, for the setting of objectives and the monitoring and review of performance and results;
   e. arrangements for the administration of the programmes.

2. to make recommendations for achieving cost-effective improvements where necessary.

The scrutiny team's report *Efficiency Scrutiny of Government Funding of the Voluntary Sector : Profiting from Partnership* was published in April 1990 (Home Office, 1990). The report contained over 100 detailed recommendations. Each government department, including grant-making departments in Northern Ireland, drew up action plans for implementing those recommendations which were accepted and contributed to the preparation of an overall government action plan. September 1993 was set as the target date for completion of implementation of the scrutiny's recommendations. The

17

final stage in the scrutiny process was the preparation of an implementation report which records the action taken by departments since April 1990 to implement the scrutiny's recommendations. The report will be published.

A statement of principles

A key recommendation in the *Scrutiny* report was that clear, general aims for government funding should be formulated and stated. This flowed from one of the findings in the report that the government had not set out its overall aims in supporting voluntary work. This was identified as a cause of concern to many voluntary organizations, who felt that the government thought that the voluntary sector was 'a good thing', but that there was no clear indication of what sort of role the government saw for the voluntary sector and what sort of funding arrangements it was likely to favour in the future. Those organizations thought that the voluntary sector would gain in strength, and would know where it stood, if departments' decisions on what to support, and how, were taken within the framework of a declared policy.

Effect was given to this in the announcement of the publication of the *Scrutiny* report by the then Home Secretary, the Rt Hon. David Waddington QC, MP.[5] The announcement endorsed the importance of the voluntary sector:

> The Government values highly the great contribution made by voluntary bodies to individuals, the communities in which they live and work, and their environment. Effective voluntary organisations channel the energies of individuals to help themselves and others. They meet people's needs imaginatively. They encourage individual and community responsibility. Government already supports the voluntary sector on a very large scale. In 1988-89 Government grants exceeded £2 billion. This money must be used for good purposes; and it must be used efficiently. The report of the Efficiency Scrutiny of Government Funding of the Voluntary Sector provides a basis for improving arrangements to secure this. The Government will continue to provide funds for efficiently managed voluntary organisations which provide worthwhile services, yield practical benefits and meet other valuable objectives. Support for the voluntary organisations involves a partnership between the public sector, the corporate sector and individual donors. We have made tax concessions to encourage this. Voluntary bodies should be encouraged to raise more money from private and corporate donations: it would, clearly, be damaging to the whole nature of voluntary effort if voluntary bodies were to become over-dependent on public funding.

18

The announcement also included a definitive statement of the principles by which government funding will be governed. The principles are:

- to merit support an organization must be able to achieve a direct practical effect, such as helping people, improving the environment, or providing skills for the unemployed;
- organizations must uphold accepted ethical standards;
- any support must help achieve the overall policies of the funding department;
- an organization's use or encouragement of volunteers will be an important fact in determining the support it achieves;
- any campaigning by a funded body must be ancillary to its objectives, as required by charity law;
- funding will normally be for specific services or for limited term projects and will be subject to review as policies evolve with changing circumstances;
- funding of an organization's core administrative costs will be considered when the organization has a continuing role in the achievement of particular policy objectives or provides services for other voluntary organizations;
- departments which are responsible for funding will monitor results and have regard to the voluntary organization's efficiency and costs.

An opportunity for a new, strategic framework

What relevance had the Efficiency Scrutiny for the further development of partnership between government departments and the voluntary sector in Northern Ireland? As noted above, the scrutiny covered *all* funding programmes, and thus the *Scrutiny* report, its recommendations, the government action plan and the implementation report extended to Northern Ireland. But perhaps the most important influence of the scrutiny was the opportunity which it provided to develop a *specific*, government strategy on support for the voluntary sector in Northern Ireland.

Given the diverse nature of the voluntary sector and the scale of public funds it receives, it was not unexpected that the scrutiny should identify the need for government departments to establish strategies for supporting voluntary bodies which should clearly reflect the priorities of each department. As part of their response to the *Scrutiny* report, government departments in Northern Ireland agreed to prepare a strategy which would give an unequivocal statement of support for the voluntary sector. This would contain an overall Northern Ireland strategy as well as one for each discrete area of business. It would deal with partnership not only in the sense of funding, but

19

also in terms of the involvement of the voluntary sector in the policy-making process. A draft *Strategy* was prepared and issued for widespread consultation in 1992.

At the same time, a separate interdepartmental exercise was in train within government to consider two reports on community development in Northern Ireland which had been submitted to the Secretary of State for Northern Ireland by the Community Development Review Group (CDRG, 1991a,b). The Review Group had highlighted the important role played by community development in Northern Ireland and had identified the absence of an explicit commitment to the principle of community development and a clear understanding of what is entailed in community development practice.

A community development process was, of course, already implicit in a number of key government programmes and priorities, and departments and their agencies rely heavily upon harnessing the energy of local communities to ensure that policies and programmes are successfully implemented. There was, however, no strategic overview of the existing investment. The Community Development Review Group's reports provided an opportunity to build on what was already being done; to make support for community development explicit; to provide a sharper focus within government on community development practices and principles; and to put in place a mechanism through which a number of key issues in this field would be considered on an interdepartmental basis.

There was a convergence in the culmination of the process of analysing comments on the draft *Strategy* and of the community development review. The draft *Strategy* had been well received by the sector, but a number of respondents had commented on the absence in it of any significant reference to community development and had stressed the importance of linking the *Strategy* with a statement on community development. Departments involved in the interdepartmental review of community development took the view that their support for community development was closely, even inextricably, linked to their support for the voluntary sector and that the outcome of the review should be reflected in the *Strategy* in its final form. As a result, the *Strategy* published in February 1993 reflected the outcome of two separate, but closely related exercises within government, one the implementation in Northern Ireland of the Efficiency Scrutiny recommendations, the other the response to the Community Development Review Group's reports.

The *Strategy* was launched by the Secretary of State for Northern Ireland in February 1993. In his foreword, the Secretary of State reaffirmed the importance of partnership between government and voluntary and community groups. He said:

The Government is committed to working in partnership with them and to continuing to support the voluntary sector so far as the inevitable constraints upon the availability of resources permit. I believe that the strategy set out in this document will make the partnership even more productive. I welcome the inclusion in it of a clear statement of the importance which we attach to the work of community groups, and to the process of community development that can make so significant a difference to life within the Province.

The *Strategy*, a 'first' for Northern Ireland, is wide-ranging. It breaks new ground by providing:

a. a clear statement of the strategic aims of Northern Ireland departments in supporting the voluntary sector. These are:
    i.   to encourage, promote and support an independent, vigorous and cost-effective voluntary sector in the province;
    ii. to encourage and promote voluntary activity;
    iii. to ensure that maximum benefit is obtained from the resources which they make available to the voluntary sector;
    iv. to build on the experience of the voluntary sector in the development and advancement of departmental policy objectives, recognising the value of its independent perspective;
b. a statement of the common and agreed principles underpinning all departments' support for the sector;
c. a statement of the action which departments will take in pursuing the scope for securing greater consistency among their grant-making procedures and in developing good practice;
d. a sectoral strategy for each area of business - for example, health and personal social services and rural development.

On the community development front, the *Strategy* contains a statement of principle on government's support for this process in Northern Ireland. This:

i.   recognises and endorses the value of community development and the role of community groups in Northern Ireland;
ii. acknowledges the need to enhance the effectiveness and efficiency of departments' existing commitment to community development;
iii. announces that action will be taken to provide a sharper focus within Government on community development and to address a range of specified issues on an interdepartmental basis, including the need to ensure coherence as far as possible between existing departmental programmes and to develop inter-sectoral strategies and funding arrangements for new programmes.

A further, important advance made by the *Strategy* was the recognition within it of the role of the voluntary and community sector in the policy formulation process. The *Strategy* makes clear that partnership between the government and the voluntary sector is not only about funding, important though that is. It is also about involving the voluntary sector as early as possible in the policy-making process; about building on the experience of the sector in the development and advancement of departmental policy objectives; and about taking into account the impact on voluntary organizations and volunteers of changes in those policies and plans. The *Strategy* contains a number of commitments on how the sector will be involved.

A new focus for voluntary activity

A key initiative in the *Strategy* was the announcement that a Voluntary Activity Unit would be established within the Department of Health and Social Services to provide a clearly identified focal point for voluntary activity in Northern Ireland. The *Strategy* also announced that action would be taken to strengthen the existing mechanism for interdepartmental consideration of issues affecting the voluntary sector, and to facilitate as appropriate and through that mechanism, discussion with the sector on issues of a cross-departmental nature.

It is interesting to note that the 1980 policy review by the Co-ordinating Committee on Social Problems had not endorsed the need for a Northern Ireland equivalent of the Home Office's Voluntary Services Unit. In the intervening years, however, the number of issues in the voluntary activity field which required interdepartmental consideration and action in Northern Ireland had increased significantly. In particular, the implementation in Northern Ireland of the report of the Efficiency Scrutiny by an overall Northern Ireland Action Manager supported by a team of departmental action managers had set an agenda for continuing work to develop good practice. The interdepartmental review of community development in turn had pointed to the need for a focus on community development, and had also set a well-filled agenda of key issues in this field which had to be addressed on an interdepartmental basis. The need was demonstrated and the time was considered right to establish a Voluntary Activity Unit charged both with keeping the *Strategy* under review in the light of experience of its operation and with lead responsibility for community development.

The establishment of the Voluntary Activity Unit on 14 June 1993 was announced by the Secretary of State for Northern Ireland in his opening address to the Northern Ireland Council for Voluntary Action's Conference in June 1993 *Partners or Adversaries - the Voluntary Sector's Developing*

Relations with Government and the Significance of the European Framework.[6]
He confirmed that the precise aims and role of the Unit would be defined in
a strategy statement developed in consultation with the voluntary sector. The
Unit added to its remit in December 1993 responsibility for policy on, and
preparation and administration of, charity law. These had rested previously
with the Department of Finance and Personnel.

The role and aims of the Voluntary Activity Unit

A draft *Strategy Statement* (DHSS, 1993a) on the role and aims of the
Voluntary Activity Unit was issued for consultation on 22 December 1993.
This dealt among other things with the structure and accountability of the
Unit; its contribution to the achievement of the strategic aims of Northern
Ireland departments for the support of the voluntary sector and for community
development; and the mechanism for ensuring interdepartmental consideration
of key issues in these fields.

The role of the Unit includes the critical one of contributing to the
achievement of the strategic aims set in the 1993 *Strategy*. It does this by:

a. co-ordinating and keeping under review government policy towards the
   voluntary sector and on community development in Northern Ireland;
b. facilitating liaison among government departments, through bilateral
   contacts on and the provision of an appropriate mechanism for interdepartmental consideration of, these issues;
c. actively promoting the interests of the voluntary sector with other
   departments;
d. encouraging other departments, through the issue of voluntary sector
   proofing guidance, to have regard, when new policies are being introduced or existing policies developed, to the need to consider whether any
   change will have a particular impact on the voluntary sector and, where
   it does, and public consultation is possible, to ensure that the views of
   the sector are sought;
e. monitoring the impact of the voluntary sector proofing guidance;
f. increasing the effectiveness of the voluntary sector in Northern Ireland
   by:
   i. supporting organizations which provide resources and support to the
       wider voluntary sector;
   ii. encouraging efficient and effective practice; for example, by
       encouraging research, developing methods for monitoring and
       evaluation, and fostering the development of new training and
       management initiatives;

iii. ensuring that departments pursue the scope for securing greater consistency among their grant-making procedures;

g. increasing and promoting the giving of time (through volunteering) in the voluntary, statutory and private sectors and money (through charitable donations);

h. acting as a channel of communication between Government and the voluntary sector in Northern Ireland and as a point of reference to voluntary organizations seeking support from central Government.

The draft *Strategy Statement* breaks new ground in three particular areas, because of the Unit's conviction that its relationship with the voluntary sector should be based on openness and transparency. The first area is the commitment to publish an annual report on the Unit's activities. This will include a report on the administration of the Community Volunteering Scheme[7], and on the exercise by the Department of Health and Social Services of its responsibilities relating to charities, as required by Section 34 of the Charities Act (Northern Ireland) 1964.

The second area of new ground lies in the arrangements for new interdepartmental machinery and the involvement of external interests in aspects of its operations. The *Strategy Statement* announced that an Interdepartmental Group on Voluntary Activity and Community Development would be established, replacing the existing Interdepartmental Voluntary Action Group. Chaired by the head of the Voluntary Activity Unit, the Group has representation from all Northern Ireland departments and the Central Community Relations Unit involved in support for the voluntary sector and community development. It provides a forum for interdepartmental consideration of issues affecting the voluntary sector and those in the community development field.

The Voluntary Activity Unit is keen to facilitate access to the Group by groups involved in voluntary activity and community development. To achieve this, the statement indicates that the Unit will draw up, on an annual basis, a forward workplan for the Group identifying the issues which will be considered. External interests will be consulted on this and given an opportunity to suggest additional items. The aim of this is not to set the agenda for those interests, but rather to ensure that key issues of common concern to the statutory and voluntary sectors are identified for interdepartmental consideration in a particular period. External interests will also be consulted by the Group, wherever possible, in carrying out its workplan and sub-groups with representatives from those interests may be set up to address specific issues.

The third area of new ground is the Voluntary Activity Unit's intention to explore the possibility of drawing on the experience of staff from other

Northern Ireland departments and to consider a staff exchange scheme between the Unit and the voluntary sector.

Think Voluntary

The importance of having regard to the impact of new policies on the voluntary sector was stressed in the 1993 *Strategy*, which contained a list of questions which all departments were asked to consider when new policies are being introduced or new policies developed. Updated guidance, including a new *Think Voluntary* leaflet (Home Office, 1993), was issued to all Northern Ireland departments in November 1993. In addition, guidance for those involved in the preparation of legislation in Northern Ireland now incorporates a reference to the need to consider the impact on the voluntary sector when framing legislative provisions.

The European dimension

The partnership between government and the voluntary sector is, of course, also influenced by European issues, and the voluntary sector may also be affected by changes in policy and procedures arising from EC directives, or proposals for EC legislation. Four particular recent developments are worthy of note.

At national level, the government has established a Government/Voluntary Sector Forum on Europe as an important meeting place for the exchange of views. The Forum is not confined to EC issues, but is also competent to address the wider Europe, including Central and Eastern Europe, the Baltic States and the former Soviet Republics. Its aims are:

a. to inform interested parties (participants and, through them, others) of European legislation and other relevant issues which affect the generic interests of the voluntary sector;

b. to contribute to the development of responses towards proposed EC legislation; and

c. to contribute to the development of government/voluntary sector thinking on Europe.

Both the Voluntary Activity Unit and the Northern Ireland voluntary sector are members of the Forum. The voluntary sector can, therefore, contribute to the development of thinking at national level based on its experience in European issues and of sharing a land border with another member state.

The *Think Voluntary* leaflet referred to above makes clear that the same questions about implications for the voluntary sector should be asked whether proposals originate within the UK or from Brussels.

An important development supported by government was the recent establishment within the Northern Ireland Council for Voluntary Action of a European Unit, with funding provided under the EC Structural Funds. The Unit's aims are to develop a resource for the Northern Ireland voluntary sector on Europe; to enable the voluntary sector to influence European policy more effectively; to assist its preparation for the incoming Community Support Framework (1994-1999); and to increase the benefits of European programmes for Northern Ireland.

But perhaps the most significant development, both in terms of government's readiness to involve the voluntary sector in policy formulation and of the further acknowledgement of the sector's contribution to the achievement of economic and social cohesion, was the development of the *Northern Ireland Structural Funds Plan 1994-1999* (DFP, 1993). The plan was prepared in consultation with a wide range of local organizations throughout Northern Ireland, which were invited to put forward their proposals for activities which they thought should be eligible for assistance in the next round of funding. The voluntary sector responded to this, arguing the need for a community infrastructure which recognized the critical importance of the voluntary sector and the work it undertakes. A second stage in the process involved consultation on a draft of the key sections of the plan, which reflected many of the ideas and proposals put forward by local groups.

The *Structural Funds Plan*, which was submitted to the European Commission in Brussels on 3 November 1993, has as its strategic aim 'to promote economic and social cohesion both within Northern Ireland and relative to the other regions of the European Community'. The plan identifies six strategic themes, one of which is community infrastructure, constituting the areas of activity which need to be the focus of Structural Funds assistance if its strategic objectives are to be achieved. On community infrastructure, the plan says:

Positive action is ... needed to overcome community alienation by promoting reconciliation between communities in Northern Ireland and by tackling sources of disadvantage which sustain community divisions. While Targeting Social Need can play a significant part in improving employment and employability in areas of greatest need, it is also necessary to invest in voluntary and community activity which can help local people to engage actively in building and sustaining a community infrastructure and thereby make an important contribution to economic development. The principles, practices and methods of community development can greatly assist in this process (para 4.15).

The plan contains a Physical and Social Environment Programme whose objective is to foster internal social cohesion by improving the physical and social environment within Northern Ireland to ensure that the whole community is more able to take advantage of economic growth potential. This will be tackled in four ways and through four sub-programmes - the promotion of community reconciliation; the regeneration of urban areas; the targeting of social need; and the development of community infrastructure.

The Community Infrastructure Sub-Programme, which will be administered within the Department of Health and Social Services by the Voluntary Activity Unit, will seek as a primary objective to enable local communities in areas of acute hardship and disadvantaged groups to contribute effectively to policy formulation in their areas by providing voluntary and community groups with the necessary skills in management, planning, monitoring, evaluation, auditing, fundraising, and group work. It will also aim to develop area integrated development initiatives to ensure an effective balance and plurality of provision and to support the development of independent advice giving services.

Negotiations are currently, (Spring 1994), in train with the Commission to agree a new Community Support Framework. This will describe the areas eligible for EC funding and allocate the funding to the various sectoral programmes. Once agreement is reached, voluntary and community groups will be able to take advantage of the many opportunities which the Structural Funds will provide to benefit from significant additional resources, not just through the Community Infrastructure Sub-Programme, but also across other operational programmes and sub-programmes.

Towards the future

A clear, strategic policy framework for the support of the voluntary sector and for community development is now in place. The Voluntary Activity Unit is now in operation and is consulting on its precise role and aims. A new Interdepartmental Group on Voluntary Activity and Community Development has been established. What more needs to be done? What issues are still on the policy agenda or need to be brought on to it?

The 1993 *Strategy* is not, of course, set in concrete. The relationship between government and the voluntary sector is a developing one and subject to change. As departments' policy objectives adapt to meet changing needs, so also do the concerns of and the services offered by the voluntary sector.

It is essential, therefore, that the detailed procedures recommended by the *Efficiency Scrutiny* and now in operation in Northern Ireland and the *Strategy* itself are kept under review in the light of experience of their operation. This task will fall to the Voluntary Activity Unit.

The *Strategy* did not provide solutions to all the issues of concern in the community development field. Rather, it defined an agenda of issues which will now be taken forward by the Interdepartmental Group on Voluntary Activity and Community Development. These include:

a.   the need to ensure coherence as far as possible between existing departmental programmes which have a community development dimension;

b.   the development of inter-sectoral strategies including funding arrangements for new programmes;

c.   the establishment of appropriate monitoring and evaluation arrangements to measure the effectiveness, efficiency and equity of community development practices and principles;

d.   the development of processes required to clarify the methods and skills which are considered appropriate to community development;

e.   the identification of the educational and training needs of those in the voluntary, community and statutory sectors who are involved in or with community development activities.

A key issue is the need to ensure that the principles and practices in the *Strategy* bed down in the grant procedures operated by departments' agents. The *Strategy*, of course, deals with relationships between central government departments and the voluntary organizations which they fund, as did the *Efficiency Scrutiny*. But perhaps the closest interface between the voluntary and statutory sector is to be found at local level, between voluntary groups and a wide range of agencies. The *Strategy* contains a commitment that all departments will exhort their agents to adopt comparable principles in their relationships with the voluntary sector and action on this will be critically important.

On the health and personal social services front, the Department of Health and Social Services will be issuing new guidance to health and social services boards and trusts on their relationships with the voluntary sector. This will have regard, among other things, to the significant changes which have taken place in those relationships through the introduction of the Health Service and *People First* reforms and the resultant movement from a grants to a contract culture within a purchasing and contracting framework.

More work needs to be done in involving local communities in policy formulation in their areas. In his opening address at the Northern Ireland

Council for Voluntary Action's Conference *Partners or Adversaries* in June 1993[8], the Secretary of State for Northern Ireland acknowledged that:

> It is in local communities that voluntary and community groups feel that to effect real change, they must be able to contribute to policy formulation and be part of the decision-making process. The Strategy endorses the view that the experience of local community groups in identifying local needs, skills and strengths, and responding in imaginative and effective ways can be a significant factor in the formulation of social and economic policies.

As noted above, the objectives of the Community Infrastructure Sub-Programme specifically include the need to involve local communities in policy formulation for their areas and to develop integrated area development partnership initiatives.

Action is in train at national level to consider how rules and regulations which hamper voluntary effort can be cut down, and an eighth Deregulation Task Force on Charities and Voluntary Organisations has been set up to look specifically at the burdens placed on the sector. It will report to ministers on priorities for the repeal or simplification of existing and proposed regulations and enforcement methods. It will be important to consider the implications of this exercise for the voluntary sector in Northern Ireland.

An area where further developments can be expected in the near future is the promotion of volunteering, which is attracting a high profile nationally. The encouragement and promotion of voluntary activity is, of course, also one of the strategic aims of government departments in Northern Ireland. In October 1993[9], the Prime Minister announced a new initiative called *Make a Difference*, which will build on the wide range of work being done already by volunteers including those involved in employee volunteering schemes, local voluntary organizations and those who, in less formal ways, help each other in their communities. This is a UK initiative and the Voluntary Activity Unit will be working with the voluntary sector to ensure its full application in Northern Ireland.

On the charity front, the Voluntary Activity Unit is considering what changes are required in charity law in Northern Ireland. It will publish a consultation paper on proposed amendments to charity law leading to a proposal for a Draft Charities (Northern Ireland) Order.

Action on all these fronts should ensure that we continue to develop the framework within which voluntary activity can be encouraged and promoted. Such a framework deals with partnerships and relationships and defines the nature of them. Over recent years these have changed significantly. We have, for example, seen the emergence of new partnerships between the voluntary, statutory and private sectors, an increasing emphasis on efficiency and effectiveness and the introduction of a contract culture. But, as we look to the future, what about the broader, more fundamental issues such as the boundaries between the statutory and voluntary sector? What about the scope, role, and very nature, of voluntary activity itself? These are important issues which merit careful reflection and on which it will, I suggest, be helpful to have an informed debate. The publication in October 1993 of Barry Knight's report *Voluntary Action* (Knight, 1993), for example, has contributed to this process by stimulating a debate on the future of the voluntary sector.

Conclusion

I end where I began, with the *Strategy for the Support of the Voluntary Sector and for Community Development in Northern Ireland.* It is an important document which has been welcomed by the voluntary sector. But its success and its enduring effect will depend on the extent to which its statements of principles and practice are translated into concrete action, which will in turn result in tangible benefits for the voluntary and community sector and, through it, for people in need in some of our most deprived areas in Northern Ireland.

Notes

1. The *Strategy* was launched by Sir Patrick Mayhew QC, MP on 22 February 1993.
2. The Co-ordinating Committee on Social Problems, which is no longer in existence, was established in 1975 and chaired by the Department of Health and Social Services, with terms of reference which included the examination of social problems with an interdepartmental content.
3. The Central Personal Social Services Advisory Committee was established under Article 24 of the Health and Personal Social Services (Northern Ireland) 1972 Order to advise the Department of Health and Social Services on the provision of any service with which that committee is concerned and to undertake such investigation as the Department thinks fit.
4. The Interdepartmental Voluntary Action Group was set up in 1985 to provide co-ordinating machinery for purposes such as sharing information on grant-making and ensuring consistency in the government's relations with voluntary bodies.
5. Home Office news release (4 April 1990) - *Efficiency Scrutiny of Government Funding of the Voluntary Sector.*

6. This address by Sir Patrick Mayhew QC, MP is reproduced in *Agenda for Action*, NICVA, 1993.
7. The Community Volunteering Scheme is designed to generate a variety of volunteering opportunities primarily, but not exclusively, for unemployed people of all ages through which new skills may be learnt or existing skills maintained or developed. It is administered by the Voluntary Activity Unit as part of its responsibility for the promotion of volunteering.
8. *Agenda for Action*, see note 6.
9. Press notice (19 October 1993) from 10 Downing Street - *Prime Minister's speech to the Per Cent Club*.

References

Beveridge, William Henry, Baron (1948), *Voluntary Action: a Report on Methods of Social Advance*, Allen and Unwin, London.

Central Personal Social Services Advisory Committee (1979), 'Report of the Sub-Committee on Support for Voluntary Organisations', [unpublished].

Co-ordinating Committee on Social Problems (1980), *Tomorrow's Resource: a Review of Government Policy towards the Voluntary Sector in the Field of Social Welfare*.

Community Development Review Group (1991), *Community Development in Northern Ireland - Perspectives for the Future*, Community Development Review Group/Workers Educational Association, Belfast.

Community Development Review Group (1991), *Funding for Community and Voluntary Groups in Northern Ireland*, Community Development Review Group/Workers Educational Association, Belfast.

Department of Finance and Personnel (1993), *Northern Ireland Structural Funds Plan 1994-1999*, HMSO, Belfast.

Department of Health and Social Services (1974), *Support for Voluntary Organisations*, Circular HSS 15(OS) 1/74.

Department of Health and Social Services (1985), *Co-operation between the Statutory and Voluntary Sectors in the Health and Personal Social Services*, Circular HSS(SS) 1/85.

Department of Health and Social Services (1993), *Draft Strategy Statement on the Role and Aims of the Voluntary Activity Unit*.

Department of Health and Social Services (1993), *Strategy for the Support of the Voluntary Sector and for Community Development in Northern Ireland*, HMSO, Belfast.

Griffiths, H., Nic Giolla Choille, T. & Robinson, J. (1978), *Yesterday's Heritage or Tomorrow's Resource?: a Study of Voluntary Organisations Providing Social Services in Northern Ireland*, New University of Ulster, Coleraine.

Home Office (1978), *The Government and the Voluntary Sector: a Consultative Document*, Voluntary Services Unit.

Home Office (1990), *Efficiency Scrutiny of Government Funding of the Voluntary Sector: Profiting from Partnership*, HMSO, London.

Home Office (1993), *Think Voluntary*, Voluntary Services Unit and Public Relations Branch.

Knight, Barry (1993), *Voluntary Action*, Home Office for CENTRIS Research Project: Voluntary Action in the 1990s, HMSO, London.

Ministry of Health and Local Government (NI) (1949), *Welfare Services Act (NI)*, Circular Letter No. W28.

Wolfenden, John, Baron (1978), *The Future of Voluntary Organisations: the Report of the Wolfenden Committee*, Croom Helm, London.

3 A partnership of dilemmas and contradictions: unresolved issues in government–voluntary sector relations

Nicholas Acheson

In February, 1993 the government published its *Strategy for the Support of the Voluntary Sector and for Community Development in Northern Ireland.* It contains, for the first time in a public document, a clear statement of policy towards voluntary organizations and the paragraph on their perceived role and importance is worth quoting from:

> Government Departments in Northern Ireland acknowledge the intrinsic value of the voluntary sector and its capacity to generate and harness goodwill and motivation and to translate these into action in response to a wide range of needs. They also recognise the important role played by the voluntary sector in the social and economic life of the Province where, in the context of Northern Ireland's special circumstances, it provides a forum for reflecting the views and concerns of individuals and communities to Government ... They endorse voluntary activity as an important way in which the energies of individuals and groups can be channelled to help themselves and others; and of encouraging individual and community responsibility as local people identify and address social, economic, environmental and cultural issues which affect their lives (DHSS, 1993).

This chapter offers an exploration of the meaning of this statement and looks at some of the ways in which the government project since 1979 of reforming and restructuring the welfare state has interrelated with the special circumstances of Northern Ireland. It is argued that government experience in applying its policies to Northern Ireland has exposed some of the unresolved contradictions within public policy in respect of the voluntary sector where the evidence suggests a number of different objectives are being pursued which are, in practice, not easy to reconcile.

The Conservative Party project during the 1980s to roll back the state has undergone a distinct change in emphasis since the last general election. The task now is not so much the replacement of state provision by other agencies, in particular the private sector, but rather to implant a 'rationalistic' system of management into public services controlled by a quasi market, rather than by more traditional methods of direct accountability to an electorate or to recognized interest groups. The concept of the 'mixed economy of welfare' has been recruited to the task of making public services more efficient and better targeted. Expectations of the voluntary sector have changed out of all recognition as a result. This changed environment of public services, delivered through a multiplicity of providers in some sense competing for business, has not only given voluntary organizations a new role, but has also, in a much more general sense, pushed them to centre stage in the public policy debate.

While government rhetoric in the early 1980s saw the voluntary sector and voluntarism as a substitute for state intervention, they are now seen more in terms of being a means towards greater flexibility, innovativeness, and efficiency. A language of substitution has been replaced by a language of partnership. Government's determination to break up public service monopolies has led to an enormous increase in the sums of public money being invested in voluntary organizations. By 1989 expenditure on the voluntary sector in the United Kingdom as a whole had increased to about £2.1 billion per annum. The growth had been piecemeal and ad hoc, department by department, and it may have been partly to gain a sense of order that 1989 and 1990 saw the publication of a number of key documents which sought more closely to define government policy.

Two white papers, one on charity law reform (Home Office, 1989) and one on community care (DH, 1989) and the report of the Efficiency Scrutiny of Government Funding of the Voluntary Sector (Home Office, 1990), together with the Home Secretary's statement in the House of Commons in April 1990 outlining the principles which would underlie government support for the voluntary sector, set out the basis of the new agenda.

In a parliamentary written answer given on the publication of the *Scrutiny* report, the Home Secretary referred to the fact that grant aid to the voluntary sector exceeded £2 billion and added:

> The Government values highly the great contribution made by voluntary bodies to individuals, the communities in which they live and work, and their environment. Effective voluntary organizations channel the energies of individuals to help themselves and others. They meet people's needs imaginatively. They encourage individual and community responsibility (Hansard: 4 April 1990, col. 639).

His statement went on to emphasize that government support for voluntary bodies would focus on practical results, on opportunities for volunteering and would be increasingly based on specific projects over time limited periods.

Taylor (1992) has pointed out that the ministerial statement laid considerably less emphasis than did the *Scrutiny* report on the need for government grant to cover the core costs of infrastructural organizations necessary to underpin the continuing independence and cohesion of the voluntary sector. On the basis of what ministers have said, the government looks less interested in these issues than in the perceived gains in efficiency and consumer choice that voluntary organization managed services might offer. The same priorities seem apparent in the Northern Ireland *Strategy*, quoted at the start of this chapter, where the emphasis is on funding practical projects which will help to achieve the overall policies of departments. It shall be argued that this emphasis may create particular problems in the Northern Ireland context. But, before turning in more detail to the local implications of these policy changes, two general features of the relationship between the state and the voluntary sector should be elucidated.

Those charged with the responsibility of making sense of these changes in practice can easily lose sight of the radical departure in policy they represent. The social settlement at the end of the Second World War in which a consensus was established, and which lasted for forty years was based on the view that it was the role of the state to intervene to ensure that the social and health needs of citizens were met and consequently the voluntary sector had a residual, if any, role. Wilford (1989) has argued: 'The major accomplishment of the voluntary sector during the first postwar phase had been to survive, retaining a subsidiary position, mopping up pools of unmet need'.

Ironically perhaps, the reformers of public administration of the 1980s have looked to the voluntary sector to remedy perceived inefficiencies in state services which were established by their predecessors of the 1940s to remedy inefficiencies in the then voluntary sector. The nature of the debate has of course changed. The architects of the National Health Service were concerned to overcome the fragmented nature of services in the voluntary sector. Now, that same fragmentation is seen as a virtue enabling a quasi market to operate, maximizing both innovative ideas and efficient use of resources. It remains to be seen whether the wheel will once again turn full circle in another forty years.

However, the consequence of the new faith in the voluntary sector has been to move it firmly to centre stage in the shaping of social policy and in the planning of welfare services. But it is noticeable that the debate which has followed has been couched in very instrumental terms. The issue has been the extent to which voluntary organizations can actually promote government

35

policy objectives. Government itself, as we have seen from the Home Secretary's written answer, quoted above, has clearly stated that funding of voluntary organizations must be related explicitly to government objectives.

Such instrumentalist values are implicit in an approach to welfare which stresses the value of rational management. Tasks must relate to outcomes which in turn must be related to overall objectives in explicit ways. However, what this rational model fails to capture adequately is the place voluntary organizations occupy in the social structure. It has never been argued by government that the existence of the voluntary sector can be wholly justified through its ability to deliver government funded services in approved ways. While the community care debate has been dominated by discussion of the relevance of voluntary organizations to government welfare goals, exemplified by the white paper, *Caring for People* (DH, 1989), and its predecessor, the Griffiths Report (DSS, 1988), quite other arguments have also been advanced by government itself on the place and proper role of the sector.

In contrast to the instrumentalist approach, the white paper of 1989 on charity law reform said the following:

> The importance of the voluntary sector does not ... lie just in its capacity to deliver services funded by the Government; nor is it any part of the Government's policy to place on voluntary organisations the burden of delivering essential services for which it is right that the Government should remain responsible. The Government seek a free, vigorous and creative partnership in which each partner is able to make its distinctive contribution. What the voluntary sector has essentially to offer is its practical grass roots experience, its ability to respond flexibly and swiftly to changing needs and circumstances and perhaps above all its capacity to innovate (Home Office, 1989).

One might think that the first part of this passage is somewhat defensive; after all, who other than the government itself could have created the impression that it did think the value of voluntary organizations lay in their ability to deliver services? But implicit in the passage is the recognition that the voluntary sector's place in society is owed to something other than its perceived capacity to deliver government programmes. Indeed the charity law reform white paper suggests this is the case, notwithstanding the award of grants for specific services.

Thus far, the argument that this change in emphasis is of some importance might appear a little far-fetched. Indeed government has tended to argue in, for example, the community care white paper, that the other virtues of voluntary organizations are 'add-on' attributes. Things are, of course, not quite that simple.

Two quite distinct arguments can be advanced to show that the picture being presented does not quite add up and both throw light on the relationship between the state and the voluntary sector.   The first has to do with the nature of welfare itself and the importance welfare has assumed in contemporary industrial societies as a means of maintaining social cohesion. Such functionalist arguments have been advanced by both the Left and the Right.   From the Left the neomarxists have argued that 'social policies are fundamentally an aid to the effective control of the labour force' (Room, 1979, p. 197).   Welfare, in this view, deflects fundamental social criticism and reinforces the false-consciousness of the working class.   Gough (1979, p. 52) has noted: 'They [social services] have the aim in part of maintaining and adapting the "reserve army of labour", a potential labour force, and in part of maintaining and controlling groups that threaten social stability'.   From the Right behavioural arguments are advanced to stress the need for welfare policies to reform and discipline the socially irresponsible.   Whatever version of such arguments one adopts, it seems indisputable that the need to promote social cohesion in complex industrial societies is an important role of the modern state and that welfare policies are in fact an important, though not the only, means of achieving this.

Thus the more voluntary organizations become important in social policy, the more their potential role in promoting social cohesion will be seen as important.   The complexity of this role is apparent in the light of a second set of arguments around the relationship between the state and civil society.

A crucial defining feature of voluntary organizations is that they derive their legitimacy from the free association of citizens outside the structures and purposes of the state.   Civil society is rich with these associations to a greater or lesser extent in any liberal democracy and the fact of their existence can be taken as evidence of a society's commitment to the values which underlie them.   Because of this, promoting voluntary organizations and voluntary activity can itself be seen as an important means of securing the values which underpin the operation of a market economy and the compliance of citizens. This has always been explicitly recognized by the Conservative Party ideologues whose views have been informing public policy for the past thirteen years.   A good example is offered by Margaret Thatcher herself. Speaking in 1981 at a meeting of the Women's Royal Voluntary Service (WRVS), she argued that voluntary organizations were significant in maintaining a free society:

> They are not just a way of giving help and caring, vitally important though it is, and the wonderful work that you do; they are an example that we are a free people, and continue to be that and do things our own way.   And when we are free, this is the important thing, we do rise to our

responsibilities and carry them out far better than any Government. And so I could say that the great volunteer associations are really a vital part of the defence of our freedom of action (Loney, 1986, p. 135).

If it is the case that the level and diversity of voluntary activity is evidence of the health of civil society and if it is part of the function of government to secure the legitimacy of the institutions of the state in the eyes of citizens, then it clearly follows that it is in a government's interests to promote voluntary action as a good in itself. Put rather more crudely, for a government keen to parade its democratic credentials and its claims to promote and protect a pluralist social order, the existence of many and varied voluntary organizations is clearly grist to its mill. Promoting voluntary organizations as a significant source of help for those in need will also reinforce philanthropy rather than social citizenship as the value underpinning welfare and may thus in turn legitimize a view of the state as residual and non-interfering.

However, these considerations pose some problems for a government which is also keen to recruit the voluntary sector to the task of delivering various welfare programmes on its behalf and has overseen a substantial transfer of resources to the sector during the past decade. The difficulty lies in striking the right balance between incorporating the voluntary sector as a means of delivering the state's programmes in an efficient manner, while at the same time keeping it sufficiently independent for it to remain a credible source of legitimacy for a pluralist society. The greater the role of the voluntary sector in providing welfare on behalf of the state, the more acute the dilemma.

This issue becomes particularly acute, and perhaps therefore more visible, in circumstances where the very right of the state to exist at all is in question. What is the legitimizing role of the voluntary sector and what strategies are available to the state to control it? And how has the current government, which has a particular interest in the role of the voluntary sector in promoting social cohesion, tried to manage? The evidence from Northern Ireland on how these questions have turned out in practice is particularly important because it uncovers fundamental problems which in more 'normal' societies are less obvious and can easily be overlooked.

The government's public attitude to the voluntary sector is set out in the passage quoted at the start of this chapter. The voluntary sector is not valued only because it can deliver government-funded programmes. Echoing the charity white paper, the 'intrinsic' value of the sector is recognized. More noticeable and unique to Northern Ireland in terms of the importance it assumes, is the recognition that voluntary organizations serve to fill the democratic deficit resulting from the virtual collapse of politics. The sector provides a forum for reflecting the views and concerns of individuals and communities to Government'. Given this recognition, it is perhaps surprising that the emphasis of the document remains to support projects which provide practical benefits in line with government departmental objectives. There is little evidence in the *Strategy* document of the dilemmas government faces in managing the legitimizing role of voluntary organizations in communities which are actively hostile to the state.

The experience of voluntary organizations in Northern Ireland illustrates both the existence of these dilemmas and how government has dealt with them. The argument will be that where there is a clear conflict over the legitimacy of the state, government will be more interested in using its relations with the voluntary sector to control the conflict than to achieve welfare goals, even where the sector's role in welfare is being otherwise promoted.

Before turning to the evidence, the reader should be reminded of some of the salient features of the voluntary sector in Northern Ireland. First, while it often is seen as operating in an ideological space which is neutral to the fundamental conflicts and divisions within Northern Irish society, and undoubtedly has played a role in ameliorating conflict on the ground, the voluntary sector also reflects and reproduces the deep sectarian divisions in society. As these divisions have their focus on the very legitimacy of the state itself, voluntary organizations can be, and are, drawn into this conflict.

An insight into how these factors interrelate is offered from the Northern Ireland Social Attitudes Survey. A striking feature of the conflict in Northern Ireland is the level of consensus on certain issues both between and within the two main communities. One of these is the communitarian attitude to welfare; here there is clear agreement in both communities, and in all classes, that it is the state's role to protect people's health and welfare, and there is a majority in favour of increasing taxation to increase social spending (Wilford, 1992, p.105ff). Health is the highest priority for spending in both communities. There is little tendency to blame people for being poor. The most popular explanation of poverty is that it is an inevitable part of modern life and a substantial minority believe it to be the result of social injustice. Commenting on these findings, Evason (1991, p. 71) notes:

> Equally firmly, the population rejects efforts to integrate the concepts of poverty and inequality. There is little support for blaming the victims of poverty for its occurrence. While some would explain poverty as the result of social injustice, the most favoured interpretation is one that locates poverty within a structural perspective, but shorn of overt political overtones.

If true, this represents a considerable change from the 1970s. Northern Ireland respondents to an EC wide survey of attitudes to poverty conducted in 1976 were more likely to blame the victims than to offer any other explanation and a much smaller minority than in the 1990 survey blamed social injustice (Ditch, 1983, p. 292).

Insofar as attitudes have changed, they have clearly changed against the grain of government thinking over the past ten years. One might then hypothesize on this basis that voluntary organizations are unlikely to be willing recruits to a government agenda that they replace state-run services.

What can be said with some certainty is that the level of agreement between the two main communities about the nature of social problems and the role of the state in dealing with them is high and that it is this which provides the shared ideological space which allows voluntary organizations to operate as they do.

It would be wrong, however, to conclude that voluntary organizations can act collectively to help resolve the political conflict in Northern Ireland because it is also true that they are embedded in the sectarian divisions of society and tend to reflect and reproduce these divisions. Various studies have shown that, although the picture is varied, there is a large degree of sectarian division within the voluntary sector and this is reinforced and perpetuated by the wider forces which keep the two communities apart (Whyte, 1990, p. 38).

This complex picture of a high level of consensus on the role of the state in welfare among deep sectarian divisions over which state should be underpinning welfare offers insights into the ways in which the voluntary sector is itself an arena where welfare as a source of legitimacy is continually being fought over.

At well over £100 million a year, government expenditure on the voluntary sector is huge and has grown rapidly over the past ten years. Voluntary organizations have become major suppliers of government funded services and a large salaried bureaucracy has emerged to manage these programmes. This has a direct interest in maintaining, and if possible enlarging, this level of funding. This level of funding has given the government a great deal of power to determine how the voluntary sector will operate, a power it has used to define not just what welfare activities voluntary organizations can engage in, but also who can be involved.

The major government-funded programme delivered almost entirely by voluntary organizations is the Action for Community Employment scheme (ACE). This is a wage subsidy scheme aimed at providing short-term employment and training to people who have been unemployed for more than six months. The scheme has more than 10,000 places and costs over £50 million a year to run. ACE has had an extraordinary impact on the voluntary sector over the past ten years and provides the arena in which the potential role of the voluntary sector in legitimizing the political order is most clear. It is worth speculating, perhaps, that similar issues may emerge over social service provision as the community care reforms, in which voluntary sector will play an increasingly important role, begin to take effect over the next few years.

First, the ACE experience has shown how voluntary sector involvement in government welfare programmes on a large scale has tended to increase the sectarian division of welfare. The evidence for this is in other chapters in this book. One consequence of this may be to undermine the ability of the sector as a whole to expand the area of social consensus that it has operated in in the past. The government's rather lukewarm commitment to investing in the voluntary sector infrastructure, as opposed to project funding, may exacerbate this tendency and weaken links between project-funded organizations operating independently of one another in each community.

Although nowhere mentioned in the government's *Strategy for the Support of the Voluntary Sector*, since 1985 it has been policy that grant aid is subject to the condition that the recipient body does not in any way promote the standing of paramilitary organizations. The policy originated in a parliamentary written answer (Hansard, 27 June 1985), subsequently press released by the government, in which the then Secretary of State for Northern Ireland, Douglas Hurd, stated that, while it was government policy to encourage voluntary activity which had the 'genuine aim' of improving conditions in areas of need, it was not in the public interest to grant aid organizations which had 'sufficiently close links with paramilitary organizations to give rise to a grave risk that to give support to these groups would have the effect of improving the standing, or furthering the aims, of a paramilitary organization, whether directly or indirectly'.

The implication of the wording of this statement is that where this risk is judged to exist, then the stated welfare goals for which the grant sought would be payable are not genuine. Grant aid has been cut off from organizations for this reason probably less than thirty times and in a minority of cases it has been restored, but it is quite clear that where this has happened, the perceived problem has not been what was being done, but who might be involved and on what terms. Thus the activities which have been affected have included pre-school playgroups, Irish language classes, a photography workshop and advice services.

Furthermore, the policy also operates as a warning to groups to police their own operations, and in particular who becomes involved, for fear of losing grant aid. A high degree of dependency on government funding leaves organizations very vulnerable to pressure of this sort. It has to be said that recently this mechanism has been used less and less but, significantly, government has retained the right to withdraw or to refuse funding on these grounds in a decision-making process which is not open to public scrutiny.

While there are examples of organizations in Protestant areas losing their funding, most have been in areas where there has been a high level of support for Sinn Fein. It seems likely that the operation of the policy is linked to the government's determination to use its financial muscle to isolate Sinn Fein. Thus Rolston (1990) has argued that the issue at stake is legitimacy, but the question remains as to why government should wish to control who gets involved in voluntary activity when it also has an interest in promoting such citizen activity in general. In other words what is the perceived link between voluntary involvement and the larger question of legitimacy of institutions?

It seems likely that the policy is informed by a particular view on what it is to be a socially or politically involved person, a view which lies at the heart of government policy towards the voluntary sector. It was most clearly articulated by Douglas Hurd when he was Home Secretary and it may not be coincidence that 'political vetting', as the policy has come to be known, originated during Mr Hurd's time at the Northern Ireland Office. Writing in *The Independent* newspaper when he was Home Secretary, Mr Hurd (1989) said:

> The idea of active citizenship is a necessary complement to the enterprise culture. Public service may one day have been the duty of an elite, but today it is the responsibility of all who have the time or money to spare. Modern capitalism has democratised the ownership of property and we are now witnessing the democratisation of responsible citizenship.

Commenting on this passage, Barnett (1989) has noted the word 'responsible' in the last sentence, where the qualification suggests that this definition of active citizenship means a way of channelling people's activity in socially and politically approved directions.

While the term 'active citizen' seems to have disappeared with Mrs Thatcher's departure from Downing Street, the concept remains very much alive. It provides a way of reconciling the need to recruit voluntary organizations to the task of delivering government-funded programmes, while at the same time promoting their diversity and independence as a means of achieving social cohesion and the legitimacy of social and political institutions. Behind the attraction of the idea lies the view that social problems are essentially behavioural and concern groups of people whose behaviour does not conform to social norms. Voluntary organizations will provide the means of reforming people through encouraging active participation and of canalising energies. Deakin (1990), whose argument this is, goes on:

More fundamentally, voluntary organizations provide the crucial means by which communities can move towards escaping the dead hand of uniform state control, as the alternative way by which essential services can be delivered within the neighbourhood.

Thus it is not just a question of controlling what voluntary organizations do and encouraging them to provide essential services, it is also a question of controlling who gets involved and on what terms. In return for his or her activity, the citizen in this view is accorded enhanced social status and this enhancement will in turn reflect on whatever other views and activities such a person might either hold or participate in.

In Northern Ireland where whole communities dispute the legitimacy of the state, it has therefore come to be seen as crucially important to control the allocation of social status, lest successful local voluntary action enhances the legitimacy of those opposed to the existence of the state. One way of doing this is to stop grant aiding organizations perceived as providing opportunities for participation of people who themselves are seen as a threat. The more the government seeks to involve and promote voluntary organizations in the delivery of services on the basis of departmental policy objectives, the more visible will their legitimizing role become. Hence the more politically important and the more necessary to control. The impact of the ACE scheme and the episode of political vetting illustrate what may happen when the dilemma becomes explicit. In this case control over access to social status was more important than any welfare gains, although matters are not always so clear cut. It has to be said that the policy may be more difficult to implement in other areas of administration. A feature of the ACE scheme is that its goals are directed towards the long-term unemployed participants, rather than at the 'community benefit' to which their participation is meant to contribute. Closing down an ACE scheme becomes relatively easy since the employees can be transferred to other more acceptable employers.

The central thesis of this chapter has been that, although the government has promoted the role of the voluntary sector as a means of meeting the welfare needs of the population and has a clear interest in pointing to the existence of a vibrant voluntary sector as evidence of the 'normality' of life in Northern Ireland and the legitimacy of the state as a protector and promoter of plural values, it also must seek to exercise control over voluntary organizations as providers of 'citizenship entitlements', lest it inadvertently promote the legitimacy of those seeking to overthrow the state. When the dilemma becomes explicit, as it has done in Northern Ireland, the temptation for government must be to adjust its welfare goals in the light of perceived, or real, threats to state security.

43

Experience gained in Northern Ireland is likely to assume greater importance during the later 1990s, when a further strengthening of the view that voluntary organizations have a key role in promoting social cohesion can be expected. It is important because it illustrates the centrality of this political dimension to voluntary action and the way the state must always seek to impose limits on the nature and extent of that action. But this control can never be total without sacrificing the democratic values underpinning the market economy which give a significant place to the freedom of association, the freedom from which the legitimacy of all voluntary action is derived.

These issues will continue to play a central and quite visible role in voluntary sector relationships with government in Northern Ireland so long as the political conflict continues. The tone of the debate over the past few years, particularly following the publication of the *Scrutiny* report, suggests it may become more subtle than it has been. Government's public acknowledgement of the role of voluntary organizations in providing feedback on public opinion in the absence of local politics, and its recognition of the role of community development in its 1993 *Strategy* document is evidence for this. It will be instructive to watch how the relationship develops.

So long as a government remains in office which holds that voluntary activity and voluntary organizations are important ways both of delivering basic services and of offering citizenship entitlements to people, the dilemmas discussed in this chapter will continue to have real consequences. The way they have worked out in practice in Northern Ireland with its deep divisions over the legitimacy of the state will continue to offer important insights.

References

Acheson, Nick (1989), *Voluntary Action and the State in Northern Ireland*, NICVA, Belfast.

Barnett, Anthony (1989), 'Charlie's army', *New Statesman and Society*, 22 September.

Deakin, Nicholas (1990), 'Towards the 21st Century: Challenges for the Voluntary Sector' in *Proceedings of the 1990 Conference of the Association of Voluntary Action Scholars*, Centre for Voluntary Organisation, London School of Economics, London.

Deakin, Nicholas (1991), 'Government and the voluntary sector in the 1990s', *Policy Studies*, vol. 12, no. 3, Autumn.

Department of Health (1989), *Caring for People: Community Care in the Next Decade and Beyond*, HMSO, London.

Department of Health and Social Services (1993), *Strategy for the Support of the Voluntary Sector and for Community Development in Northern Ireland*, HMSO, Belfast.

Department of Social Security (1988), *Community Care: an Agenda for Action* (Griffiths Report), HMSO, London.

Ditch, John (1983), 'Social Policy in "Crisis"?: the Case of Northern Ireland' in Loney, M., Boswell, D. & Clarke, J. (eds), *Social Policy and Social Welfare*, Open University Press, Milton Keynes.

Evason, Eileen (1991), 'Perceptions of Poverty' in Stringer, P. & Robinson, G. (eds), *Social Attitudes in Northern Ireland*, Blackstaff, Belfast.

Gough, Ian (1979), *The Political Economy of the Welfare State*, Macmillan, London.

Home Office (1989), *Charities: a Framework for the Future*, HMSO, London.

Home Office (1990), *Efficiency Scrutiny of Government Funding of the Voluntary Sector; Profiting from Partnership*, HMSO, London.

Hurd, Douglas (1989), 'Freedom will Flourish where Citizens Accept Responsibility', *The Independent*, 13 September.

Loney, Martin (1986), *The Politics of Greed: the New Right and the Welfare State*, Pluto Press, London.

Rolston, Bill (1990), 'Political Vetting: an Overview' in *The Political Vetting of Community Work in Northern Ireland*, NICVA, Belfast.

Room, Graham (1979), *The Sociology of Welfare: Social Policy Stratification and Political Order*, Blackwell and Robertson, Oxford.

Taylor, Marilyn (1992), 'The Changing Role of the Nonprofit Sector in Britain', in Gidron, B., Kramer, R.M. & Salamon, L.M. (eds), *Government and the Third Sector: Emerging Relationships in Welfare States*, Jossey-Bass, San Francisco.

Whyte, John (1990), *Interpreting Northern Ireland*, Clarendon Press, Oxford.

Wilford, Richard (1989), 'The State and the Voluntary Sector: an Overview' in *Poverty and Policy in the 1990s: the Role of the Voluntary Sector*, Bryson House and Department of Politics, Queen's University of Belfast, Belfast.

Wilford, Richard (1992), 'The Thread of Social Welfare' in Stringer, P. & Robinson, G. (eds), *Social Attitudes in Northern Ireland: the Second Report, 1991-1992*, Blackstaff, Belfast.

4 The European Union and the development of supra-national policy toward the voluntary sector

Stevie Johnston

For certain groups working in the voluntary and community sector in Northern Ireland, the European Community/Union has been increasing in relevance and importance in recent years. It is seen as offering alternative social and economic policies to those which have dominated the political agenda in the United Kingdom since the Conservatives came to power in 1979. The Community not only presents a different political vision, it also has the potential to deliver real resources to develop projects which do not fit easily into mainstream government funding programmes. In Northern Ireland, as elsewhere in Europe, Community policy and programmes have often been more relevant to the needs of marginalized people than those of local institutions (Tsiakalos, 1992, p. 115). New opportunities for lobbying through the various Community institutions have been created. Some groups have been active in setting up European networks to maximize this lobbying potential. The impact of lobbying, when successful, is immense as changes to Community rules apply across all twelve member states. As European Community law is autonomous, the European Court has been used by pressure groups to challenge national policies which breach Community treaties. This is of particular importance to organizations in the United Kingdom which find constitutional challenges to their national government difficult because there is no written bill of rights.

These are some positive reasons why some people in the voluntary and community sectors are interested and involved in the development of the European Community. For many other groups Europe is seen as a distant bureaucracy irrelevant to their day to day needs. This chapter looks at some of the underlying reasons for this perception, why the situation is changing and what more can be done to ensure that the voluntary and community sectors can utilize the full potential of Europe, both as a resource for their work and as a means of helping to generate policy flexibility and change.

One of the key reasons why groups have not been quicker to grasp the potential of Europe's social dimension has been that the Community itself is unclear as to what its social policy role should be. What today is known as the 'European Community' was originally set up essentially as a free-market mechanism. There is wide acceptance that the Treaty of Rome was highly non-interventionist (Brewster and Teague, 1989, p. 54) in nature and that this philosophy has influenced the development of the Community. Even the Maastricht Treaty failed to deliver a clear social policy framework (Jackson, 1992). Instead, what has emerged is a somewhat vague social dimension. The Commission has promoted the need for a social aspect to the European Community and, by a 'dynamic interpretation' (TUC, 1992) of those articles which contained specific social provisions and by calls for high levels of employment, has encouraged the development of the social dimension. However it remains marginal to the main thrust of the Community, which is to establish an internal free market for goods and services within Europe. Even this limited social dimension has come in for criticism, particularly from the United Kingdom Government. In the European Council the United Kingdom has used its power of veto to block nearly all social legislation proposals coming from the European Commission and from the Parliament, leading to virtual deadlock on social policy initiatives during most of the 1980s. Thus it comes as little surprise that, at national and regional level, the United Kingdom Government has done little to promote Europe's potential as a means to develop social initiatives, although it does emphasize the potential of the single market for business opportunities.

A key concept in the Commission's efforts to sustain and enhance the development of the social dimension has been that of solidarity (Spicker, 1991, p. 17). To the present United Kingdom Conservative administration solidarity conjures up collectivist, even Marxist, visions of fraternity. In other Community states the term has both collective and individual dimensions. Common action, mutual responsibility and shared risks, *à la* Beveridge, are regarded as the best means in which to organize social goods. This has influenced the thinking behind the Community's social dimension. Titmuss's concept of institutional welfare states that society shapes need and therefore has a responsibility in meeting these needs. In a similar way the Community accepts that dislocations are created by the free market in Europe and, in a spirit of solidarity, it must provide a means to address these. This it has done through the Structural Funds and, more recently, through the Cohesion Funds, which were created in response to the extraordinary dislocations which will result from the single market.

Within these funds, and their various programmes, the potential exists to deliver real benefits to the voluntary and community sectors. The Community Structural Funds, and perhaps more importantly the Community Initiatives, have among their aims promotion of employment, training, equal opportunities, rural development, local economic regeneration and, in Northern Ireland, community relations. Community Initiatives are those programmes which the Commission runs directly with the aim of advancing Community policies which, either by their nature or member states' unwillingness, are unlikely to occur through national spending of the Structural Funds. These initiatives are key community development issues in which the voluntary and community sectors could have an extensive role in programme delivery.

Although the Commission has actively sought consultation with non-governmental organizations, (NGOs) and has been willing for them to play leading roles in programme delivery, the bulk of the resources from Europe are delivered through national governments who may have different priorities for these funds than those of the Commission. They may even regard the funds as part of, and not additional to, their mainstream spending programmes. This results in nearly all the Structural Funds being allocated to, administered and spent by, government departments themselves. Inevitably the policy agenda of the national government comes to dominate this spending. In the United Kingdom the government's agenda has been to resist the notion of social solidarity.

It should be remembered that belief in the existence of a collective society was rejected by Mrs Thatcher whose policy agenda continued to have a significant influence over the next administration. The dominant view on the subject of human organization and the role of the state is that:

> Society is seen as a competition of atomised individuals: the task of social policy is to ensure that each individual has sufficient resources, health and education to compete effectively within the market place. Beyond this the state should not intervene in social policy. Market processes are sufficient to achieve social objectives (Spicker, 1991, p. 8).

It is hardly surprising that the United Kingdom Government actively promoted enterprise development as the corner-stone for its spending of the 1989-1993 Structural Funds and played down their potential for social policy advancement, so limiting the voluntary and community sector's ability to develop through access to them.

Northern Ireland's Objective One status formally acknowledges that the Community's solidarity and cohesion policies have a part to play in its development, so opening up an opportunity which NGOs have grasped to the best of their abilities within the national policy framework. This special status was sought on the basis that Northern Ireland's conflict made it a special case for help, even though it did not fit the criterion that gross domestic product (GDP) should be below 75 per cent of the European Community average. It was 78 per cent in 1989. This special recognition found concrete application in Community funds being used to support the Community Relations Council and other community relations projects.

In the lead-up to the formulation of the 1994-1999 plans for the Structural Funds the policy environment changed significantly. While Objective One status had originally been granted somewhat reluctantly, using the conflict argument, this time the government allowed not only Northern Ireland to be given special recognition but also extended it to Merseyside and to the Highlands and Islands. The formulation of the Northern Ireland plan also entailed a wide-ranging consultation to which the voluntary sector actively responded, in particular through the European Affairs Committee of the Northern Ireland Council for Voluntary Action which co-ordinated opinions, formulated proposals and suggested amendments throughout the process. The final document (*Northern Ireland Structural Funds Plan, 1994-1999*) shows how much policy space has been created in Northern Ireland in relation to the advancement of social policy through the European Structural Funds. Although the document stresses the belief that economic revitalization should be the predominant factor in meeting the needs of all the community, its strategic aim is promotion of 'social and economic cohesion both within Northern Ireland and relative to other regions of the European Community' (DFP, 1993, p. 68). Furthermore it acknowledges that targeting social need should form part of the priorities for structural fund spending to address socio-economic differentials between Northern Ireland's communities (p. 87). The Plan goes so far as to suffix its strategic aims with French translations e.g.: 'Internal Cohesion' (*Stabilité à l'intérieur.*)

The policy space with regard to social policy results from a number of factors. The following list is not in order of importance. It is widely agreed that economic policies and priorities are inadequate and have failed. Northern Ireland 'achieved' the GDP level to allow it, as of right, to be an Objective One region, with its GDP falling to 74.3 per cent of the European Community average in 1990. A further fact is the increasing maturity of the civil service in dealing with Europe. There has been a steady stream of Northern Ireland civil servants on secondment to Brussels and locally-based civil servants have had more dealings with the Community. Information flow has improved with a number of agencies now providing information on European issues. In particular the opening of the Northern Ireland Centre in Brussels has increased awareness of the opportunities Europe offers and has lent the technical expertise to realise these possibilities. Furthermore, it has become increasingly acceptable to policy makers that European Community funds should be used to advance social policies where they contribute to the advancement of the government's objective of welfare pluralism.

European programme funding and the voluntary and community sectors

The democratic deficit in Northern Ireland provides the non-governmental sector with a prominent role in the delivery and evaluation of social policy. Local authorities have a few minimal powers as most of their functions have been given to central government and to quangos. They have not been active in responding to matters of policy over which they have little influence. Non-governmental agencies, however, have specific interests which they have a duty to protect and, by developing European networks and alliances, they have sought to influence policy on their members' behalf. The voluntary and community sectors have played leading roles in a number of European networks on women's, rural and poverty issues amongst others and have developed a rapport with senior Commission officials, not least when Jacques Delors met with representatives from the sector on a visit to Northern Ireland in 1993. Through these networks and contacts their representatives have been able to highlight positive aspects of Community programmes and also to raise concerns over the ways in which other Community policies, or lack of them, have created, or have led to, serious disadvantages for socially excluded groups. The Commission, and in particular its president, share some of these concerns, particularly in relation to the onset of an unfettered single market with few regulatory controls. However, the Commission is limited in its competence to deal with many areas of social policy. Indeed during the 1980s Community expenditure on social policies accounted for 5 per cent of its total spending (Hitiris, 1991, p. 257) compared to 60 per cent on agriculture (Hitiris, 1991, p. 83). The scope for policies to be introduced which would run counter to the free market ethos of the single market is limited. Because the United Kingdom has opted out of the Social Chapter the potential for the Community's social dimension to impact in Northern Ireland, apart from its Structural Fund commitments, is further reduced.

The national policy environment in the United Kingdom has not encouraged voluntary and community groups to benefit from European funding. Even when programmes to address social need have been negotiated, there have been difficulties with their implementation. Research carried out into the barriers which community groups face in accessing European Community funds, (Mallaghan, 1994) has highlighted some areas of difficulty. To access European funds, groups need to have considerable knowledge both of the Commission's priorities for the use of its funds and/or of the programmes which they operate. They also need to know how the United Kingdom

Government intends to use these funds in Northern Ireland in furtherance of its own policy. They then often have to persuade local officials, many of whom have no knowledge of European Community funds, to provide matching resources for a project and to guarantee that, should the project fail, they will repay the Commission the money that it invested. Even for groups which reach this stage there are still considerable problems such as cash-flow and accounting procedures. Payment on projects is sometimes delayed and groups have to be able to cope with cash-flow difficulties and to have complex arrangements for allocation of costs to meet the accounting requirements of both the European Community and the matching funder. Target outputs have to be met for specific periods. These are based, not on perceived need, but on the evaluation, or accounting requirement, of the funding programme. Transnational partners sometimes have to be found, often from other Objective One regions, with complementary programmes which allow for an exchange of participants and expertise. If the evaluation or accounts of their transnational partner are deficient then the local group must quickly find new partners or face closure.

The Commission has been aware that all this was a daunting task and has allocated a special pool to provide 'technical assistance' to those trying to access its funds. However, during the last round of Structural Funds, the United Kingdom Government was reluctant to make these funds directly available to groups, arguing that money spent on this would reduce sums available for the actual running of projects (Mallaghan, 1994).

Those obstacles have resulted in smaller and medium-sized groups having considerable difficulty in accessing funds. Some have come to believe that groups which had established contacts in Europe had an inside track to funds and that those in receipt of one type of Community funding had the best chances of drawing on other programmes. Indeed this was the case. As with any sphere of business, once groups had established a track record of being able to handle the complexity of the programmes, had networked with other projects in other member states and had made contact with key officials, new opportunities did occur. Simply by being on certain mailing lists, groups already operating in Europe received unsolicited offers to become transnational partners for projects. The view that 'to those that have shall be given' was at odds with the message the Commission wished to present when it stressed the central community development concepts of participation and partnership. The result was 'an atmosphere of frustration and unrealised expectations' (CDRG, 1991, p. 44).

These practical problems which influenced the spending of the 1989-1993 funds were documented and sent both to the Commission and to the Northern Ireland Government. The situation for the next spending period, 1994-1999, may improve. The *Structural Funds Plan* for this period has written into it many technical assistance measures and an assurance that there will be 'adequate' advertising of programmes (DFP, 1993, p. 171). Also of great significance has been the establishment of a European Affairs Unit for the voluntary sector based in the Northern Ireland Council for Voluntary Action (NICVA). Financial help for groups at the early stage of project planning would contribute positively to the quality and quantity of schemes operating under the Structural Funds.

The technical assistance is of little benefit if the policy environment is totally unsympathetic. Consultation for the 1989-1993 plan was poor, resulting in limited opportunities for groups to find points of contact between Community Programmes, the Structural Funds framework for Northern Ireland and the social needs of people in their areas. The 1994-1999 plan has allowed for a much better consultation. Its strategic objective of internal cohesion, the strategic theme of community infrastructure and the naming of community and voluntary groups as financial beneficiaries for many of its measures, suggest that NGOs should benefit to a greater degree from this round of funds and that they will not have to bend proposals to meet the programme's criteria rather than their community's actual needs.

With a better policy environment, clearer information and better technical assistance the central question is the level of overall funds that the sector will be able to access. Initial figures suggest that over £250 million will be available in various forms for human resource initiatives from which the sector could benefit. However, in the last round of funds voluntary sector expenditure of the European Social Fund accounted for only 7.5 per cent of spending with the vast majority being spent by government itself. It should also be remembered that public sector expenditure is some £8 billion per annum in Northern Ireland, with £3 billion as a subvention from the United Kingdom treasury in contrast to the £1 billion from Europe over six years. As the voluntary and community sectors have in the past tried to tap European Community funding programmes, there may now exist a danger that spending on voluntary and community priorities will increasingly only be available within this limited European funding framework. However, this fear would overlook the priority that government accords to the development of the voluntary and community sector, and the significant future role that government sees for the voluntary sector in particular. The availability of European funding at this time of public expenditure stringency is expedient.

Subsidiarity

Long before nationalists started to use the concept of subsidiarity as a means to try and limit the powers of the Commission, Jacques Delors had been advocating its use so that decisions would be made as close as possible to the people. Expenditure by voluntary and community organizations fulfils this principle. By arising out of the communities they represent the organizations are well placed to identify needs and gaps in provision. The Commission can be reasonably certain that resources allocated to target needs are being delivered to those sections of society who are least benefiting from the single market, such as the socially excluded. There has been criticism that European Structural Funds have not filtered through to these groups and that it is the better-off who benefit most from European Community programme expenditures (Community Workers' Co-op, 1992).

As financial beneficiaries in the 1994-1999 spending round, voluntary and community organizations will be able to offer programmes in the fields of employment, training, volunteering, urban and rural redevelopment, disability, pre-vocational education, youth work, community relations, and local economic development, targeting social need and developing community infrastructure. They may wish to be directly involved in the administration of the programmes themselves, in the way that the National Council for Voluntary Organisations ran the English European Social Fund programme for voluntary sector interests. Indeed after some of the difficulties experienced in accessing European Community funds, particularly the Commission's 'Community Initiatives', it is possible that, if the sector had control of budgets, with its first-hand knowledge it could target and deliver funds to best meet needs, to encourage innovation and to promote a greater sense of local control.

The greater role for the voluntary and community sector and the recognition given in the current plan to community development, in a wider sense than just community relations, (on which the last plan focused), are reflected in government's creation of a Voluntary Activity Unit and Community Development Section within the Department of Health and Social Services. It is thought likely that these bodies will have access to the Structural Funds to meet likely commitments on 'targeting social need' although this theme is required to run across all departments and not only in relation to European funded programmes. Many reasons can be given for this change in emphasis in government policy. The failure of the enterprise initiatives to deliver economic growth or reduce community differentials; lobbying by the Community Development Review Group for greater recognition of community development as a positive force; and the effective response by the voluntary and community sector to the draft 1994-1999 CSF all played a part. Government has not been responsive to similar pressures in the past and personnel changes amongst Northern Ireland ministers alone cannot fully account for the policy shift on community development and the recognition that the economic model is not working. But there is a growing recognition that concepts such as partnership and participation (which are central to many of the innovatory measures the European Community funds promote) have a very real role to play in the government's impetus towards welfare pluralism and citizen consumerism and that they bypass traditional modes of contact between the citizen and the state.

The new European approach to social policy contains many of the pluralist concepts that the United Kingdom is keen to introduce into its own social welfare system. Government has failed to recognize, or has chosen for political reasons to play down, these similarities. Much of the debate on social policy in the European Community has focused on issues of industrial citizenship. There has been much less debate on the models of welfare adopted by other member states which have influenced the Commission's social policy proposals.

Community social policies have been regarded in the United Kingdom as socialist-inspired and over regulatory and have often been portrayed in a negative light. Professor Robert Pinker (1991, p. 280) considers the differing views of the role of the state which mirror the positions on the social dimension of the United Kingdom Government and of the European Commission:

> Neo-liberals who see negative liberty as sufficient in itself view almost all forms of statutory welfare as a threat to freedom, and dismiss the concept of social justice as lacking in specificity and moral authority. Collectivist advocates of positive liberty link freedom to act with ability to act and link this ability in turn with rights and access to certain basic social services.

Recent neo-liberal United Kingdom governments have branded statutory welfare as a threat to freedom and have tarred the European Community's social dimension with the collectivist brush. Solidarity, the fundamental concept underpinning the social dimension, is interpreted as Marxist. In fact the original six members, who have most influenced the Community's social dimension, have had mixed economies of welfare. The rhetoric of a United Kingdom at odds with European Community social policy, belies the fact that since 1979 British social policies have been moving closer to the pluralist models of continental Europe, as the Conservative Government has actively encouraged the growth of occupational, private and voluntary sectors as potential alternatives to statutory provision (Pinker, 1991, p. 295).

The continental countries have had forty years to develop this pluralistic system. This has allowed for debate and for models of good practice to develop in relation to appropriate roles and responsibilities of central and local government, and voluntary organizations, in service provision. Paradoxically in the United Kingdom the radical pace of change has resulted in more power being concentrated in the hands of central government. This sits uneasily with the concept of subsidiarity, as understood by the Commission, as meaning that decisions should be taken as closely as possible to the people, and it helps explain why the United Kingdom has chosen to interpret it as minimum interference from the centre.

Robert Pinker (1991, p. 297) goes on to discuss the possible outcome of the social policy debate for the Community and Britain:

> The rest of Europe seems to have settled for a middle-ground version of pluralism in which the state continues to play a major role either directly or indirectly. It remains to be seen whether British social policy continues to move towards a more radical model of pluralism in which privatisation programmes reduce the role of the government to a residual status, despite the evidence of electoral resistance to these objectives.

The question for the voluntary and community sector must be whether it wants, and is ready, to act as an agent for advancing welfare pluralism, particularly with the government advocating its radical implementation. The sector has not had forty years to sort out roles and responsibilities. Furthermore, it becomes increasingly difficult to define what government is and where its policies reside, and consequently to decide the nature of non-government organizations and where their responsibilities end and government's responsibility begins. For example are housing associations non-government bodies? Their expenditure accounts for more than one third of the total expenditure on the voluntary sector in Northern Ireland, but their function is clearly to meet needs previously met directly by government. What is the status of local development or rural partnerships, made up from local community workers, local business people, and representatives of central and local government? The current European Community Support Framework will be used to create more of these sorts of bodies. Access to Community resources will encourage the voluntary and community sector to develop activities and programmes which may conflict with roles occupied by the civil service, by local authorities or area boards, particularly in the field of training. There is a very real danger that, unless the sector develops only in areas of unmet need, it will merely replace services currently offered by government, thereby undermining the additionality principle. The British Government has come under constant attack over the additionality principle from Commission officials.

Government can of course argue that it is advancing programmes which aim to bring spending closer to the consumer of social goods and is thereby increasing his or her control over them in line with the philosophy of the Citizens' Charter. Although this would find some agreement among those advocating greater citizens' control over decision making, its consumerist bias does not have a rights base and so does not guarantee minimum or equitable distribution of services.

Accountability

Accountability is closely linked with the concept of democratic control. In Northern Ireland there is little democratic control or accountability in relation to central government and its non-departmental agencies. There is also little democratic control over the Commission and there is no role either for elected local representatives. This results in part from the fact that national governments were unwilling to cede their sovereignty to the European Parliament to oversee the Commission. Voluntary and community organizations have, therefore, a key role to play in commenting on Community policy and on the way its programmes operate. However, these organizations are also main beneficiaries of European money and are certain to become increasingly dependent on Community funds. Furthermore, they are also extremely diverse and have no elected forum for developing responses to European issues. The European Affairs Committee of the Voluntary Sector reports back to NICVA Executive which has a representative function for the sectors and this provides a means for channelling the views of voluntary and community organizations to Europe and to the government. In theory the differing policy outlook of the government, the Commission and the sector should create a dynamic tension which may ensure critical assessment of policies and spending. However, the growing emphasis on partnership must call into question the rigour of this as an evaluation process. Voluntary and community organizations were represented on only a few, relatively minor, committees during the period of the 1989-1993 Structural Funds. By contrast, the plan for the 1994-1999 period (DFP, 1993) calls for twice yearly meetings of a formal body, the Northern Ireland Community Support Framework Monitoring Committee, (NI SCFMC) and for the creation of sub-committees for each of the seven sectoral programmes. The Monitoring Committee will have an important role to play in ensuring the effective implementation of the Community Support Framework. The main part of its membership will be drawn from Northern Ireland government departments but one third of its members will represent the voluntary and community sector. This arrangement will guarantee consultation and communication but it remains to be seen how relationships between the two sides develop.

What is lacking is a more developed role for local representatives. There is growing scepticism about politics, and party politics in particular, and one may observe some movement away from politics as the main arbiter of power.

The adversarial model is still the principal means for the scrutiny of policies, for proffering alternatives for the legitimization of policy through universal suffrage and of the subsequent use of power. In the past abuse of these powers has led to local elected representatives in Northern Ireland having their responsibilities curtailed. This puts Northern Ireland in a somewhat unique position within the European Community, since normally much of the contact between the Commission and local areas is through elected local authorities who act as the legitimate brokers of power and in furtherance of the subsidiarity principle.

The new Structural Funds arrangements will allow possibilities for this policy vacuum to be filled. Local authorities now have the powers to raise two pence in the pound on local rates to support economic development. This will raise relatively small sums but has the potential to create a multiplier effect, not only by drawing in additional resources but also in instilling among policy makers and administrators the confidence to play a significant role in local regeneration in similar ways to that already undertaken by local authorities in other Community countries. The naming of local councils as financial beneficiaries in many sections of the *Structural Funds* document would indicate that the time is ripe for them to develop innovative schemes to benefit their communities. The creation of the Community's new Committee of the Regions should help to strengthen their position within the overall Community framework, giving them an avenue for formal representation at its heart. By acting in partnership, local councils and the voluntary and community sectors could co-operate fully to use Europe's potential as a vehicle for change. Local government has elected authority, while the voluntary and community sectors have firsthand assessment of community need, and policy and administrative expertise on the functioning of European institutions.

Another relationship which has the potential to advance social policy in the European arena is that of the voluntary sector and the trade unions. In the Treaty of Rome it was always envisaged that social partners would play an important role in influencing Community policies. The social partners were to be drawn from both sides of industry and from non-governmental organizations. However, because social policy was first developed mainly in terms of industrial citizenship, the social partnership was seen primarily in terms of the trade unions and the employers' organizations. Now however, the non-governmental sector is being given the renewed regard within Europe which was initially intended. This opens up scope for joint efforts between the voluntary and community sectors and trade unionists to advance out of the social policy vacuum that was a feature of the Community's development in the eighties.

To make an alliance effective the issue of welfare pluralism will have to be addressed. Welfare pluralism threatens traditional models of employment through competitive tendering leading to privatization and in turn to the introduction of lower pay and 'atypical' working, such as part-time and temporary contracts which undermine workers' rights. The Commission is addressing these issues and indeed European Directives drafted in the seventies are being used to oppose the introduction of competitive tendering in public services in the United Kingdom.

The difficulty for the voluntary sector is that, while it would in general be supportive of efforts to ensure that decent wages and conditions are given to those who are moving from state services to private sector providers, it itself is increasingly competing for government contracts. Voluntary sector management committees are becoming the employers of staff who, in the past, would have worked directly for local or central government. As public expenditure is squeezed to reduce the cost of the welfare state, voluntary sector employers will come under increasing pressure to deliver contract targets on declining budgets. Inevitably this will lead to conflict with unionized workforces who would expect the voluntary sector, with its strong value base, to offer the terms and conditions that workers would have had if they had been employed by a statutory agency. Voluntary agencies may be unable to get government departments to agree that contract costs should allow them to employ people in line with European standards, if they exceed those set by national legislation. If so, it will be difficult to meet these standards. The position will be particularly severe for voluntary sector groups who are competing against private sector firms, whose key aim is profit. However much they support in principle Europe's attempts to advance workers' interests, as contractors retained by a government hostile to the Social Chapter, they will attract little sympathy, and fewer contracts, if they try to introduce good practice based on European standards. The result may be that what would once have been regarded as a natural alliance may now be difficult to forge. The rapid shift to welfare pluralism in the United Kingdom will put further stress on the relationship. The shared value of solidarity will need to be negotiated so that it can embrace corporatism and self-help.

Conclusion

Government policy aims to centralize policy control while encouraging diversity in provision. It promotes altruistic responses to social need but has no commitment to generalizing good practice to the point where it becomes a state responsibility. Partnership is encouraged at local level, particularly in the field of economic regeneration, as a feasible response to the ailments of declining areas. However, the partnership principle is not extended to the formulation of the policies which will determine the economic environment in which these local responses will operate, even though this will be the determining factor in their potential for success. Europe will continue to emphasise the concept of partnership in relation to the use of its funds. However, the degree to which this can impact on national policy and priorities will be limited mainly to flexibility in the delivery of social goods.

Operating in this environment it will be essential that all those committed to addressing social exclusion co-operate to the full. In the absence of an effective means in the domestic arena, the European setting offers perhaps the best mechanism to challenge some of the United Kingdom Government's ideology and social policies.

Individual groups, unions or councils may be looking after the needs of their particular area and may believe, perhaps with some justification, that this will lead to incremental change in policy. However this will never build an alternative paradigm. Rather it will tend to reinforce the belief that individualistic responses can effectively fill the needs gaps created by insensitive policies. A forthcoming green paper on the future of the Community's social policy should address social exclusion by setting out a clear statement of rights on what constitutes a minimum standard of life and on the implications this has for the supply and quality of services for all the Community's citizens. While respecting the subsidiarity principle, the Community needs the ability to ensure that any basic rights standard is applied for all its citizens if social dumping is to be avoided. The voluntary and community sectors will be well placed to monitor if welfare pluralism is causing some groups to fall below these standards and, in turn, to lobby for the Community to act if, and when, this occurs.

References

Brewster, C. & Teague, P. (1989), *European Community Social Policy: its Impact on the United Kingdom,* Institute of Personnel Management, London.

Community Development Review Group (1991), *Funding for Community and Voluntary Groups in Northern Ireland,* Community Development Review Group/Workers Educational Association, Belfast.

Community Workers Co-op (1992), *Reform of the Structural Funds,* Dublin.

Department of Finance and Personnel (1993), *Northern Ireland Structural Funds Plan 1994-1999,* HMSO, Belfast.

Hitiris, T. (1991), *European Community Economics,* 2nd edn, Harvester Wheatsheaf, Hemel Hempstead.

Jackson, P. (1992), 'A social Europe?', *Poverty Today,* no. 18, July/September.

Mallaghan, A. [1994], *European Funding: a Game of Snakes and Ladders,* Community Technical Aid (NI), Belfast. [Forthcoming]

Pinker, Robert (1991), in Wilson, T. & Wilson, D. (eds), *The State and Social Welfare,* Longman, Harlow.

Spicker, Paul (1991), 'Solidarity' in Room, G. (ed.), *Towards a European Welfare State?,* SAUS, Bristol.

Tsiakalos, G. (1992), 'Combating Social Exclusion, Fostering Integration' in *Conference Papers 2-3 April 1992,* Brussels Commission of the European Communities, Brussels.

TUC (1992), *Unions after Maastricht,* Trades Union Congress, London.

5 Managing community relations and conflict: voluntary organizations and government and the search for peace

Mari Fitzduff

Following the reemergence of sectarian violence in 1969 in Northern Ireland and particularly in the aftermath of the riots in Belfast and Derry in August 1969, the Labour British Home Secretary, James Callaghan announced the establishment of a Ministry for Community Relations and a Community Relations Commission (Community Relations Act, 1969). Thus began the history of the involvement of the British Government in attempts to foster improved community relations between the two major religio/politico communities in Northern Ireland.

This chapter looks at that history which has not always been one of co-operation and has, at different times, suffered from confusion, open rivalry, and, for many years, from indifferent neglect. It also asks how possible it is for a government, which is seen by many as a part of the problem, to be effectively involved in promoting the work of reconciliation. It looks at the role of the voluntary sector in assisting the development of community relations work, and the limitations for it in undertaking such development.

Community Relations Ministry and Commission 1969-75

The Ministry of Community Relations was the first organization to be established in the wake of Callaghan's visit to Northern Ireland in August 1969. It was charged with the promotion of policies which would improve community relations. It was also made responsible for administering a major financial programme of social intervention, i.e. making money available to statutory bodies and voluntary organizations (including community groups) for what were considered to be worthwhile projects. The Ministry was also given responsibility for financing the activities of the Community Relations Commission.

The Community Relations Commission was established about a month after the establishment of the Ministry and was charged with the promotion of activities relevant to the field of community relations. The terms of reference for the Commission were almost identical to those of the Race Relations Board of Great Britain (Race Relations Act, 1968). It was to be concerned with promoting harmonious community relations through various programmes, advising the minister on community relations issues and carrying out research that was deemed relevant to its objectives.

In approaching its task of promoting community relations, the Commission decided to adopt as its main strategy the initiation of local community development programmes across Northern Ireland. Its analysis of this as the preferred approach was based on the belief that communities which lacked self-confidence were less likely to relate unaggressively to one another. Furthermore, it believed that the problem, particularly for people in more socially marginalized communities, of relating to the people/structures of power, contributed to feelings of helplessness and resentment which in turn contributed to community tensions. The Commission's belief was that the process of community development, i.e. empowering people in communities to participate in decision-making about issues and structures affecting their lives, could help address these problems, and thus assist in resolving existing and developing conflicts (Hayes, 1992).

Community development as a philosophy and in practice was an approach which was then, in the late sixties, becoming popular as a method of assisting development in some Third World countries, and it was one in which the first director of the Commission had been involved. The decision to use it to assist the management of a situation which appeared to be developing into a major religio/politico conflict was however both unique and relatively untested.

The Commission subsequently channelled most of its resources into this oblique approach, although in addition it did allocate some of its resources to deliberately bringing people together from across the religio/politico divide. The latter was done through various conferences, some school programmes, and through some set-pieces of reconciliation work, which included on a few occasions bringing together some republicans and loyalists who were active in the conflict. The Council also conducted various research programmes through which it hoped to inform its programmes and those of the Ministry.

Almost from the beginning the problematic nature of the relationship between the Ministry and the Commission was evident. While the Ministry was given the power to define the development of policy on community relations, there is little extant evidence to show that it actually took this role

64

seriously. In addition, the Ministry appears to have failed to engage with the Commission in developing policy on agreed approaches to the problems of a community which was becoming more divided and violent at an alarming rate.[1] Despite the intended advisory role of the Commission, it was rarely consulted.

> Apart from the utterances of some of its Ministers it [the Ministry] never indicated its strategy, it never defined its objectives, and it never took anyone into its confidence regarding what it was trying to do (Griffiths, 1974, p. 16).

The Ministry's intended policy development role appears to have been abrogated almost totally in favour of its two other roles, i.e. its assumption of responsibility for the administration of the Social Needs programme, and for the financial affairs of the Commission. Undaunted by its own lack of clear policy, it continued to retain considerable control over the resources of the Commission, maintaining a hold over even minor expenditure which ensured that the Commission felt extremely limited in developing its programmes.

In the years of their existence, the Ministry and the Commission never appear to have been able to develop any adequate *modus vivendi* about policy or resource allocation. There appeared to be no agreement between them about the causes of the conflict nor about effective and appropriate approaches to managing it. The Ministry eventually admitted to scepticism about the community development approach of the Commission and to suspicion about the possible radical nature of some of those programmes which it saw as threatening in that they assisted communities to question the propriety of some existing statutory and departmental decisions.

The Commission for its part (in the words of its then director) claimed that:

> The Ministry began to implement a policy of choking off the supply lines so as to hinder the development of the Commission whilst at the same time building up the strength of its own empire by taking advantage of every opportunity open to it (Griffiths, 1974, p. 13).

In the event, both the Ministry and the Commission had a short life, the shortness assisted no doubt by the continuing acrimony between them. A proposal to the Ministry for a substantial expansion of the community development programme of the Commission was dismissed, not surprisingly in view of the Ministry's scepticism and suspicions about the use of community development. The chairman of the Commission subsequently resigned, and this was followed a few months later by the resignation of the director, in April 1972.

The Commission itself survived until the Sunningdale Agreement in April 1974, when it was abolished by the newly formed Assembly for Northern

Ireland as one of the first acts by the incoming Minister for Community Relations Mr. Ivan Cooper (NI Assembly, 1974). The main reason generally suggested for such a decision was that the Ministry (and in particular the civil servants servicing it) was not alone in becoming increasingly suspicious of the possible radical nature of some of the Commission programmes whose outcomes they felt to be uncertain or possibly counter-productive (Hayes, 1972). The newly elected politicians of the power-sharing executive were also unsure as to the best use of such community development programmes, becoming increasingly convinced that they as elected representatives should shoulder the major responsibility for hearing people's concerns, and translating such concerns into structural action, without the use of what they saw as an independent body. Hence the statement made by Ivan Cooper in abolishing the Commission, that it had become an impediment to the process of communication between government and people and that, while it might have been needed under a Unionist controlled government, now that a power-sharing executive had been achieved, such a body was no longer necessary (NI Assembly, 1974).

Ironically, one month later, on 28 May, the power-sharing executive was brought down by a strike by Ulster loyalists who disagreed with the inclusion of a Council of Ireland as part of the legislation which set it up. In the following year the Community Relations Commission was formally abolished (Community Relations Amendment, 1975) and thus came to an end the first attempt by the British Government to set up an agency to address community relations in Northern Ireland.

Assessments of the success or otherwise of these first government attempts at promoting community relations vary. There appears to be agreement that the process of community development remains an important method of facilitating participation between government and communities. This belief has continued to underpin many programmes initiated since that time which concentrate on local community involvement in approaches to addressing social need. Organizations and programmes now currently endorsing and resourcing this approach include the Northern Ireland Voluntary Trust and the various government initiatives such as Belfast and Foyle Action Teams and Making Belfast Work.

Furthermore, the statement by the government, in February 1993 (DHSS, 1993), endorsing the principles of a community development approach and suggesting their use by all government departments when developing their programmes, appears to show that government had finally accepted the type of process initially highlighted, and first developed, by the Commission.

However, the success of community development in contributing to an improvement in community relations, still remains a matter open to question and led to much debate particularly in the early years of the 1990s (Fitzduff,

1989a). The thesis that it can assist such an improvement is now, however, receiving some strong endorsement from several recent studies, and in particular the evaluation of the District Council Community Relations programmes set up in 1990. This evaluation is eliciting some clear evidence which suggests that community relations work, in all of its forms, is more effectively developed where existing community development programmes are flourishing (Knox & Hayes, 1993).

The hiatus years 1975-86

The demise of the Community Relations Commission was followed by over a decade of relative neglect by the government of community relations work. After the collapse of the Assembly, the order which officially abolished the Commission also settled responsibility for community relations within Northern Ireland on the Department of Education which was formally charged with 'formulating and sponsoring policies for the improvement of community relations in Northern Ireland'.

Although the Department appears to have failed to come up with any discernible overall policies or strategies to ensure the effectiveness of the work, it did carry out its funding responsibility from 1974 to 1990 by continuing to resource the few existing voluntary agencies concentrating on community relations work. These included such organizations as Corrymeela and the Central Churches Coordinating Committee. By 1986 this funding was running at approximately £400,000 per annum (Frazer & Fitzduff, 1986). In addition, it resourced secondments for training teachers to work in community relations, as well as a variety of educational and holiday programmes to facilitate contacts among children and young people.

In 1976, district councils (financed by the Department of Education) were charged by government with responsibility for supporting and encouraging community groups, including groups of a community relations nature. This was to be done through the development of community services departments and the hiring of community service officers. Because of the limited availability of resources, much of which went on funding community centres, and the sensitive nature of the work itself which was either threatening or divisive to district councils, most of which were rent by sectarian tensions, few district councils made any effort to develop their remit in community relations.

An exception to this was a programme undertaken by Belfast City Council in 1983. The Council was offered an allocation of £100,000 per annum for three years to be spent on improving community relations. This became known as the Belfast Areas of Need (Community Relations) programme. An assessment of the scheme showed that there were different opinions about what the work should entail, and about what work was effective. The chief result of the scheme was a general increase in support for the idea of improving community relations, although most people involved in the scheme felt that there was a lack of adequate theory or practice to fulfil its objectives effectively (Darby et al., 1986).

Renewal of interest in community relations work

The mid-eighties saw some signs that the government might again be considering addressing more seriously the more effective development of community relations work. In 1986 an internal DENI report[2] looked again at the possible usefulness of further developing community relations work. Around the same time, in 1985, SACHR undertook to commission a report on the present state of the work, and its potential for future development (Frazer & Fitzduff, 1986).

The latter reported on the underresourced, underdeveloped and unstrategic nature of much of the work. It also outlined the beginnings of a theoretical framework for its development, and suggested some practical structures that should be considered if the government intended to take the work seriously. Among these suggestions were the creation of a specialist community relations unit within the Secretary of State's office and the creation of an independent community relations body.

The suggested functions for the specialist community relations unit included advising the Secretary of State and other ministers on all aspects of promoting better community relations; working to eliminate discrimination; ensuring that all government policies, e.g. in housing, health, industry, economic development, and education, were geared to improving community relations; and ensuring that adequate funding was made available for the further development of the work.

The central functions suggested for the independent agency were that it should ensure a focal point for all organizations active in the field of community relations; develop training in community relations work; increase public awareness of the need for the work at all levels within Northern Ireland; and give advice to government, in particular through the proposed government unit.

The report suggested that there was a need for positive support from government in promoting such work at all levels, and not just at the voluntary sector level. It suggested that the major facilitative structures for or against such work were government departments themselves. It hence suggested that any government unit should be located centrally, rather than in a separate ministry, because of a conviction that locating it within a particular ministry could leave it marginalized, rather than at the centre of the policymaking of all departments.

In the event, both major suggestions of the report were implemented. In 1987, the Central Community Relations Unit (CCRU) was set up, responsible to the Central Secretariat and funded through the Department of Finance and Personnel. Although it received an overall remit for the development of community relations work, the Department of Education remained responsible for the development of community relations work with young people and children.

The newly formed CCRU immediately started a consultative process to assess what its strategic approach should be in developing community relations work. It consulted with a wide range of statutory bodies, particularly with those who had been involved in community relations work. By the time they began their consultation there was already in existence an embryo group which was lobbying for a more co-ordinated approach to community relations work. This group had members drawn from some of the varied reconciliation bodies who were concerned about the lack of any focus for such groups. In addition, between 1988 and 1989 CCRU drew together a wide ranging group of people, not only from the reconciliation sector, but also from the wider voluntary sector, and from district councils, trade unions, and business sectors to talk through some possibilities for a new external agency. This group became the major mechanism through which such an independent agency, the Community Relations Council (CRC) was eventually developed.

During the first few years of its existence, the CCRU also began seriously to address the theme, parallel to that of community relations, of cultural traditions and diversity. It concentrated on exploring whether such concepts could be reframed so that diversity could be acknowledged as a source of richness rather than being necessarily divisive. The theme was addressed in conjunction with senior managers in the cultural field - in museums, in the media, in publishing, and in educational circles generally - and gradually developed into a body which became known as the Cultural Traditions Group. These discussions were continued through a variety of large conferences. The first of these, called Varieties of Irishness, was held in Coleraine in 1989, and was followed by several others addressing the theme of diversity. The Cultural Traditions Group was also interested in ensuring that the Irish language should be seen as a cultural right, and not one necessarily tied to those who sought a particular political option.

In setting up the Council, preference was shown by the minister of the time for an organization that could encompass the two parallel themes of community relations and cultural traditions work. Such a marriage was not to prove to be a problem, as most people concerned with such a development became convinced of the value of cultural traditions work as an effective strand of community relations work, and it only remained for some minor problems of structure, style and membership to be addressed.

Eventually, in January 1990, the CRC was inaugurated. Its chairman was Dr James Hawthorne, a former controller of the BBC who had previously been chairman of the Cultural Traditions Group, and who agreed to embrace the new and wider task of chairing the CRC. The members of the Council were drawn from the statutory, private, voluntary and community sectors and one third of them were appointed by the minister.

Community relations 1990-94

The Community Relations Council had, at the time of writing, been in existence for four years. It claims its work to be 'pre-political' work, i.e. aimed at improving understanding, respect and co-operation between communities in order to achieve a just and sustainable constitutional solution to the Northern Ireland conflict. It also recognizes that the work of community relations is only one aspect of the necessary approaches to a conflict that is about many needs, e.g. community development work aimed at ensuring confident and capable community leadership, impartial security, containment of paramilitary violence and progressive political activity (CRC, 1991).

In drawing up its initial strategic plan the Council deliberately decided not to concentrate on developing more 'reconciliation' groups, or to depend upon the work of such existing groups. While recognising the valuable, and often courageous, work undertaken by many of them, the CRC was not convinced that work through such agencies could reach the wide spectrum of people necessary to ensure the effectiveness of its programmes. It therefore expanded its remit to include that of persuading groups who had not previously acknowledged or developed their capacity to assist in improving community relations, to address its development through additions to their ongoing policies and programmes, including training for such work. These groups have included work, business, church and sports groups, many groups from the voluntary and community sector, health and education boards, etc. It has also co-operated with a variety of other significant groups who have substantially been addressing community relations/anti-sectarian issues under their own auspices, e.g. the trade unions and bodies such as the Workers Educational Association who have appointed full-time community relations workers.

The CRC also decided to take a much more focused community relations approach than the first Commission. Building upon an initial and much expanded typology for such work (Fitzduff, 1989b) enabled it to engage a much wider spectrum of people, including those who had previously been cynical of the 'peace and doves' stereotype attached to the work. It became more possible to build a coalition of people and organizations addressing both the 'softer' issues such as understanding and co-operation, as well as the 'harder' issues of inequality, rights, and political and constitutional differences.

During the four years of its existence, the Council has worked with approximately 1,000 groups, assisting and resourcing their work in community relations (including cultural traditions). It has pursued an extensive programme of conferences, seminars and training workshops. Participants increasingly continue to be drawn from all sectors, and within any workshop addressing sectarianism can be found trade council members, youth sector and church workers, district councillors (from all political parties) ex-paramilitaries, educationalists, and community sector workers of all kinds.

Several other initiatives have also greatly helped the overall development of community development work. The work of the Department of Education has helped to ensure that programmes within schools designed to increase understanding among children and young people (including substantial contact programmes) are now part of every schoolchild's curriculum. A substantial European funded programme (under the auspices of CCRU) has ensured that there are now many more venues available for such contact work and many of the existing reconciliation bodies are now much better resourced, and therefore able to address their goals more effectively.

In addition, a district council community relations programme begun in the 1990s means that every district council now has at least one full-time community relations worker addressing needs in its area. As each of these programmes has had to ensure an overall commitment from what are often very divided councils, their very existence has marked a substantial sign of progress in the field.

While much remains to be done, the indications overall for the possible success of the work appear to be positive. Despite evidence that segregating patterns of living are still continuing, and that violence is still being used to achieve political leverage, there are some pointers that the work of many bodies now involved in community relations is bearing some useful fruit. Among the most significant of these are the open and committed involvement now of many major institutions to anti-sectarian work; the substantial development of mutual understanding programmes in schools, and the existence of twenty-one integrated schools most of which have developed in the last four years; the much more vigorous involvement of the churches in community relations work; the increasing ability for cultural traditions work to encompass respect for a plurality of traditions including the Irish language, support for which has become much less contentious; the increased capacity for local councils to co-operate; and increased cross-community cohesion in rejecting violent actions by the paramilitaries.

In addition, the recent British *Social Attitudes Survey* for Northern Ireland shows that three times as many people now - as opposed to three years ago - believe that relationships between communities are indeed improving (Stringer & Robinson, 1993). It is agreed, however, that whether such improvement can impact upon the use of violence by a tiny minority, or can help in achieving a sustainable political solution remains open to question.

Contested government - a positive role in community relations?

Most community relations work in Northern Ireland is now funded by the British Government and the European Community and the question of whether or not there can be a positive role for a government in facilitating community relations - particularly a government which is seen by many participants to be a substantial part of the problem - remains a moot one for some people. Agreement or otherwise about such a role for the government will, to a large extent, depend upon how one sees the causes of the conflict. Such an agreement is rarely easy to achieve, however, even by conflict theorists, and is of course much more difficult to achieve on the part of the conflicting protagonists.

In addressing the Northern Ireland problem, two fundamental disagreements about priorities in seeking a resolution to the conflict appear to have dominated, and limited, conflict management. The first is the difference between those parties who see the conflict as the responsibility of an exogenous party, i.e. where blame is placed upon a protagonist who is external to Northern Ireland, and those who see the problem as endogenous, i.e. relating to internal factors between the conflicting parties, and within Northern Ireland itself (Whyte, 1990). The second major difference is between those who see the problem in Northern Ireland as a structural one, i.e. built into the existing constitutional structures, and the discriminatory nature of Northern Ireland itself, and those who see the problem as a psychocultural one, whose solution could be achieved through a transformation of the relationships between the communities.

Both nationalists and unionists have, at varying times and with varying degrees of intensity, blamed external parties for the cause and continuance of the conflict. To many nationalists, the main cause of the conflict in Northern Ireland has been the continuing presence of the British Government in the region. Where nationalist political parties have differed has been in how they are prepared to remove that presence. The SDLP have been resolved on removing it through peaceful, democratic means, and through eventually persuading the Unionist/Protestant community that they should join a united Ireland. Republican paramilitaries on the other hand use violence to persuade the British to leave Northern Ireland. While both sections of nationalists have begun in recent years to accept that a 'Brits out' policy may not be adequate to the complexity of a situation where the majority of the population within the region see themselves as British, for many their essential view of Britain as their protagonist remains, if in some cases somewhat muted, and perhaps increasingly since the Downing Street Declaration of 15 December 1993.[3]

Many unionists also favour an exogenous analysis and see the problem as the continuing desire of the Republic of Ireland to reclaim Northern Ireland as part of its territory. Some unionists also perceive an imperialist agenda on the part of the Roman Catholic Church in Ireland, and thus their main fear remains that of exogenous forces whose agenda they see as being carried out by the IRA, and indeed also in some cases by the SDLP.

However, there is also a school of thought which focuses on endogenous factors as the main problem. While not denying the role of external factors, it sees the main source of the problem as now being the inability of the communities within Northern Ireland to agree among themselves about how to progress with a political solution. For the most part it believes that both the British and Irish Governments will accept whatever is agreed by the communities, and that securing such an agreement should be the prime focus of the work.

Those involved primarily in community relations work have been seen as generally favouring an endogenous emphasis. For the most part they will prioritise work undertaken within and between the major communities in Northern Ireland. They believe that work addressing the ignorance, hostility and prejudice, discrimination and fear existing between communities is necessary before it is possible for communities to discuss and subsequently agree upon contentious subjects including rights, security force policing, issues of equity, and political and constitutional issues. They believe that without such work, these issues cannot be adequately dealt with and will merely continue to cause further contention and violence.

Interpretations of the conflict held by communities will vary according to time and contexts. In 1969 Catholics generally viewed the problem as an internal one i.e. the refusal by the unionists to share power and accord equality to them and, on the whole, they had little problem with the British Government's endorsement of community relations work. Unionists were probably more suspicious of it, sensing that any questioning of the status quo might leave them vulnerable in any changing situation.

However, as it became obvious that on issues of equality - in voting patterns, in housing allocation, and in job allocation - it was going to be difficult for the majority Unionist government to satisfactorily deliver on equity, the framework for interpreting the problem gradually changed. By the mid 1970s the belief that the whole structure of the state would have to shift fundamentally towards a solution that allowed for a further integration between the two parts of the island of Ireland had gained considerable ground among many Catholics. This meant that for them, work that concentrated on Catholic-Protestant relationships was discounted as naïve and insubstantial. Those who continued to beat the little resourced drum of community relations during the latter half of the 1970s and almost the whole of the 1980s were in the main disregarded as naïve. The rise and fall of the Peace People was but a more obvious manifestation of such a dismissal.

But times change, as do interpretations. Now, in the mid 1990s, while both of these exogenous interpretations still hold some sway in some quarters, (i.e. that relationships will only improve after the British have gone, or alternatively only after the IRA campaign has stopped and the nationalists have settled for an agreed internal government), there is an increasing acceptance on all sides of the need to develop internal work.

Several things have helped to ensure such an acceptance. The first has been the obviously changing position of the British Government. This change was substantially signified in the signing of the Anglo-Irish Agreement in 1985. This not only established the right of the Government of the Republic of Ireland to comment on matters pertaining to Northern Ireland, but expressed the willingness of the British Government to withdraw sovereignty when, if ever, the majority in the region so wished. The agreement has been followed through by statements from successive secretaries of state which have confirmed such willingness to leave, subject to the consent of the unionists, claiming an essential lack of national interest for the British Government in remaining in Northern Ireland. This assertion was particularly exemplified in the Downing Street Declaration of December 1993, which reiterated the essential 'neutrality' of the British Government in retaining the Union.

The Irish Government has also now accepted through the declaration that agreement among the peoples of Northern Ireland to any constitutional change is paramount and that work on securing such an agreement should be undertaken. They have said that they have no intention of pursuing any constitutional claim to the region, while retaining the hope that there will eventually be a united Ireland by consent.

Admissions of disinterest by the British Government have essentially changed the perspective for many nationalists, as such admissions suggest that their task should now be to persuade unionists that their place would be better secured in a united Ireland, or variations thereof, rather than to continue in their attempt to persuade the British to go. The arguments now left for some nationalists (some of whom, though by no means all, are still persuaded by the idea of a united Ireland), are about whether the British, having signified their own disinterest, should now force/persuade the unionists to look to a connection with the South for their future.

Perspectives have also fundamentally changed for the unionists. No longer able to rely upon the advocacy of the British Government in retaining the Union (though such connection is guaranteed as long as the majority so wish) they are struggling to come to terms with not just the internal need to fundamentally reassess their relationships *vis-à-vis* sharing power with the ever growing nationalist population[4] but also their relationships with the much feared Republic of Ireland.

The changing perspective and agendas of both communities, therefore, increasingly point to the work that needs to be done between them in coming to terms with their differing aspirations.

In addition to the substantial reframing of the problem that has occurred for nationalists and unionists alike over the past few years, and which may prove to have helped an increasing endorsement of the process work involved in community relations, there has been a strategic reassessment of what can and should be delivered through such work, but perhaps even more importantly what needs to be delivered in parallel to such work.

By the late 1980s, two decades after the start of the troubles in 1969, the Northern Ireland conflict was beginning to be seen as not one problem, but a series of problems, demanding a variety of approaches and solutions (Fitzduff, 1989; Darby, 1991). Such an analysis has provided those most involved in developing approaches to the conflict with a certain relief from the confusion and competitiveness which had beset attempts at any concerted conflict resolution strategies. Competing claims are still heard in the various arenas of conflict strategists, e.g. for a primary focus on the further diminution of the inequities which still pertain in Northern Ireland society, particularly in employment; or for a concentration on the containment of political violence; or for pursuing a political solution. More attention is now being given to the idea of resourcing and pursuing a variety of enlarged approaches. Those engaged in a psychocultural approach are being encouraged to take structural issues into account.[5] Some of those who have focused with some simplicity only on external enemies are tentatively beginning to look at their neighbours, to see if, irrespective of, or in parallel to, dealing with the external context, they should also begin to deal more directly with each other.[6]

This developing, multi-faceted, approach has also allowed for the involvement of a much wider range of groups, and on a much wider range of issues, than had hitherto been thought possible.

Given the present view, as expressed in the Downing Street Declaration, of the British Government (and to a certain extent the Republic of Ireland Government) as 'neutral' facilitators to the Northern Ireland communities in coming to an agreement on a political solution, it is likely that in the near future both governments will focus more energy and resources on facilitating reconciliation between communities within Northern Ireland and between all parts of the island of Ireland.

If there does remain a threat to the continuance of the work it is less likely to come from either government, than (remembering the fate of the Community Relations Commission) from the politicians themselves. There are unfortunately still some politicians who are tempted to view the work with some suspicion, particularly if it continues to challenge their capacity to improve or otherwise connections and co-operation between communities. It has also been argued that there may well be a fundamental contradiction between community relations work and the work of gaining votes in Northern Ireland, and in that sense some politicians may continue to view the work and its prescriptions of co-operation between communities with some disfavour. The question remains open.

Community relations and the voluntary sector

In assisting the development of an agenda for community relations work, the voluntary sector has always been seen as crucial, and early efforts at developing such work were almost exclusively undertaken by it. But the work of community relations has moved well beyond such a focus, and indeed such a dependency is probably both unfair and unrealistic.

At least three factors have made such dependency problematic. The first is the sector's own ambivalence about its relationship to the state. The second is the limited nature of the power wielded by the sector, and the third is the lack of any agreement within the sector, as indeed within many other sectors, about the endogenous or exogenous nature of the conflict, or about the need to prioritise (or combine) the psychocultural or structural approaches to the conflict.

The relationship between the voluntary sector and the state has always been an ambiguous one, particularly since the introduction of the welfare state, with its presumption of total state caring. But in the last five years in particular, the voluntary sector has been undertaking a review of its relationship to government, particularly in the light of the recent government policy of 'community care' in the health and social services field. The very success of the sector in many areas, i.e. of effective service delivery at low cost and of creative innovation in respect of of social need, is leading the sector into closer relationships with the government which is hard pressed for finance to meet its on-going social commitments.

The belief (developed by the Conservatives under Margaret Thatcher) that the cheapest form of care for those in need could most effectively be delivered by committed individual or group carers has created ambivalence among many of the voluntary bodies. Many groups suspect that the suggested framework is about a more cost-effective way for government to deliver on services, rather than about any real desire to increase the quality of delivery.

Groups themselves, many of which have grown in skill and confidence, and which have maintained their commitment to their fields, are caught between the opportunity for a more effective use of their developed skills and their possible use, or abuse, by a government whose agenda would seem to be contradictory. Government is thought to be eschewing collective responsibility for those in our community who are most in need, while advocating that such responsibility can be relocated to smaller collective groupings.

This ambivalence about the relationships between the government and the voluntary/community sector pertains also in the community relations field. A clear example of such ambiguity is some current attitudes towards the role (and expected role) of women's groups in the field of community relations.

At some implicit or expressed level there frequently appears the hope by many that it will be 'the women' who will deliver on any such breakthroughs for 'peace' in Northern Ireland. The routes by which such breakthroughs might happen are rarely specified but incorporate some of the following: that the acknowledgement of mutual social concerns will enable women to build substantive community bridges; that in their roles as wives, sisters and mothers they will persuade their men that the use of violence is counterproductive; that their collective sorrows, as they pick up the pieces of their (mostly male) bodies will inspire them to productive anger which will enable them to persuade those most capable of delivering a solution, e.g. their men, either as politicians or paramilitaries, to shake hands and produce a political solution. And it is occasionally with such hopes that some women's community development groups which cross the political divide have been funded under community relations funding.

Consideration of such funding, however, raises a variety of fundamental questions for some women's groups. The first question concerns the actual power of such groups. Asking voluntary groups to deliver on community relations produces the same ambivalence for many of them as it does for voluntary groups being asked to deliver on community care functions. In both cases, some groups suspect that they are being asked to fix a problem which they feel is not of their making. There are some voluntary sector groups who believe that, for the government to depend upon the voluntary sector to address issues of sectarianism, is an abdication of responsibility for a problem which is, many believe, ultimately caused by, and must be rectified by, the government itself.

In the second place, voluntary groups are often at the edge of assisting physical and social survival for many marginalized by poverty and exclusion. Many involved in and benefiting from such work rarely have time to lift their eyes to what is beyond their immediate daily workload, or beyond their community walls. Most women's groups feel that governments pay little attention in responding to their social and group needs for resources and facilities. Local council politicians rarely raise issues of concern to them at local council level, and in allocating community services budgets, rarely prioritise women's issues.

Accordingly, there is an understandable resistance by women's groups to add to their existing burden, (i.e. addressing social issues of immediate concern), by having to take on the fraught issue of sectarianism. And yet, just like many groups concerned with the realities and necessities of alleviating social need, many women within their groups are ambivalent about disregarding their potential ability to address sectarianism, participate in political direction making, and ultimately to help to bring to an end the political conflict.

So, although some women's groups have specifically chosen to address issues of sectarianism and reconciliation, (e.g. Women Together, Widows against Violence), other groups have had to find ways of accommodating such work as a part of, but not a prime focus of, their work. The Women's Information Group (which brings together hundreds of women from nationalist and unionist areas to address social issues) has achieved a workable compromise, satisfactory to all in the group, by setting up a particular optional working group, within which women from differing communities address issues of division existing within and between their communities.

Many other groups are understandably reluctant to develop work specifically addressing issues of political division and are fearful of such work. Groups often believe that encouraging work which addresses divisions, which elucidates differences, which attempts to develop collective principles by which to address inequality, sectarianism, paramilitarism, security force practice etc. will divide the often fragile nature of the social and personal alliances existing between them.

The principle of discreetly preserving silence on possibly divisive issues and of politely skirting around crises, is perhaps an even more necessary skill in the more marginalized areas where the community sector is often at its most vibrant, and where the results of the on-going conflict are most obvious. In addition there is the very real fear of raising such issues in areas where questioning of paramilitary methodology can result at the very least in taunts of disloyalty and betrayal, and, at the very most, in threats or murder.

In addition, any suggestion that the voluntary sector has kept itself 'pure' from the discriminatory and exclusive practices of the many other sectors in Northern Ireland is unproven. Many organizations (and it is most obvious in some of the most respected and long established agencies) are almost as burdened with exclusivity, exemplified through unbalanced staffing and customer balance as are many commercial concerns in the region. This is often obvious in the symbols used by an organization in its holiday customs, its choice of venues, or of patrons, all of which serve to continue such exclusion.

The contribution of the voluntary sector

This does not mean that voluntary groups have only as much to offer as any other sector of society in addressing issues of sectarianism, and the spectrum of work encompassed under the title of community relations. There is, in fact, a variety of factors which ensure that the voluntary sector has in many instances played a courageous and innovative role in developing this work, despite its ambivalence, and obvious limitation of its power.

The first advantage the sector has is one of location. The voluntary and community sector, by definition, is at its most useful, and is most visible, in areas where issues of social deprivation are most apparent, and where anger at such deprivations has often energized community commitment. Those areas that are most marginal economically and socially are usually also the areas that have suffered most from the violence. Unlike the more affluent suburbs of Belfast, or the more salubrious satellite towns of County Down, which generally remain relatively untroubled by many aspects of our conflict, in disadvantaged communities there is daily evidence of an on-going war with the presence of soldiers, paramilitary intimidation, sectarian graffiti, and occasional rioting. These ensure that people are unable to forget the existence of the troubles. These reminders, along with the continuing murders that have blighted so many working-class communities, compel such issues to be addressed, despite the dangers inherent in doing so. An excellent example of such co-operation was the response of the community workers on the Falls and Shankill Road interfaces in the aftermath of the killing of ten Protestants on the Shankill Road by the IRA in November 1993. These workers, who for some years had been involved in a loose standing conference addressing issues of division and conflict within and between their areas came to the fore in the days and weeks following the murders, providing much needed connections between the communities, carrying expressions of condolence and concern, which in turn ensured that the disaster did not result in extensive communal retaliation.

Communities addressing social issues often discover that such work is more effective if it is carried on in co-operation with other communities. Hence, many community groups have recognized common concerns across the community divide and have moved to address them together. One of the few (relative) certainties about resolving conflicts is that such issue-based work is one of the most productive ways to develop long-term trust between supposedly opposing groups. Such issue work often gives rise to informal opportunities for divisive issues to be addressed. Increasingly, facilitated by the work of the Community Relations Council and other groups like the Workers Educational Association such groups are now more frequently moving on to address issues of sectarianism and political differences.

In addition, the flexibility for which voluntary and community groups are particularly noted means that decisions to add on work addressing sectarianism can often be more easily made. Many such organizations are small in numbers, and are often led by the more innovative in the community who have been active in identifying a particular social niche or need.

In practice this means that many of the models of policy and programme development, and modules for training now suggested by the CRC for consideration by statutory bodies have been piloted within the voluntary sector. Current work on sectarianism within the workplace, work with public bodies, political representatives etc. has often been tried and tested initially within the voluntary sector.

While acknowledging the above developments, there remains a major factor as yet unaddressed in any serious way by the voluntary sector in Northern Ireland and that is its own relationship to the democratic process here.

It has frequently been suggested that the reason for such a vibrant voluntary/community sector in Northern Ireland is that these sectors are engaging some of the most able leaders. It is suggested that the best leaders in the voluntary sector are drawn from those who would normally pick up responsibility for political life if they lived elsewhere but who are presently eschewing it because of the disastrous image the political process has in Northern Ireland.

In addition, direct rule by the British Government since 1974 has meant that resource decision and delivery for the voluntary sector has for twenty years been decided almost unilaterally by civil servants in Northern Ireland. Hence alliances have been made with civil servants of all departments and this has proved to be of advantage to voluntary sector groups, who have become used to such co-operation. Some of these groups might not welcome a return to politician-led policy for the voluntary and community sector.

Because direct rule has provided such co-operative opportunities with the civil service there are many within the voluntary and community sector who have ignored the need to ensure the education and support of politicians for their work. This may in the end prove to have been a problematic practice. The recent setting up of a Select Committee for Northern Ireland (March 1994) which will bring some measure of public accountability for ministers and civil servants may augur the necessity for a new involvement between the voluntary sector and politicians at all levels, and such an involvement could prove to be a major link in furthering social and political development in Northern Ireland.

If the voluntary sector can more thoroughly engage, appropriately challenge and further educate its political representatives in the many aspects of its programmes which are designed to address social exclusion and need, and in particular in those existing programmes which are designed to improve community relations and address sectarianism, it may help to ensure a more creative engagement by politicians in the development of a just and sustainable solution to the conflict. This, in addition to an increased commitment on their part to address intimidation, sectarianism and the use of violent political leverage in all its forms, will help further to enhance what has been, for the most part, an honourable record over a period of twenty-five years, when the energy and commitment of voluntary groups to the process of developing their communities has been one of the abiding and positive features of a very divided society.

Notes

1. There were 13 deaths in 1969; by 1972 the number of deaths was to rise to 467.
2. This was an unpublished review of community relations undertaken under the aegis of Pat Carville of DENI.
3. The Downing Street Declaration was signed on 15 December 1993 by John Major (British Prime Minister) and Albert Reynolds (Prime Minister of the Republic of Ireland).
4. The 1991 census showed that Catholics now constitute 43 per cent of the population, as opposed to 37 per cent in 1971.
5. There are many examples in the CRC's Annual Report for 1993 of reconciliation groups now addressing issues of equity, justice and constitutional politics.
6. In 1991 Sinn Fein began to talk publicly about their need to form new internal relationships with the Protestants in Northern Ireland. This marked a significant shift away from their sole focus on the British. See e. g. McLaughlin, M. (1991), 'Protestantism, Unionism and Loyalism' (unpublished).

References

Community Relations Act (NI) (1969), HMSO, Belfast.

Community Relations (Amendment) (NI) Order (1975), HMSO, Belfast.

Community Relations Council (1991), *First Annual Report*, CRC, Belfast.

Darby, J. (1991), *What's Wrong with Conflict?*, (Occasional paper no. 3), Centre for the Study of Conflict, University of Ulster, Coleraine.

Darby, J., Moore, R., Dunn, S. & McCartney, C. (1986), 'Report on Belfast Areas of Need (Community Relations Programme)', unpublished report.

Department of Health and Social Services (1993), *Strategy for the Support of the Voluntary Sector and for Community Development in Northern Ireland*, HMSO, Belfast.

Fitzduff, M. (1989a), 'Political Exigencies and Community Development' in Deane, E. (ed.), *Lost Horizons, New Horizons*, Workers Educational Association, Belfast.

Fitzduff, M. (1989b), *Typology of Community Relations Work and Contextual Necessities*, Policy and Planning Unit, Northern Ireland Office, Belfast.

Frazer, H. & Fitzduff, M. (1986), 'Improving Community Relations', (A paper prepared for the Standing Advisory Commission on Human Rights).

Griffiths, H. (1974), *Community Development in Northern Ireland: a Case Study in Agency Conflict*, (Occasional paper in Social Administration), New University of Ulster, Coleraine.

Hayes, M. (1972), *The Role of the Community Relations Commission in Northern Ireland*, Runnymede Trust, London.

Knox, C. & Hayes, M. (1993), *Evaluation of the District Council Community Relations Programme*, Centre for the Study of Conflict, University of Ulster, Coleraine.

Logue, K. (1992), *Anti-Sectarianism and the Community and Voluntary Sector*, CRC, Belfast.

Northern Ireland Assembly, Official Report vol. 3, no. 1, 3 April 1974.

Race Relations Act (1968), HMSO, London.

Rooney, A. (1993), *Women, Community and Politics in Northern Ireland*, University of Ulster, Coleraine.

Stringer, P. & Robinson, G. (eds) (1993), *Social Attitudes in Northern Ireland: the Third Report, 1992-1993*, Blackstaff, Belfast.

Tajfel, H. (ed.) (1982), *Social Identity and Intergroup Relations*, Cambridge University Press, Cambridge.

Whyte, J. (1990), *Interpreting Northern Ireland*, Clarendon Press, Oxford.

6 Government, community development and the housing association movement

Derek Birrell

The mid-seventies saw the first major academic study on the voluntary sector in Northern Ireland, *Yesterday's Heritage or Tomorrow's Resource?* (Griffiths et al., 1978) carried out in the Department of Social Administration at the New University of Ulster. This study was focused on voluntary organizations providing social services. It identified 700 voluntary organizations and estimated that there were well in excess of 1,000 voluntary welfare organizations. It was noticeable that only 19 per cent of organizations were controlled from outside Northern Ireland showing that Northern Ireland had a largely independent and self-sustaining voluntary sector. The sector was also mainly of fairly recent origin with approximately 60 per cent of all organizations founded after 1960. The survey found considerable diversity in the size of voluntary organizations. The majority, some 70 per cent, were small in terms of the scale of their operations. The majority, 60 per cent, had a single office while the remainder had a branch structure within Northern Ireland. Approximately one-third of organizations had under twenty volunteers but some had in excess of 2,000 volunteers. Seventy per cent of organizations employed staff but this ranged from one to fifty. It was noticeable that paid staff worked almost exclusively in administration rather than in professional or service provision.

The survey also found that three-quarters of voluntary organizations were providing direct services and the remainder were classified as support service organizations or political action/pressure groups. Half of the direct service organizations were providing personal social services, child care or counselling and the remainder were mainly providing advice, residential accommodation, employment or material assistance. The survey reported that the work of almost half the organizations was aimed at easily defined categories of need: children; the community; the elderly or disabled people.

Quite a number of groups, 25 per cent, believed they were providing similar services to statutory agencies but 70 per cent felt that the services they provided were uniquely different from those provided by government and one-third also believed they were filling a gap in provision.

Griffiths et al. concluded that activity in the voluntary sector in Northern Ireland was high. The expansion in numbers between the early sixties and the mid-seventies reflected the growth in popularity of ideas of participation and self-help, increased awareness of poverty and social needs, and increased criticism of statutory services. The study indicated the main strengths of the voluntary sector as it had developed as flexibility; the enthusiasm of volunteers; a commitment to self-help; and greater choice and provision in social services. The study also identified several weaknesses: an inability to identify and measure need; undemocratic internal structures; a lack of innovation; a lack of evaluation procedures; little training for volunteers; and limited contact with other voluntary organizations.

Government strategic policies

In the early 1970s several government publications had given support for the voluntary sector in a fairly general way. A DHSS statement had noted it was a desirable end in itself for statutory bodies to be involved with voluntary organizations but made the point that the relationship had to be based on 'unavoidable financial and other constraints'. There was a suggestion that co-operation should be mainly concerned with prevention and dealing with specific problems of specific client groups. In 1974 the Department issued a circular *Support for Voluntary Organisations* (DHSS, 1974) based on the principle of co-operation. This laid down general principles and guidelines for the encouragement, mobilization and co-ordination of voluntary effort in association with the statutory health and social services. A further document in 1975 *The Regional Plan for the Development of Health and Personal Social Services in Northern Ireland* stated that there would have to be close liaison between boards and appropriate voluntary bodies and community groups which supplemented and complemented the existing statutory services and noted that the nature and organization of this effort would require to be constantly reassessed in the light of changing need.

The most significant advance in government policy was to stem directly from the Wolfenden Report (1978) on *The Future of Voluntary Organisations*. The Wolfenden Report was focused on Great Britain but included Northern Ireland in its remit and the committee took evidence in Belfast. It made particular reference to the role of umbrella organizations in Northern Ireland, for example, the Northern Ireland Council of Social Services, and noted that several such bodies acted as both resource centres and the direct provider of services. There were no specific recommendations concerning Northern Ireland but the report had a general influence on thinking about the voluntary sector. The report emphasised the special contribution of volunteers: filling and bridging gaps in statutory services; providing alternative services; the pioneering role of the voluntary sector, and the role of the sector as the main providers of advice. It also noted the limitations of the voluntary sector: its unevenness; diversity; and lack of resources. The Wolfenden Report made a range of suggestions for the future - providing the voluntary sector with more support services, more central government finance and greater collaboration with government, and particularly stressed the importance of intermediary bodies such as local councils of social services of which there were few in Northern Ireland.

The publication in 1978 of the Wolfenden Report and *Yesterday's Heritage or Tomorrow's Resource?* (Griffiths et al.) led to government action. The then minister of state, Lord Melchett announced a wide-ranging strategic review of government policy towards the voluntary sector. This review was undertaken by the Co-ordinating Committee on Social Problems, an interdepartmental group of senior officials concerned with aspects of social policy. The response to the research survey and the Wolfenden Report appeared in 1980 in a report entitled *Tomorrow's Resource (CCSP)*. This document recommended a partnership relationship between the statutory and voluntary sectors of social welfare provision. The main thrust of the report was to highlight the need to achieve a more open relationship between both sectors and a greater willingness by the statutory side to facilitate the involvement of voluntary organizations in a participative and consultative role. *Tomorrow's Resource* encouraged statutory authorities to do everything possible to involve voluntary organizations in the planning of services, particularly at local level. It also attempted to lay down guidelines for funding policy which recognized the uncertainty experienced by voluntary organizations. While grants would normally be on a yearly basis it was suggested that statutory bodies should indicate whether there would be a longer-term commitment to support. *Tomorrow's Resource*, however, set its face against a local version of the Home Office Voluntary Service Unit. The recommendations were endorsed by the government as indicating the general direction which government policy should take in the coming years.

Around the same time there were two further papers specifically related to health and personal social services. The Central Personal Social Services Advisory Committee undertook a report entitled *Support for Voluntary Organisations (CPSSAC, 1979)* which took a critical look at the support available from the DHSS and the Area Health and Social Services Boards. This report was at times very critical. It noted that some voluntary organizations appeared to have been made to feel that if they were partners they were at best inferior partners. It suggested that the relationships would be improved if boards had a better appreciation of the contribution the voluntary sector makes. The report called for the philosophy of partnership between the statutory and voluntary sector and what it really involves to be explained more fully. More specifically it called on area boards to implement consistently the DHSS standard grant aid scheme, to respond flexibly and promptly to requests for assistance, to produce information leaflets giving details of assistance, and to appoint a senior officer in each area to encourage, assist and co-ordinate the development of voluntary effort. Finally the report called on area boards to display a greater commitment to the maximum participation of voluntary groups in the planning and provision of social services.

The second paper, a DHSS circular *Planning and Monitoring in the Health and Personal Social Services* (1980) pointed to the important contribution to be made by the voluntary sector in complementing and supplementing the statutory services and asked boards in preparing their five year strategic plan to involve voluntary bodies and groups and to take full account of the contribution which the voluntary sector might be expected to make, given adequate support. It was still apparent that, despite the number of reports and recommendations and the growth of voluntary organizations, there was little evidence of actual partnerships. The paper noted the various forms of support for the voluntary sector in terms of increased financial support and also of other support through material assistance, advice and service by board officers on management committees.

This became one of the main objectives of a discussion paper published by the DHSS in 1985, *Co-operation between the Statutory and Voluntary Sectors in the Health and Personal Social Services in Northern Ireland.* This paper accepted the value of voluntary organizations and of the way in which they can complement or supplement the work of the statutory services in extending the scope and variety of provision, in offering a choice of services and in providing a service where none might otherwise be available. The paper declared its intention to move beyond statements of the principle of co-operation and identity and to canvass opinion on practical ways in which the principle might be realized to greater effect, particularly at field level. Some of the existing problems with relationships were examined, for example, the feeling by voluntary organizations that the statutory sector was sometimes unappreciative of their contribution and potential. At the same time it suggested the voluntary sector was not always so aware of the competing demands and financial constraints the boards faced. It also suggested that the lines of communication between the statutory and voluntary sectors were not what they might be. It recommended that the statutory sector should be prepared to exchange information with voluntary bodies about needs, services and assistance to help identify the ways in which each could best assist the other.

The paper noted the particular financial problem caused by the lack of guaranteed long-term funding which engendered feelings of insecurity for voluntary organizations and created particular problems in the recruitment of full-time staff. It recognized that to find a solution would not be easy as boards would be unwilling to enter into long-term commitments without clear and continuing evidence of their value. It recognized a further difficulty in that voluntary organizations had a problem in gaining access to boards at the levels at which policy decisions were made. The paper recommended that voluntary organizations should contribute to and receive copies of boards' strategic plans in order that they might be effectively involved in the realization of the goals and objectives detailed therein. Such collaboration was seen as ensuring necessary co-ordination, an exchange of information, and the effective use of total resources. The paper suggested that involvement in joint planning would require voluntary organizations to see themselves not as wholly independent but as an 'integral component of the network of provision made for the whole community' (DHSS, 1985, p. 13). However it was accepted that a standard approach might not be possible and that liaising boards would have to consider what joint planning arrangements would be best suited to their area. It was also suggested that organizations dealing with particular groups should meet together to discuss common problems, share ideas and devise complementing rather than competitive plans. There was a specific recommendation that boards should consider nominating officers with special responsibility for liaison with voluntary bodies. It also noted that apart from finance boards might provide a wide range of facilities and services in kind for voluntary bodies and suggested examples of joint use of services - e.g. joint purchasing or use of spare transport or buildings. Further help suggested by boards concerned the training of volunteers and training professional staff to work with volunteers.

The government's commitment to working in partnership with, and continuing to support, the voluntary sector resulted in a major consultation exercise in 1992 on a *Draft Strategy for the Support of the Voluntary Sector in Northern Ireland*. This was developed as part of the response by government departments in Northern Ireland to the *Report of the Efficiency Scrutiny of Government Funding of the Voluntary Sector* (Home Office, 1990). The *Strategy* was revised to include a statement on community development and was published in February 1993 (DHSS, 1993a). Government departments' aims were described as:

(1) to encourage, promote and support voluntary activity;
(2) to ensure the voluntary sector obtains maximum benefit from resources available; and
(3) to build on voluntary sector experience in developing departmental policy objectives.

Community development

The second part of the 1960s in Northern Ireland brought the Civil Rights Movement and the emergence of many local community groups. In response to the civil disturbances, the Northern Ireland Community Relations Commission was established in December 1969, marking a major initiative in community work in Northern Ireland (Frazer, 1985 and Lovett et al., 1994). The remit of the Community Relations Commission was to promote better community relations and a community development approach was adopted to achieve this. The Commission set up sub-committees to look at community problems and acted as a forum for discussion and debate on community work (Tweed, 1971). Contact was made with a large number of individuals and community groups and their confidence was retained through severe civil and sectarian disturbances. The Commission gave help and support, both financial and administrative, to many voluntary bodies but its main aim was to assist small local groups tackling a particular problem especially where there was the possibility of crossing the sectarian divide (Hayes, 1972). The early 1970s saw the emergence of powerful community action groups, for example, the Bogside Community Association, and talk of participatory democracy and a community parliament (Frazer, 1985). Griffith (1975) identified 500 community action groups which he saw as a measure of the dislocation of the fabric of society in Northern Ireland due to the conflict and its consequences. The rapid growth in this period of community action was a response to the urgency of need and a partial breakdown in statutory provision.

Hayes (1972), then Chairman of the Community Relations Commission, identified constraints on the work of the Commission including the lack of consensus, links with government, the lack of credibility of existing institutions, and the high level of violence in the society. The first short-lived power sharing government in 1974 decided the community movement was too radical and moved for disbandment of the Commission (Lovett et al., 1994). As the statutory Community Relations Commission was 'winding down', a new voluntary organization was set up, Community Organisations Northern Ireland (CONI). Although short-lived this brought together community activists and community leaders and served as a link between the work of the Commission and that community development and thinking which survived

(CDRG, 1991). A counter organization, the Ulster Community Action Group was also established as an umbrella organization for Protestant groups. A further initiative, the Standing Advisory Council of Community Groups, was established to oversee voluntary community work in the Province but this was also short-lived.

In 1976 a new phase began when government passed responsibility for community work over to district councils, marking the increasing takeover by the state. Organizations like CONI collapsed, the voluntary sector became more institutionalized and the number of local leaders declined as community work became a state dominated profession. Under the control of district councils, the emphasis in community work was on the provision of resources and facilities rather than on giving local communities more power and control over their lives (Frazer, 1985). Some community groups, in an attempt to counter the emphasis on provision of physical facilities, concentrated on encouraging creativity, developing the individual, and increasing political awareness at a local level through community arts, education and women's projects.

The government did appear to realize that local councils were unlikely to promote community developments. At this time government set up the Community Worker Research Project, designed to promote community-based development projects and evaluate the results of employing community-based workers to promote such projects (CDRG, 1991a). More significantly 1979 marked the establishment of the Northern Ireland Voluntary Trust (NIVT), set up as an independent charitable trust with a £500,000 government grant. The NIVT has had a significant impact on community development in Northern Ireland, not only through grants to small community groups but also in providing support and advice. Programme themes have included rural development, women's groups, community care, community arts and education, community relations, and local economic development. The core activity of the Trust is to empower communities to build on their sense of belonging and so bring about positive social change through community development.

The government measure with possibly the greatest impact on community development was the introduction in 1981 by the Department of Economic Development of the Action for Community Employment (ACE) scheme (CDRG, 1991a). Initially the scheme provided a 90 per cent salary for previously unemployed workers undertaking community work. Changes were introduced in 1985 leading to increased part-time work, an emphasis on training and preference for larger projects. Although significant resources, up to £50 million per annum, are being directed to the community and voluntary sector, community activists argue that it has been counter-productive in terms of community development. It has been suggested that statutory agencies and district councils have exploited the ACE scheme as a method of job substitution (Campbell, 1983).

During the 1980s a number of significant events deepened divisions between the two communities in Northern Ireland making contact between community groups difficult. The first major event was the hunger strike in 1981 and the subsequent involvement of Sinn Fein in politics. This raised fears in government circles of paramilitary involvement in community action. The other major event was the signing of the Anglo-Irish Agreement in 1985. This was greeted with total opposition by the Protestant community and the inevitable violence brought community contact to a low ebb (Lovett et al., 1994). Although the number of people involved in community development was growing, their work was fragmented and failed to cross the sectarian divide.

In 1988 a Community Development Conference was held at the University of Ulster at Magee College. A Community Development Review Group was formed to take the issues raised at this conference further and to put community development back on the policy agenda. The objective of the review was to consider the experiences of community action and development over the previous twenty years and to make recommendations in relation to the promotion of community development in the immediate future. The Review Group prepared and published two reports in 1991 (CDRG, a, b). These defined community development in Northern Ireland as a process which embraces community action, community services, community work and other community endeavour, whether geographical or issue based, with an emphasis towards the disadvantaged, impoverished and powerless within society. The message of the report, *Perspectives for the Future*, was that community development was thriving in Northern Ireland but was often fragmented, both by issue and by location. It suggested a much more concerted effort was needed to build networks, to provide support and training, and to allocate resources to core and continuing work over a longer period rather than relying on short-term funding and projects (CDRG, 1991a). The main recommendations of the review were as follows:

1) Community development should be made a priority issue. Statutory and voluntary agencies should commit themselves to adopting a community development approach.
2) Central government should make a clear commitment to community development in an interdepartmental policy document.
3) Local authorities should make a clear commitment to community development. Their most important role is funding. It is vital that grants, information and advice are available.

4) The relationship of voluntary organizations to community development should be identified through written guidelines providing a framework for their relations with community groups.

5) A framework of support for community development needs to be developed including an annual Community Development Consultative Conference and a working party to assess training and education.

6) Short-term, ad hoc funding does little to facilitate the community sector and a long-term commitment is needed. Proposals included a Community Development Fund financed by central government and administered by the NIVT.

Recently there has been a growth in issue-based community work, for example, an emphasis on 'community care' by the Health and Social Services Board and an extension of community development to rural areas. The Rural Development Council was established in September 1991 to work in this field. The RDC has elected to pursue a community development approach through a Community Support Officer and local Development Officers. There has also been an increasing involvement of women's groups in community development and community relations, and a growing emphasis on community economic regeneration and support available from government, the European Community and the International Fund for Ireland. Larger voluntary organizations have begun to adopt policies on community development, for example, the Northern Ireland Council for Voluntary Action has put a community development approach at the head of its aims and the Northern Ireland Association for the Care and Resettlement of Offenders (NIACRO) and Extern have taken similar initiatives.

In response to the *Report of the Efficiency Scrutiny of Government Funding to the Voluntary Sector* (Home Office, 1990), a draft strategy was prepared by the Department of Health and Social Services. Following the reports of the Community Development Review Group (1991) the strategy included a statement of principle on the government's support for community development. The importance of community development was clearly recognized in the *Strategy for the Support of the Voluntary Sector and for Community Development in Northern Ireland*, published in February 1993 (DHSS, 1993a). The strategy noted the following positive features:

1) A key strength of community development is its diversity; therefore it has the potential to make a major impact on a wide range of social and economic policies and programmes.

2) Community groups make a particular contribution in offering people opportunities for self-help and taking responsibility for activity which is a direct benefit to the community they serve.

3) Local community groups have a role in enhancing the ability of statutory and voluntary agencies to reach and involve people in need.
4) Local community groups encourage active participation and generate a sense of ownership and control, vital to success, over matters which affect the people involved and the communities they serve.
5) Community development methods can broaden vision and capacity for social change.

Government acknowledged the need to enhance the effectiveness and efficiency of government departments' commitment to community development and in particular to address the following issues:

1) the need to ensure coherence between existing programmes of community development;
2) development of inter-sectoral strategies, for example, funding arrangements for new programmes;
3) establishment of appropriate monitoring and evaluation techniques;
4) development of processes required to clarify the methods and skills appropriate to community development; and
5) identification of educational and training needs of those involved in community development.

The strategy proposed a Voluntary Activity Unit, which would take a lead responsibility for community development as well as voluntary action and provide structures necessary for interdepartmental consideration of key issues in this field. The (DHSS, 1993b) *Strategy Statement on the Role and Aims of the Voluntary Activity Unit* specified that one of the major aims is to promote and enhance the effectiveness and efficiency of the existing commitment to community development.

Community services

The present system of community services throughout the Province originates from the Moyle Report (1975). Under the 1973 Recreation and Youth Services Order, district councils already had responsibility for recreational facilities and community centres, but, as a result of the demise of the Community Relations Commission, it was felt the time was ripe to extend the responsibilities to include community development. Roland Moyle, Minister of State with responsibility for the Department of Education, which had taken over responsibility for community relations, convened a working party. The Moyle Report in July 1975 and the subsequent Department Circular 1975/51 in January 1976 became the basis for the new arrangements which came into operation from 1 April 1976 (McGinley, 1990). This led to the present system where district councils have responsibility for community development through their Community Services Departments. Community Services Departments are responsible for: community work; development and management of community centres and resource centres; assistance to voluntary groups for the provision of community facilities and services; consumer advice centres; compilation and analysis of social data for use by the council and community groups; preparation of Neighbourhood Amenity Plans; and itinerants' sites.

Rolston (1985) identified a reluctance by some councils to become involved in community services. Although all councils now accept government money for community services, the amounts allocated to community services by some councils is very small. There are a number of reasons for this reluctance. Firstly, elected representatives are wary about encouraging community groups, seeing this as a threat to their role. Secondly, there is the possibility of sectarianism. In the area of community services there is scope for the sectarian distribution of resources by councillors. Thirdly, cutbacks have made councillors reluctant to involve their councils in increased expenditure.

The Community Development Review Group (1991) argued that councils have adopted a disjointed and incremental approach to community services since they were given responsibility for encouragement of community work in 1976. It is interesting to note that only a relatively small part of the budget available to district councils from the Department of Education actually ends up with community groups. In 1982/83 the Department's grant to district councils for expenditure on community work was just under £1.5 million yet only £594,253 was used for funding community groups (Frazer, 1985). Most expenditure on community services goes to salaries and on the running of community centres and resource centres. Add to this the preference of Community Services Departments to work directly with community groups rather than umbrella organizations and the result is, especially in larger areas, that community groups struggle for the attention of the council's Community Services Department.

In most councils community services are linked with leisure services and this linking of responsibilities usually results in community services taking a secondary position. Belfast is the only council to have separated leisure and community services. By doing this Belfast City Council has made a major commitment to community services but it is still seen as a relatively minor part of the council's work. In the year 1990/91 total expenditure for all Belfast City Council departments amounted to £43,255,320. In the same period total rate-borne expenditure by the Community Services Department was £2,380,679, 5.6 per cent of total council spending. In addition the Community Services Department received £627,750 from the Department of

Education (NI) bringing total Community Services Department spending to just over £3 million, a small part of the council's total expenditure. Of this only £554,000 was given in direct grant aid to community and voluntary groups (Belfast City Council, 1992). Since the Belfast Areas of Need Initiative was discontinued, funding has been available from DENI for Community Services Departments. Until 1987/88 the grant approved by DENI continued to increase annually to an all time high in 1987/88 of £1,944,880. However, in recent years there has been a decline in the percentage of grant provided by DENI. In 1988/89 a drop of approximately £25,000, a cut of 12 - 15 per cent, reduced the council's level of funding to pre 1983/84 levels (McGinley, 1990). Due to the severe curtailment of funding from DENI, Belfast Action Teams have been the main providers of grant aid where it was possible to tailor projects within their spending priorities.

Housing associations

Housing associations are voluntary non-profit making organizations which supplement the work of the private sector, the public sector and the Northern Ireland Housing Executive. Up to the mid 1970s housing association activity in Northern Ireland was on a very small scale. In 1974 a Voluntary Housing Steering Committee was set up in Northern Ireland and began to lobby for the introduction of legislation to provide Northern Ireland housing associations with similar support to that afforded in Great Britain by the Housing Act 1974. Legislation mirroring the 1974 Housing Act in Great Britain was enacted in Northern Ireland in the Housing (NI) Order, 1976 (Singleton, 1983). The order enabled housing associations to register with the Department of the Environment (NI) giving them access, for the first time, to the Housing Association Grant for the provision of special needs accommodation. The Steering Committee also pressed for the establishment, with government financial support, of a Northern Ireland Federation of Housing Associations. As an interim arrangement, financial assistance was given for a Northern Ireland Committee of the National Federation of Housing Associations which became an autonomous body, the Northern Ireland Federation of Housing Associations (NIFHA) in April 1977 (Holmes, 1993). The primary function of the NIFHA is to represent the housing association movement to all those able to influence its future and in particular to statutory bodies and government agencies. In addition to the representative role it also provides an advisory and information service direct to members through conferences, seminars and workshops. There is also a professional service covering, for example, book-keeping services, staff induction and training, land and property acquisition, and self-build management. Registration, control and financing of housing associations is undertaken by the Department of the Environment (NI). Promotional work is devolved to the NIFHA. The Federation also has formal liaison machinery with the Northern Ireland Housing Executive which determines the housing need which triggers or terminates a housing association scheme. Points of contrast with the system in Great Britain include the approval of tenant selection policies by the Department of the Environment, allocation on the basis of the Northern Ireland Housing Executive selection system and rent levels set in line with NIHE property.

Compared to Great Britain, the voluntary housing movement in Northern Ireland has been more restricted by government to providing for special needs such as sheltered and specialist accommodation for the elderly. FOLD (Free the Old from Loneliness with Dignity) was the first housing association registered in Northern Ireland after the passing of the Housing (NI) Order, 1976. FOLD's overriding objective is to provide sheltered accommodation for the elderly, provision of which is lacking in Northern Ireland. The James Butcher Housing Association was also founded in Northern Ireland in 1976. Most of the accommodation is sheltered for older people and aims at fostering independence and peace of mind for relatives and tenants. The James Butcher Association also provides HELPLINE, a 24-hour community alarm service for those in sheltered housing and LIFELINE is provided, in conjunction with Help the Aged, for 8,000 elderly people in non-sheltered housing. In recent years housing association activity has been extended concentrating on new initiatives, for example, both FOLD and the James Butcher Housing Association are presently promoting 'Housing with Care' and aim to contribute to 'Care in the Community' initiatives. Recently housing associations have been tackling a wider range of needs, for example NIH Housing Association is to amalgamate with James Butcher to form a stronger association and meet a wider range of needs such as housing for general family accommodation and schemes for persons with special needs, for example, mentally ill, young persons leaving statutory care and persons suffering from alcohol or drug addiction.

In 1981, the Northern Ireland Federation of Housing Associations produced a report 'New Directions' for the voluntary movement in Northern Ireland. Suggested initiatives, some of which are being implemented, included improvement for sale and co-ownership. Legislation mirroring the provisions of the Housing Act, 1980 in England and Wales was enacted in Northern Ireland in the Housing (NI) Order, 1983. Despite the dramatic increase in finance made available to the voluntary movement, Singleton (1983) noted that progress was slow. Problems included procedural delays in Housing Action Areas and government cuts of housing expenditure. These problems had been overcome and record numbers of new homes were being achieved. In 1992, forty-eight housing associations were on the register of the Department of the Environment (NI) giving them access to grant funding from the Department. Housing associations started 1200 new homes in 1993/94 since the registration of associations in 1976 (Smith, 1994). In 1994/95 registered housing associations will receive £45 million in funding from the Department of the Environment (NI). The Northern Ireland Co-Ownership Housing Association (NICHA) will receive £5.2 million and the remaining £39.8 million will go to other associations to continue their work in meeting special housing needs (Smith, 1994). New challenges face housing associations with the introduction of 'mixed funding' (McDonald, 1993). Formerly housing associations enjoyed the shelter of funds such as revenue deficit grants and repair grants. Now assumptions will be tested and shortfall will have to be made up by compensating savings elsewhere or by rental increases.

An important feature of the voluntary movement in Northern Ireland was the creation of community-based housing associations. These associations were viewed as one way of bridging the gap between local people and the 'remote' Northern Ireland Housing Executive and central government. Locally-based housing associations devote time and effort to their communities which a large organization such as the NIHE cannot possibly match. This is a powerful argument for their retention (Singleton, 1983). In the late 1970s thirteen community-based associations (Smith, 1993) were formed in Belfast with finance from the Department of the Environment's Housing Association Branch and guidance from the NIFHA. Community-based housing associations are often located in small tightly knit communities, but rarely bridge the sectarian divide in terms of committees or tenants. Creation of the community-based housing associations also contributed to an intensive public debate on the merits of redevelopment versus rehabilitation. Planners eventually agreed that large scale redevelopment was destructive and unacceptable and that a rehabilitation strategy should be adopted in designated Housing Action Areas (HAAs) throughout Belfast (Smith, 1993). Some community-based housing associations are directly responsible for implementing HAA proposals having drawn up the action plans themselves. For example, Belfast Community Housing Association was formed in 1977 to improve the Lagan Village area which was deteriorating and suffering from housing blight. Its area of interest is defined by a single HAA, the Lagan Village HAA drawn up by the Association itself and brought into operation in August 1981 (Singleton, 1983) based largely on rehabilitation but with a small element of infill new build. Sixty per cent of the present housing stock is in its ownership. The continuing aim is to provide good rehabilitated and new housing for people in need and to improve the area for residents.

Through their involvement in all aspects of housing provision, design, development, construction, management and maintenance, community-based housing associations are uniquely placed to exploit their experience. They are well equipped for the task of meeting housing needs within and beyond their designated areas of operation. They also have the capability and potential to diversify into other fields of activity which would benefit the communities in which they operate (Smith, 1993).

The Northern Ireland Co-Ownership Housing Association was set up in 1978 when the building industry was in recession. The Labour Government hoped co-ownership, a form of equity sharing, would stimulate the industry by making home ownership available to people who would find it difficult to pay a full mortgage. Co-ownership is an equity sharing scheme largely unique to Northern Ireland. The principal difference between the operation of the scheme in Northern Ireland and the rest of the United Kingdom is that in Northern Ireland it is undertaken by a single specialist housing association (Singleton, 1983). Co-ownership enables applicants initially to buy as much as they can afford with the option of buying the rest back from the NICHA at any time. Buyers purchase a minimum of 50 per cent of the value of the property through a mortgage and/or savings and pay rent to the NICHA for the other part of the property. Although 50 per cent is the minimum, up to a maximum of 75 per cent can be purchased with the rental amount being reduced accordingly (Simm and McCallum, 1993).

By 1993 the NICHA had provided accommodation for some 11,500 families, couples and single people (Simm and McCallum, 1993). In 1993 the NICHA (Smith, 1994) assisted 520 applicants in purchasing the house of their choice. There is no doubt that co-ownership has been generally successful. However, the financial issue became controversial in the early eighties with the NIFHA arguing that financial allocation to the voluntary movement had been distorted by the inclusion of grants for co-ownership (Singleton, 1983).

In May 1990 the Northern Ireland Housing Executive commenced a review of its rural housing policy. To aid the process a consultation booklet 'Leading the Way' was published in November 1990. Responses to this were taken into account in finalising the review which culminated in the launch in June 1991 of *The Way Ahead* (NIHE, 1991). During the process a joint NIHE/NIFHA working group met regularly. In addition to direct contributions by housing associations to the Executive, this provided a forum for the development of new rural housing policy initiatives. Critical to this will be the drive by the housing associations to provide special-needs housing in smaller towns and villages (Gallagher, 1993). Community-based housing associations embracing rural catchment areas will have a particularly important role in complementing the work of the NIHE in meeting rural housing needs. The creation of a separate Rural Housing Association is a particularly important recent development in meeting the more dispersed and isolated housing need (Gallagher, 1993). With a province-wide remit the Association will obtain vacant dwellings for improvement for letting or sale and will also undertake some small-scale new build schemes. Housing associations have a particularly important role to play in facilitating a 'bottom-up' approach in developing tailored housing solutions (Gallagher, 1993).

References

Belfast City Council (1992), *Images of Community Development in Belfast*, Belfast City Council, Belfast. A report on the work of the Community Services Department of Belfast City Council.

Campbell, T. (1983), 'ACE - undermining real employment?' *Scope*, no. 66, pp. 8-9.

Central Personal Social Services Advisory Committee (1979), *Report of the Sub-Committee on Support for Voluntary Organisation*.

Community Development Review Group (1991a), *Community Development in Northern Ireland: Perspectives for the Future*, Community Development Review Group/Workers Educational Association, Belfast.

Community Development Review Group (1991b), *Funding for Community and Voluntary Groups in Northern Ireland*, Community Development Review Group/Workers Educational Association, Belfast.

Co-ordinating Committee on Social Problems (1980), *Tomorrow's Resource: a Review of Government Policy towards the Voluntary Sector in the Field of Social Welfare*.

Department of Health and Social Services (1974), *Support for Voluntary Organisations*, Circular HSS 15 (OS) 1/74.

Department of Health and Social Services (1985), *Co-operation between the Statutory and Voluntary Sectors in the Health and Personal Social Services*, Circular HSS (OS) 1/85.

Department of Health and Social Services (1993a), *Strategy for the Support of the Voluntary Sector and for Community Development in Northern Ireland*, HMSO, Belfast.

Department of Health and Social Services (1993b), *Strategy Statement on the Role and Aims of the Voluntary Activity Unit*, HMSO, Belfast.

Frazer, H. (1985), 'Community Work in Northern Ireland: an Overview', Paper presented at the ECDE Conference, Galway.

Gallagher, S. (1993), 'Rural housing: the associations' challenge' in *Northern Ireland Federation of Housing Associations Directory, 1992-1993*, NIFHA Corporate Media (NI) Ltd., Holywood.

Griffiths J. H. (1975), 'Paramilitary groups and other community action groups in Northern Ireland today', *International Review of Community Development*, no. 33/4, pp. 189-206.

Griffiths, J. H., Nic Gioll a Choille, T. & Robinson, J. (1978), *Yesterday's Heritage or Tomorrow's Resource?: a Study of Voluntary Organisations Providing Social Services in Northern Ireland*, New University of Ulster, Coleraine.

Hayes, M. (1972), *Community Relations and the Role of the Community Relations Commission in Northern Ireland*, Runnymede Trust, London.

Holmes, E. (1993), 'The Northern Ireland Federation of Housing Associations' in *Northern Ireland Federation of Housing Associations Directory, 1992-1993*, NIFHA Corporate Media (NI) Ltd., Holywood.

Home Office (1990), *Efficiency Scrutiny of Government Funding of the Voluntary Sector: Profiting from Partnership*, HMSO, London.

Lovett, T., Gunn, D. & Robson, T. (1994), 'Education, conflict and community development in Northern Ireland', *Community Development Journal*,. vol. 29, no. 2, pp. 177-86.

McDonald, H. (1993), 'The new financial regime' in *Northern Ireland Federation of Housing Associations Directory, 1992-1993*, NIFHA Corporate Media (NI) Ltd., Holywood.

McGinley, A. (1990), 'District Councils and Community Services: Who Really Cares?' in Deane, E. (ed.), *Lost Horizons, New Horizons: Community Development in Northern Ireland*, Workers Educational Association, Belfast.

Northern Ireland Housing Executive (1990), *Rural Housing Policy Review, Leading the Way: a consultative paper*, Belfast.

Northern Ireland Housing Executive (1991), *Rural Housing Policy, the Way Ahead: a Policy Statement*, NIHE, Belfast.

Rolston, B. (1985), 'Community services in Northern Ireland: the last ten years', *Critical Social Policy*, no. 14, p. 83.

Simm, J. & McCallum, D. (1993), 'Co-ownership works and how!' in *Northern Ireland Federation of Housing Associations Directory, 1993-1993*, NIFHA Corporate Media (NI) Ltd., Holywood.

Singleton, D. (1983), 'The voluntary housing movement in Northern Ireland: progress, problems and prospects', *Housing Review*, vol. 32, no. 5, pp. 155-59.

Smith, J. (1993), 'Community-based associations: one man's view' in *Northern Ireland Federation of Housing Associations Directory, 1992-1993*, NIFHA Corporate Media (NI) Ltd., Holywood.

Smith, T. (1994), Talk presented at the fourth annual dinner for housing association chairmen, April 1994.

Tweed, B. (1971), 'Community work comment in Northern Ireland', *Social Work Today*, vol. 2, no. 15, pp. 2-4.

7 The Protestant churches and social welfare: voluntary action and government support

Duncan Morrow

Protestantism and the dissenting tradition have long been identified as important factors in shaping the nature of the voluntary tradition in the English-speaking world. In Northern Ireland the defence of Protestant liberty, including, one supposes, the right of free association, has long been given as one of the main justifications for Unionism. As such, Protestantism and voluntarism are closely tied together with many aspects of social and political life at a conceptual level. The Victorian Age left a legacy, in Northern Ireland as much as elsewhere, of a myriad of voluntary groups concerned with social welfare and relief, community building and even political campaigning. Many of these groups had, and have, direct church connections, connections which have shaped their actions, their appeal and their structure.

During the twentieth century, church-related groups, often historical pioneers in their fields, have lost their pre-eminence. Some organizations, such as Barnardo's, have lost their previous attachment to churches. Others, like the YMCA, have learnt to operate within a secular environment. However, the churches have continued to provide both new organizations and personnel for other groups and continue to be active in the provision of welfare and social services in the voluntary sector.

In Northern Ireland, the continued importance of the churches in secular life and the absence of any broadly-based secular alternatives have meant that the profile of the churches in the sphere of voluntary action has been higher than elsewhere. Furthermore, as we shall see, the nature of voluntary action within the churches often encompasses a wide range of activities which are lost within single-issue and campaigning groups. What is certain is that any survey of the voluntary sector in Northern Ireland is likely to be incomplete without a thorough analysis of the churches.

101

The Protestant churches and society in Northern Ireland

Churches remain important in Northern Ireland in a way that is no longer true in England, Scotland and Wales. Up to 80 per cent of people in Northern Ireland maintain some church connection, and the churches remain important social centres. This high level of church loyalty must be qualified. Attendance is higher among Catholics than Protestants and there are sharp differences between the rural areas and Belfast in particular. Moxon-Brown (1983) found that 39 per cent of Protestants in Northern Ireland attended church weekly, although the figure for Belfast was 33 per cent. In working-class areas attendance is considerably lower. A Church of Ireland survey in 1985 (COI, 1985a) found that only 16 per cent of its nominal membership attended church weekly in the inner city of Belfast, falling as low as 4 per cent in Whiterock. There is evidence that Protestants leaving Belfast do not re-establish contact with churches in the suburbs. The three Belfast presbyteries lost 68,416 people between 1963 and 1986 while the presbyteries around the city gained only 20,853 in the same period (Irish Inter-Church Meeting, 1991). Nevertheless, despite decline the churches remain the largest institutions within the community in terms of attendance and geographical reach.

In church terms, Protestantism is a single name covering a plural phenomenon. These differences in doctrine, liturgy, culture and historical experience are often hidden if Protestantism is defined in political terms, the religious dimension of an ethnic division in Northern Ireland. Defining Protestantism as 'non-Catholic' has a political validity which the churches have been unable to shake off, but it hides the contribution of Protestantism itself to the structure of public power in Northern Ireland.

The multipolar nature of church structures means that there is no single church which corresponds to the community. No church leader or assembly can ever speak for more than one part of the community. Leaders who try to do so, such as the Reverend Ian Paisley, do so on the basis of votes cast in secular elections. The churches, as churches, do not, and cannot, exercise monopoly social control. The clear authority of Catholic moral and social teaching does not exist for the Protestant churches (Hickey, 1984, p. 16). Decentralization is crucial to Protestant self-understanding. Final authority for Protestants is vested in the individual conscience and a personal reading of scripture in a more explicit way than in Catholicism.

> There cannot be a Protestant social order in the way there can be a Catholic social order as developed from *Rerum Novarum* [1891] on. There were particular Protestant emphases - the importance of individual conscience, the vocation of the committed Christian in society, the

importance of personal charity, the reform of the individual, suspicion of the concentration of power, the importance of social righteousness, particularly manifested in concern about drinking, gambling and Sunday observance. All of these emphases can be seen, to a greater or lesser extent, in the Protestant churches in Ireland (Stevens, 1992).

The three largest Protestant churches illustrate these differences. The largest, the Presbyterian Church, is rooted in Scottish Calvinism although influenced by the Baptist-inspired revival movement which took place in the United States in the nineteenth century. The result is an often uneasy combination of liberalism and conservative evangelical theology and a culture of doctrinal debate, numerous committees and thorough administration. Presbyterians are concentrated in the north and east of the province, particularly in County Antrim, and in the business communities of the cities. The Church of Ireland, once the established church, retains a sense of ministry to the whole island of Ireland. Anglicanism has traditionally been associated with English authority. The Church is in a minority in all parts of Ireland but is more evenly spread than any other Protestant church, both geographically and in terms of class. Methodism is a later arrival which had particular success in County Fermanagh. Methodism's roots as a working-class revivalist movement have left the church with a traditional interest in social reform.

Diversity is reflected in the approach to social welfare among the Protestant churches. Each church has inherited piecemeal commitments which reflect earlier concerns. For example, the Presbyterian Church in Ireland has a special Shankill Road Mission, a mission to the deaf, a residential trust for old people and a number of other organized social welfare activities. The Church of Ireland has a Social and Family Welfare Association and the only Protestant adoption society in Northern Ireland. The Methodist Church has a number of shelters for homeless people. Its East Belfast Mission and Grosvenor Hall in central Belfast are reminders of the working-class roots of the movement.

Protestant churches, voluntary action and the Northern Ireland state

The situation of the Protestant churches in Northern Ireland reflects not only a diverse internal structure but also a general willingness to support the state. The close association of religious belief and political outlook is reflected in church attitudes at an institutional level.

The willingness of the Protestant churches to hand over responsibility for welfare provision and education to the British or Northern Irish state, a state to which most of their members felt loyal, contrasts sharply with the quasi-representative role adopted by the Catholic Church, many of whose parishioners are openly hostile to the state. Protestant churches were not required to be defensive bulwarks between their parishioners and the state. Unionist and Orange Order patronage meant that the Protestant churches had a much lower public profile as community protectors (Farrell, 1976). Their influence was implicit rather than explicit. The ideological influence of Protestantism has been clearer than any structural or organizational monopoly. For Catholics the opposite was true. There is no Protestant equivalent to the Society of St Vincent de Paul nor the thorough welfare structures of Catholic dioceses.

These relationships have clearly shaped the different patterns of Protestant and Catholic voluntary action. By handing over primary responsibility to the state, Protestant churches have not faced the charges of monopolistic authority levelled at the Roman Catholic Church. However, the different relationships have appeared to give substance to loyalist jibes about Catholic 'priest domination'. Both church structures and the actual relationship to the state have shaped these impressions.

Sectarian politics, which put a premium on community defence against external enemies rather than internal class divisions, shaped the profile of the churches in another way. Although Belfast was Ireland's most industrialized city, class politics have been consistently subordinated to religious divisions. Even the Northern Ireland Labour Party (NILP) in the 1960s was unable to master sectarian antagonisms and violence (Wright, 1973). In the voluntary sector, the result has been a relatively weak trade union movement. Even organizations like the Workers Educational Association (WEA) arrived late and never successfully established a popular movement for social education. As a result, nearly all community welfare functions not administered by the state have a church dimension. The churches have retained a 'monopoly of respectability' even in the working classes where church attendance is low.

Religious tradition continues to have a significance even for those not in the churches, especially in the field of voluntary action and the provision of community facilities. The presence of the churches in every social group in the province and the absence of any significant rivals for organizational strength have established the churches as the only thinkable vehicles of vertical integration within the Protestant community. But church leaders, at least in the three largest Protestant churches, have not seen it as their task to articulate the political views of 'their people'. They have instead emphasized moral education and the task of the churches to encourage 'good citizenship'.

The Protestant experience is shaped by the political and social realities of Northern Ireland and, at the same time, the experience of what it is to be Protestant is, in part, shaped by the churches. Under Unionist hegemony, the churches have not had to be explicitly political, leaving that to secular politicians, nor have they had to stand between the state and their community. Protestantism remains one of the hidden glues of society and politics in Northern Ireland.

The economic experience of the Protestant churches

The Protestant community as a whole has never been dominated by the experience of poverty and political exclusion as has the Catholic community. While it is true that a Protestant urban and rural poor has always existed, it has done so side by side with a prospering middle and upper class. Industrial unemployment, although higher than in many places in Great Britain, was always lower than among Catholics. Many Catholics, on the other hand, perceive poverty as a central experience of Catholic life in Northern Ireland. The growth of a substantial Catholic middle class as a result of educational change and the welfare state has been central to the changing relationship between Protestants and Catholics in Northern Ireland since the 1960s.

Economic contraction in the 1970s and 1980s found the Protestant community relatively unprepared. Throughout the 1980s, the Community Development movement has bemoaned the lack of social cohesion in Protestant, as opposed to Catholic, areas (Hamilton et al., 1991, p. 23). Paul Sweeney, director of Northern Ireland Voluntary Trust (NIVT) until 1994, has noted an 'innate resistance on the part of Protestants to declare themselves in need' and remarks on considerable differences between Catholic and Protestant groups in regard to funding applications.

> Protestants exhibit: a real reluctance to come forward; meticulous adherence to the detail of their request. The constitutionality and representative nature of the groups will be well established. The request will be modest and seldom commensurate with the level of need. There will be a strong emphasis on accountability and propriety and the request will be supported by patrons and testimonials (Sweeney, 1991, p. 8).

The Protestant churches are present throughout the community, through all classes and levels of urbanization. There is, however, a sharp contrast between the well-organized and coherent nature of the Protestant churches in middle-class and in rural areas and Protestantism in working-class areas where the remnants of Protestant values remain without the structures within which to place them.

105

The nature of Protestant church voluntary action

Because the churches are simultaneously legal institutions and communities of believers, the influence of the churches cannot be limited to those organizations which maintain a formal institutional link. At a basic level groups like Christian Aid, the YMCA and the Corrymeela Community have their *raison d'être* in Christian faith. Other groups, as diverse as Barnardo's, Child Poverty Action, Oxfam and the Richmond Fellowship, have direct origins in Christian belief and practice. A fully inclusive picture of church involvement in the voluntary sector would have to include the huge number of groups whose active core is sustained by people motivated by personal Christian faith. Among clergy some 40 per cent claimed to be involved in voluntary organizations in a personal capacity (Morrow et al., 1991, p. 21).

The impact of the churches is most visible if one adopts a wide definition, which includes membership of community-building and community-sustaining organizations. Protestant churches remain the focus of important social networks throughout Northern Ireland. At a basic level, these networks are invisible except in close interpersonal ties. This is particularly true in rural districts, where the organization of formal groups is less developed and creates considerable difficulties in measuring the 'importance' of the churches. Even in urban areas, the churches have a number of important functions for those who have no regular worshipping attachment to church. The buildings attached to churches have long been central community resources for young people, for women's groups and for sports clubs. Church halls are often the only gathering points for cultural and political activities such as campaigns against the closure of a local hospital or school carol services (Morrow et al., 1991). Only pubs and drinking clubs can claim a similar centrality.

The visible network has taken the form of numerous groups attached to local churches which provide a social and community infrastructure for the congregations. There is widespread participation in church related activities. A recent survey showed that 90 per cent of all churches had active choirs (Morrow et al., 1991, p. 13). An average choir size of twenty-five people would mean that over 27,000 people were engaged in church singing in Northern Ireland. There are thousands of church-related uniformed youth organizations, youth clubs, women's groups, bowling clubs, badminton clubs, mother and toddler groups, and prayer groups. Church youth organizations may involve as many as 100,000 young people (Belfast News Letter, 26 November 1991). The fact that these groups are not publicly financed and do not employ professional workers makes them statistically invisible in much research. There is no badminton clubs lobby group!

The churches are also huge voluntary economies in terms both of money collected and distributed and of commitment of time and skills. For example, in four months in 1985 the Presbyterian Church raised £270,000 in its own Ethiopian Famine Appeal (PCI, 1985). In 1990, Presbyterian congregational income in Northern Ireland was £25m (PCI, 1991a). If we understand the term voluntary to mean 'freely given', the Protestant churches have some claim to be the origin of modern voluntarism in British and Irish society. In this sense too, they retain the spirit of voluntarism more effectively than most other social organizations.

Protestant churches, voluntary action and the state since 1979

Since 1979 the biggest change in church community action has been their increasing involvement with state-funded programmes. Both the Church of Ireland and the Presbyterian Church have, with government backing, appointed professional social workers. The churches have become involved in the management of government job creation programmes known as 'Action for Community Employment' (ACE) schemes. This has led to a much higher profile for the churches in the economy than ever before and represents a substantial change in the nature of church local action, for it is the first time that churches have acted as employers on this scale. However, church involvement in voluntary work is almost entirely institutional and touches the congregational life of the churches only marginally. ACE management does not involve congregational participation. Instead clergy tend to chair committees made up of a few leading lay people. In many ways this is similar to the involvement of the churches with the management of schools where the churches act as acceptable intermediaries between local communities and the government. Church ACE schemes are not notably more spiritual than others.

Controversy surrounds the Catholic Church and its seeming monopoly on ACE schemes in parts of west Belfast. Statistics suggest that Protestant churches in total are at least as active in the development of ACE schemes. Of a total of 1,042 ACE posts in church-managed schemes based in the Belfast-Lisburn-Newtownabbey area in 1991, 426 (41 per cent) were employed in schemes managed by the Catholic Church while 616 (59 per cent) were in schemes managed by Protestant churches, either as single denominations or together. This reflects the total division of ACE employment under church management throughout Northern Ireland.

Table 1   ACE schemes under church management (1991)

Management (by denomination)	No of posts	% of church managed
Roman Catholic	691	29.3
Presbyterian	188	8.0
Church of Ireland	149	6.3
Methodist	63	2.7
Inter Protestant (Pres, C of I, Meth)	103	4.7
Other Protestant (single group)	360	15.3
Inter-community (Prot - RC)	529	22.4
Para-church (YMCA, Project House)	274	11.6
TOTAL	2357	100.0
Protestant	863	36.6
Roman Catholic	691	29.3
Inter-community	529	22.4
Para-church	274	11.6

Some schemes in which the churches are deeply involved (for example the Flax Trust or Gobnascale Family Centre) are not listed as church-managed by the Department of Economic Development because of the structure of that involvement. The figures reflect a narrow interpretation of the term 'church-managed'. However, even on this definition, church-managed projects employ up to a quarter of all ACE workers in Northern Ireland. Of course, church-management does not indicate the denomination of workers. This is especially true for cross-community managed projects, but may also be valid in other cases.

There is a clear difference between the number of schemes under Catholic management and the number of schemes under the management of any one of the larger Protestant churches. Indeed, the Catholic Church on its own manages nearly four times more people under ACE than does the Presbyterian Church. Here the structural difference between Catholicism and Protestantism becomes of central importance. If one excludes the schemes in which the main Protestant churches are involved, either together or in partnership with the Catholic church, the single Protestant church with the most ACE employees under its sole control is the Elim Pentecostal Church.

Table One shows that a statistical Protestant majority breaks up into numerous parts which are virtually unlinked to one another. Local conditions and initiatives predominate. There is no 'typical' structure. Instead there is a wide variation in organization and management. No Protestant church attains the universal presence of the Catholic Church. As a result, the social visibility of any single institution is much less. However, despite the fact that ACE schemes are as prevalent in Protestant churches as in Catholic churches, there is no sense of cohesive community or community leadership around such schemes in Protestantism. Instead there is a group of independent actors, related only through the source of funding. The Catholic Church can be said to provide a sense of social cohesion, but the corollary is that Protestants regard Catholicism as dominant and alien to them. The Protestant churches have a more 'democratic' appearance but, as a result, there is very little social cohesion within the Protestant community except around opposition to Catholicism and Republicanism.

The second area where the government has increased its involvement with the churches has been community relations. Again, the government has sought to tap the potential of the churches as grassroots bodies. Historical antagonism and residential segregation have meant that cross-community approaches have traditionally been a very low priority for the churches. There is some evidence that in the latter half of the 1980s government has provided the main impetus for change in churches. In general, church congregations and parishes continue to operate independently of one another. The vast majority of voluntary bodies operate within one congregation or another.

> The churches in Northern Ireland have not regarded inter-community relationships as a matter for particular programmes of action. Churches have seldom produced proposals for new initiatives which involve congregations and parishes at a systematic level. Even ACE programmes undertaken on an interdenominational basis tend to be limited to a small number of people. Serious discussions about the relationship of Christianity to the question of inter-community relationships have been limited to small groups and to particular congregations and parishes. Discussions on the task of the churches in a divided society have seldom taken place except between clergy (Morrow et al., 1991).

In general, the churches have seldom engaged in ecumenical work without government prompting. Within the Presbyterian Church in particular, most movement has appeared to be away from any relationship with Catholics. In 1989, the General Assembly voted not to join the Council of Churches for Britain and Ireland, largely on the basis that the Catholic Church was present on the same body as a full member. A significant proportion of Presbyterian clergy (in one survey, 43 per cent) would not share worship with Catholics (Morrow et al., 1991, p. 20).

The political pressure from government for an increased commitment from the churches has been growing. The establishment of the ACE programme in 1980 and of the Community Relations Council in 1990 has led to a number of initiatives. The Churches' Central Council for Community Work (CCCCW) has been rescued from near-terminal decline by government funding (PCI, 1990). The committee has since organized a number of initiatives to encourage cross-community ventures (Lee, 1990). Furthermore, nearly a quarter of church-managed ACE schemes are on a cross-community basis. To this can be added the 'para-church' managed schemes, operated by the YMCA which has made a major commitment to community relations work. These schemes are spread throughout the province.

Protestant churches and social thought in Northern Ireland

Secular writing, whether as social science or fiction, often portrays the Protestant churches in Northern Ireland as the last bastions of reaction. For many political radicals this is closely linked with political conservatism, with some allowance for eighteenth century Presbyterian radicalism. Nevertheless, one must not forget that socialism in Britain owed more to Methodism than to Marx. Yet churches are often perceived by community workers to be rivals, not allies, marked by a deep social conservatism.

> ... Areas where Protestant fundamentalism is quite strong are not immediately receptive to the challenging doctrine implied in the community development social change process ... (Morrow et al., 1991, p. 6).

Certainly, majorities in the churches have been vocal opponents of much of the contemporary liberal social agenda. Recently, the question of changing male-female relations and especially the ordination of women as clergy within the churches, has caused considerable turmoil. Although the three largest Protestant churches in Ireland now ordain women, significant elements within each church have been resistant to these changes. Culturally, in comparison to other public institutions, the church is often seen as a crucial conservative force in relation to the role of women in society.

Examination of church documents and surveys shows the ideological position of the Protestant churches to be rather complex. In a survey of clergy in Northern Ireland, between 70 and 80 per cent in each of the four main churches said that social and community outreach projects were important, or very important, in their parishes. Fewer than 3 per cent said that such projects were of no importance to them (Morrow et al., 1991, p. 15).

Furthermore, over 50 per cent of all ministers in all denominations saw specific possibilities of developing community work within their own parishes.

A reading of church reports through the 1980s suggests that Protestant churches have not been uncritical supporters of Conservative social policy. For example, the Presbyterian Church, which has a strong fundamentalist wing, had this to say on the subject of the church and the welfare state:

> As the church we must affirm the truth of the worth of each human being as created by God. We must assert to Government as a fundamental truth that anything which undermines this in terms of policy or legislation is blasphemous, as it would be an express denial of the purpose, will and character of the creator God. In this would be included such things as the exploitation of the weak and disadvantaged, economic measures whereby the gap between the 'have' and 'have-nots' grows even wider and the rewarding of wealth and privilege with large tax concessions at the expense of those on low incomes ... (PCI, 1991b)

Similarly the Methodist Church and the Church of Ireland comment annually on social and political issues. Writing in 1985 the Synod of the Church of Ireland stated:

> The problem of unemployment has to be tackled at two levels. The first is within the present economic and social structures of society. It is too easy to underestimate the contribution of individual and congregational efforts, of the local attempts to create employment and the need for moral concern and effort. Justice and mercy demand a more impressive and sensitive example from those who have most (COI, 1985b).

At a rhetorical level the churches are neither disinterested in the development of social thought nor are they always conservative. However, social welfare has only occasionally been a priority issue in congregational life. The conservatism of the churches can be detected less in public policy pronouncements than in the absence of radical experiments or development of social and community programmes from within. As Gallagher and Worrall (1976, p. 103) say:

> Truth to tell there is little convincing evidence that during these fifty years (of Unionist rule) any of the Irish churches demonstrated much in the way of insight into the social and economic implications of the gospel.

Instead, the Protestant churches became associated with clerically-controlled, and rather confined, schemes and a regularly repeated emphasis on strict personal morality (Stevens, 1992). The private moral agenda has predominated over the social in public perceptions.

Conclusions

The Protestant churches are integral to any organic understanding of society in Northern Ireland. They straddle the public and private spheres more universally than any other bodies. The decline in church attendance has not seen the emergence of any rival organizations except, perhaps, paramilitary groups. As a result, urban working-class areas which are Protestant by tradition but largely avoid church attendance, are characterized by atomization. Although economic history clearly plays an important role, Protestantism itself contributes to this, firstly through the general lack of a single focusing institution within the community and secondly through an emphasis on personal morality and effort.

In non-conformism, voluntarism is a basic principle. This voluntary base has now been supplemented by state funding, making the churches important parts of the so-called 'voluntary sector'. In church terms this has meant a decline in voluntarism and an increase in professionalism. Most of the new thinking on social and community involvement has been generated by 'para-church' groups, such as the Corrymeela Community or the YMCA rather than by the major churches.

Notes

1. These figures, together with those in Table 1, were provided on request by the Department of Economic Development, Community Projects Division.

References

The Belfast News Letter, 26 November 1991, p. 2.

Church of Ireland (1985a), *Report of the Diocesan Episcopal Commission*, Diocese of Connor, Belfast.

Church of Ireland (1985b), *Role of the Church Committee Report*, General Synod, Dublin.

Farrell, Michael (1976), *Northern Ireland, the Orange State*, Pluto Press, London.

Gallagher, Eric & Worrall, Stanley (1976), *Violence in Ireland*, Veritas/ Christian Journals, Dublin and Belfast.

Hamilton, A., McCartney, C., Finn, A. & Anderson, T. (1991), *Violence and Communities*, Centre for the Study of Conflict, University of Ulster, Coleraine.

Hickey, John (1984), *Religion and the Northern Ireland Problem*, Gill and Macmillan, Dublin and London.

Irish Inter-Church Meeting (1991), *The Challenge of the City: the Report of the Working Party on the Challenge of the Urban Situation in Ireland Today*.

Lee, Simon (ed.) (1990), *Freedom from Fear*, Institute of Irish Studies, Queen's University, Belfast.

Morrow, D., Birrell, D., Greer, J. & O'Keeffe, T. (1991), *The Churches and Inter-Community Relationships*, Centre for the Study of Conflict, University of Ulster, Coleraine.

Moxon-Brown, Eddie (1983), *Nation, Class and Northern Ireland*, Gower, Aldershot.

Presbyterian Church in Ireland (1985), '[Report of the] Board of Finance and Administration' in *Annual Reports 1985*, PCI, Belfast.

Presbyterian Church in Ireland (1990), '[Report of the] Board of Social Witness' in *Annual Reports 1990*, PCI, Belfast.

Presbyterian Church in Ireland (1991a), 'The Church and the Welfare State' in *Annual Reports 1991*, PCI, Belfast.

Presbyterian Church in Ireland (1991b), '[Report of the] Board of Finance and Administration in *Annual Reports 1991*, PCI, Belfast.

Stevens, David (1992), 'The Social Thinking of the Churches in Ireland', Irish Council of Churches, (unpublished typescript).

Sweeney, Paul (1991), *Community Work in Protestant Areas*, NICVA, Belfast.

Wright, Frank (1973), 'Protestant ideology and politics in Ulster', *European Journal of Sociology*, vol. 14, pp. 213-80.

8 Voluntary action, rural policy and social development

Jimmy Armstrong and Avila Kilmurray

This chapter will discuss a range of issues related both to objective factors which influence and impact rural dwellers, and to the importance of the rural community consciousness. It must be remembered that many complexities and contradictions emerge from any examination of rural development whether in Northern Ireland, or elsewhere.

Analyses of rurality in Northern Ireland are often at odds with the perceptions of rural communities themselves. This dichotomy was reflected in the conclusions of Colin Thomas (1986), drawn from his study of change in the Braid Valley (County Antrim) area of Northern Ireland:

> ... Perceptions of rural society's structure and pattern compiled from an urban vantage point and coloured by primarily material considerations inevitably yield only partial understanding of sociocultural processes and attitudes that emanate from the countryside itself. An interpretation which rests solely upon apparently objective criteria and descriptions of rural-urban migration, employment linkages, consumer behaviour, traffic flows and recreational activities would give the overwhelming impression that free standing rural communities no longer exist: they are seen to be subsumed in spatially more extensive, urban-oriented settlements which control, or guide, all human activities ... However, examination of cultural associations, whether defined by kinship, religious affiliation or social action space, tend to present a more morcellated view of rural populations, and also one that is far less dependent upon urban interaction. Attachments to, and support for, local institutions therefore indicate equally valid evidences of community consciousness, differing from urbanised relationships both in scale and purpose ...

Thomas suggests that the latter may be considered more appropriate tests of community cohesion and identity as they emerge from the rural perspective rather than being a necessary response to material considerations such as sources of employment and services.

Rurality and disadvantage

Despite the insights of Colin Thomas cited above, it still remains difficult to draw sharp lines of division between urban and rural areas within Northern Ireland. The evidence would suggest that while such a distinction is at times difficult to establish, nevertheless there are core areas of extremely urban and extremely rural conditions, with an intermediate zone of continuously changing blends of the two. This rural-urban continuum concept, particularly associated with the work of Paul Cloke, (1988) can be held to be appropriate to Northern Irish circumstances on the basis of the following categories:

(a) The urban areas consisting of Greater Belfast, Derry and the district towns - which account for a small proportion of the land area but account for 55 per cent of Northern Ireland's population, and much of its manufacturing base.

(b) The extreme rural areas which are characterized by a very low population density, containing 65 per cent of the land area but only 15 per cent of the population. These areas are also indicated by a high level of dependence on employment in primary industries: farming, fishing and forestry.

(c) The intermediate areas which have a shifting blend of rural and urban occupational patterns and varying population densities.

In the late 1980s the Policy Planning Research Unit (PPRU) defined the distribution of disadvantaged areas in Northern Ireland to facilitate the resource allocation decisions of the International Fund for Ireland (IFI). Using the 1981 population census results and levels of male unemployment as the primary indicator, 181 rural electoral wards were identified as disadvantaged. Nineteen additional wards were added to this category when three other variables were taken into account - these related to housing standards and levels of car ownership. On the basis of this analyses the spatial distribution of rural disadvantage can be described in terms of the following regions:

The Glens of Antrim
The Sperrins

Fermanagh
The Loughshore (Lough Neagh)
South Down and South Armagh.

These areas between them contain some 11.9 per cent of Northern Ireland's population, but account for 43 per cent of the land area, with population density being about one quarter of the Northern Ireland average.

While there is an urgent need to review the map of rural disadvantage in the light of the 1991 population census figures, it is unlikely that the general distribution of rurality will have changed much from previous estimates. Data published in January 1990 showed that unemployment in the regions specified above was two to three percentage points higher than the Northern Ireland average, while the Regional Housing Survey carried out by the Northern Ireland Housing Executive in 1986, and updated by a more recent study of rural housing policy, underlined the fact that rural housing unfitness is a much greater problem than urban unfitness, and that one rural dwelling in ten continues to lack at least one basic amenity (Armstrong, 1990).

The pattern of deprivation experienced by specific disadvantaged rural areas may well vary from area to area - thus South Armagh has a high population density, with the proportion of the population aged sixteen and under higher than the Northern Ireland average. However high rates of unemployment, small farms and a pattern of dispersed settlement across poor quality land, results in a high dependence on social security benefits and high rates of emigration. West Fermanagh, in comparison, suffers from a demographic imbalance with a low proportion of young people in relation to an above average elderly population. Some 15.6 per cent of the population are over the age of sixty-five, as compared to an average of 11 per cent for Northern Ireland as a whole. Some 73 per cent of households in West Fermanagh are still designated farm households, although with the exception of small pockets of medium quality land, most of the farming in the region is carried out on land that has been classified as medium to poor in quality (Kilmurray, 1989).

Whatever the particular aspects, the overall extent of deprivation in many areas of extreme rurality has now been established through both academic studies and the campaigning work of many local community groups and some voluntary organizations. Not least was the contribution to the rural policy debate made by the Rural Action Project (Northern Ireland) - a voluntary sector project funded under the EC Second Anti-Poverty programme over the period 1986-90. This programme verified the conclusions of the Arkleton Trust some ten years previously, that while the concept of 'disadvantage' is both subjective and entirely relative, disadvantaged rural areas in Western Europe are to be found mainly on the geographical periphery (Arkleton,

1979). In Northern Ireland such areas occur on the periphery of a peripheral region of Europe.

Community action to redress rural disadvantage

Despite persistent and deeply rooted problems of rural poverty and disadvantage, collective community action to address these issues appeared limited in comparison to the highly publicized urban community organizing of the 1970s and 1980s in Northern Ireland. This is not to say that community groups did not exist in many rural areas, but they tended to prioritize issues of community care and social concern rather than to emphasize more long-term developmental priorities. In addition to this, work undertaken in rural settings was often low key in nature, and more concerned with local credibility rather than involvement in, or impact on, the official decision-making process at either local authority or governmental level. In the chronicles of community action rural communities appeared less articulate than their urban counterparts, with their demands often being mediated through locally elected councillors, local clergy and established community figures rather than by the 'community activists' who represented urban areas.

It is interesting to examine the experience of one such rural community in the Creggan area of County Tyrone, an area in the Sperrin Mountains that falls into the category of extreme rurality. In 1972, when many working-class communities in the Greater Belfast area were dealing with vast movements of population due to sectarian intimidation, a meeting was called in Creggan school to discuss the formation of another football team and the provision of a field or base for the new team. The meeting felt that a community association should be established to consider the demand for a football club, but also the need for a community centre and the provision of increased public housing in the area. The social priority which emphasized the needs of the young football players would absorb the time, energy and fundraising abilities of local community activists for some four years, with considerable achievements despite the fluctuating fortunes of the team.

In 1976, however, the issue of local accommodation reemerged as a matter of concern. Depopulation of this rural community was being aggravated by the lack of Housing Executive dwellings for young married couples. A meeting was called to consider this issue and the fact that planning regulations made it difficult to build in the area. Research was carried out, and representations were made to the Housing Executive. Despite the fact that some eighteen people were identified as wanting to reside in Creggan, and three landowners expressed a willingness to sell sites to the Housing

118

Executive, the campaign achieved little. In the face of this setback the community committee disbanded.

1978 marked a revival of community action in the Creggan area, and in November a meeting reviewed both achievements to date and priorities for the future. Amongst the achievements were the fact that the association owned more than two acres of land, which included a playing field, car park and site for a community centre. In addition a youth club had been started. The priorities included the building of the community centre as a focus for the people of the area. The association was formalized in January 1979 by the adoption of a constitution and the receipt of an initial grant of £150 from Omagh District Council.

A detailed description of the developing role of the Creggan Community Association can be found in the Association's own publication, *Out of the Embers - a History of Creggan through its People* (Haughey, 1988). It is appropriate here to record that the work of the Association followed the path of moving through a process of concern for local young people and pensioners to the identification of the infrastructural and economic needs of the area. The story of Creggan Community Association remained however largely unknown outside the confines of its own local authority area. It relied heavily on the voluntary commitment and sense of self-sufficiency of the residents of the immediate community. This pattern of rural community action is quite different from that experienced in the Shankill area of Belfast or the Creggan area of Derry.

The late 1970s saw the development of community initiatives in at least two other rural communities with the establishment of the Community Worker Research Project (1978-82). This provided funding for a community worker to be employed in the Crossmaglen area of South Armagh and in the Knockninny area of rural Fermanagh, together with community projects in some twelve other urban or district town locations.

It is interesting to note that the evaluation report published by the Department of Education (NI) on this programme did not consider rural community development as a specific category for discussion; instead the focus was placed on neighbourhood work; economic development; research and welfare rights (Caven, 1982). In the event however, the two rural projects were particularly concerned with economic development - an interest that obviously reflected local concern with high rates of unemployment, under-employment and emigration. While much was achieved by community action in both Crossmaglen and Knockninny, the evaluation also reflected on some of the difficulties. A number of comments highlighted important points:

An aim low, score high approach as an initial strategy might have resulted in more on-the-ground concrete developments which would have provided positive reinforcement to the efforts of both worker and community and perhaps led to the more ambitious schemes having greater success at a later stage (Para. 4.4.5.).

The evidence from the two main economic projects indicates another characteristic of work in this area - that sometimes things move very slowly and projects may lie inactive for a considerable time while administrative problems are sorted out elsewhere or legal hitches are unravelled ... (Para. 4.4.7.).

The detailed description of the work of both the Crossmaglen Community Association and the Knockninny Community Development Association reveals the very wide range of activities undertaken by the respective community workers. In the case of Crossmaglen these can be summarized as:

1. carrying out a survey of local skills in the area;

2. establishing and servicing a Crossmaglen Development Association;

3. supporting a group of women who sought to establish a soft toy manufacturing enterprise;

4. undertaking the development of Crossmaglen Town Square - with long-term financial implications;

5. developing a direct labour co-operative in the area;

6. the refurbishment of a local youth club;

7. producing a calendar depicting community involvement in Crossmaglen;

8. contributing to a magazine about the Crossmaglen area;

9. attempting to involve town traders in providing Christmas decorations in the town;

10. helping the Community Association in its negotiations with the district council concerning the provision of a community centre in Crossmaglen;

11. assessing need for new housing in the area; and

12. providing a general advice role for the area in relation to welfare benefits, housing and rent problems (Caven, 1982).

The experience of the Crossmaglen community worker in participating in a complex range of community tasks is common to community action in the rural context.

120

Despite the fact that the Community Worker Research Project did not result in the elaboration of specific arguments concerning the nature of rural development, the legacy of the Project may be seen in the extension of the community development initiative in Crossmaglen beyond the early 1980s due to the support of the Newry and Mourne District Council. The development worker from the Knockninny Community Development Association joined the staff of the Northern Ireland Voluntary Trust (NIVT), carrying with him his interest and commitment to rural community development.

Between the conclusion of the Community Worker Research Project in 1982, and the establishment of the Rural Action Project (NI) in 1986, one of the few sources of funding and support for community action in rural areas was charitable trusts, and specifically the Rural Awards Programme administered by the Northern Ireland Voluntary Trust. A small number of local authorities took an informed interest in community development and were encouraged through the Rural Awards Programme to provide additional support for rural groups in their district council areas. However, in the case of district councils much depended on the priorities of their respective chief executives and community services officers - where the latter had been appointed. Encouraged by the Northern Ireland Voluntary Trust, the Northern Ireland Rural Association (NIRA) was set up in the mid 1980s in an attempt to bring together representatives of both interested statutory bodies and local community associations in rural areas. This under-resourced organization, however, was largely dependent on the energy and enthusiasm of Des Bustard, an officer with the Northern Ireland Voluntary Trust.

In seeking to combat rural disadvantage throughout the 1970s and 1980s there appeared to be a tension between local awareness of the scale of the problems to be addressed and the extremely limited resources available to rural communities. This tension was aggravated by the need of rural community activists to be seen to succeed in view of the basic caution of many rural dwellers. Anticipated local cynicism engendered by failure - or lack of apparent achievement - made community action a more daunting undertaking for activists in rural areas compared to their urban counterparts. Nevertheless an expansion in the establishment of mother and toddler groups, pensioners' clubs, youth and sporting clubs, and local history societies, all indicated that voluntarism and social concern in rural communities continued to flourish despite the fact that many of the underlying structural problems appeared virtually insoluble. For a number of vital years the NIVT Rural Awards Programme and the Northern Ireland Rural Association offered a public recognition of the worth of such work in rural areas, and highlighted the need for public policy to address rural issues.

121

Perceptions of policy making in rural areas

Despite the on-going investment of local effort and energy into the provision of services in rural communities, many community activists perceived their work as being a vain attempt to plug gaping holes left by the withdrawal of essential services by the public authorities. Lack of a clear central government policy in relation to rural development resulted in an impression that many communities located in areas of extreme rurality had been consigned to history and were regarded as being expensive to maintain and unviable in terms of their declining population. Indeed, for such communities, there often appeared to be little alternative to the vicious cycle of population decline, lack of employment opportunity, decreasing provision of services and modern housing, and the haemorrhage of both emigration and migration. On a micro scale these rural communities seemed to reflect many of the problems long noted at the macro level where patterns of change initiated in the last century have accelerated in recent decades to create economic, social and environmental concerns for the whole society. These problems show themselves at their most acute with regard to agricultural production which is still crucial to many rural dwellers and communities in Northern Ireland.

Since the first load of American grain arrived in Liverpool in the last century free market prices for farm produce have declined in the face of competition from low cost producers in the new world. Since the second world war farm input prices have risen faster than produce prices, leading to a persistent decline in product margins. Despite the intervention of both national governments and the European Community (EC) to protect farm incomes against the worst effects of these trends, farming has been continuously in retreat. The number of farms in Northern Ireland has decreased steadily at the rate of one to two per cent per annum. In addition to this the progressive introduction of mechanization has encouraged farmers to substitute capital for labour. Thus between 1981 and 1988 full-time employment on farms decreased by more than 8 per cent. Further, in the first half of this century, the once extensive employment provided by flax growing and linen production in Northern Ireland reached its peak, and then totally collapsed, leaving many rural areas with a displaced non-farming workforce.

The progressive decline in farming, with little or no counter balancing growth in other sectors, resulted in high rates of unemployment in rural areas (2 to 3 per cent above the already high Northern Ireland average) and under-employment on farms where some 50 per cent are not capable of providing full-time employment for one person. Economic growth, where it has occurred, is still concentrated in the larger urban or district town centres. This growth has, however, remained limited, with one economic commentator noting:

The essence of the economic problem in Northern Ireland is that it is an economy with a rapidly growing labour force tied to a slow growing national economy ... Equally worrying is the fact that recovery in the national economy since 1982 has largely excluded Northern Ireland (Gudgin, 1989).

In the context of these overall economic concerns the fate of small rural communities often seemed low in the list of government priorities, particularly when the concerns of the communities themselves often went unreported. Furthermore the growth centre strategy adopted by successive governments in Northern Ireland had only a limited effect on residual rural areas outside the immediate rural hinterlands of district towns (five to ten miles). The 'trickle down' benefit effect of economic development in these selected towns did little to arrest the decline of communities in remoter rural areas.

Another policy issue of concern to both rural society, and society as a whole, has been the interaction between the rural economy and the environment. The Matthew Report (1964) noted that 'the Ulster countryside is the province's greatest asset'. However, farming techniques and the need for accommodation in rural areas have often been found to be at variance with the need to protect the environment. In the past various types of grant support have been used to encourage farmers to increase output with increased fertilizer use; to increase their land area through reclamation; or to invest in new buildings and machinery to increase output per head. In the process waterways have been polluted with nitrogen, phosphate and silage effluent; hedgerows and stone walls have been removed; valuable moorland and wetland habitats have been spoiled and massive steel clad buildings have intruded (uncontrolled) on to the landscape. Conservationists have often questioned the role of the Department of Agriculture (NI) in this process. Similarly, local rural dwellers have often vented their fury on the planning authorities who were seen as blocking local development. Ken Maginnis, member of parliament for the rural county of Fermanagh, when addressing a conference on rural development in 1989 lamented 'When are the planners or the Department of Agriculture going to assist nature instead of hindering people?' (Maginnis, 1990). This has been echoed by many rural communities over the years. However speaking at the same gathering John Greer, Department of Architecture and Planning, Queen's University, Belfast contended that:

Planning controls have been in force for a relatively short period of time - 30 years - and the planners' problems stem from a lack of understanding (by the public) of the purpose of planning and from the belief that a person who owns land can use it as he pleases. This results in a lack of sympathy with any policy which interferes with the individual's right to develop as he pleases (Greer, 1990).

Nevertheless, the rural view of the planner as being unaccountable and essentially in opposition to local development is firmly rooted.

The third policy issue that concerned rural dwellers over recent decades has been the fact that economies of scale obtained by concentrating services in fewer locations have encouraged the centralization of major services such as shopping, entertainment, health, education and housing provision. This trend has made it more difficult for people, particularly elderly people, children and many women, to obtain ready access to the services they need. It has also been demonstrated by research that it is the superior access to services which has been the most frequent influence on families deciding to move from the country to the town. The dilemma was again posed by Ken Maginnis:

> Let's admit it - education in rural areas costs more; care of the aged costs more; so does the provision of water, power and sewerage. The government could do a much better job if we all lived in estates in the town. Sadly, that was the very policy which, as well as denuding the countryside, has changed the character and ethos of many of our towns, again for the worse (Maginnis, 1990).

The 1980s saw a number of vigorous community campaigns in various rural areas to protest about the closure of local schools, post offices or small hospitals - often to little avail. While contrary to the trends found in many other parts of the United Kingdom, the rural-urban migration, and consequent rural depopulation, has continued in the more remote rural areas of Northern Ireland.

From the viewpoint of the small, often remote, rural community these deep structural problems were made worse by the apparent inaccessibility of policy makers. For political reasons in Northern Ireland local authorities had little influence, and even less power. Too often it seemed that the competing needs of deprived urban areas and the often hidden nature of multiple deprivation in the countryside, combined to relegate rural needs to the agricultural agenda.

Community action for policy change

The launch of the Rural Action Project (NI) as a four year action research programme (1985-89) funded by the European Community and by the Department of Health and Social Services (NI), offered an opportunity to draw together the needs of specific rural communities and to seek to influence the government decision-making process in relation to rural policy. The objectives of the Rural Action Project (NI), as outlined in its 1986-87 Annual Report, were to reflect this dual approach:

(a) To experiment with innovative approaches to meet the needs of rural dwellers in the pilot areas.

(b) To encourage more direct participation by the local community in both planning and development decisions through the adoption of a community development approach.

(c) To experiment with mechanisms which would lay the basis for coordination between statutory, voluntary, local authority and community effort.

(d) To identify the major social, economic and community needs experienced by rural dwellers and to seek to increase public awareness concerning aspects of poverty and deprivation in rural areas.

(e) To implement a system of evaluation to meet the requirement of funders; to inform policy makers at all levels; and to disseminate the benefits of its experience to other community groups and researchers in the same field (Kilmurray, 1991).

The Rural Action Project was established through the co-operative efforts of four voluntary organizations - the Northern Ireland Rural Association, the Northern Ireland Voluntary Trust, the Northern Ireland Council for Voluntary Action and Strabane Citizens' Advice Bureau. Its work was concentrated in four rural areas: South Armagh; the Glens of Antrim; West Fermanagh and the Strabane rural district.

Although the short four year duration of the project limited the work that it could undertake, a series of local interventions were planned in consultation with existing rural community groupings in the four selected areas. The programmes of action prioritized included addressing issues as diverse, yet interrelated, as community planning, farm diversification, work with rural women, information and advice provision, and support for basic community development. The possibility of progressing from one issue to another in rural communities proved to be more effective than adopting a multifaceted approach, with overambitious objectives. The importance of local credibility and small scale perceived 'success' was as crucial to the work of the Rural Action project as was suggested in the earlier evaluation of the Community Worker Research Project (1978-82).

What was novel about the Rural Action Project approach was the recognition of the need to highlight the experiences gleaned from the local work, and to place them in a policy context. An assessment of the Project pointed out:

> ... What became very clear from the Rural Action Project was the need to give the local work a sense of place, both in terms of acknowledging its potential importance for central decision making and in recognizing that what is achieved must be relevant to locally identified needs and priorities. If essential change is to come about in rural communities it will require a synthesis to be achieved between appropriate external policies and the confidence of the local communities to cope with the demands of such change ... (Kilmurray, 1989).

Confidence varied depending on the stage of development of local community activists and the level of support that they received locally. For many of the rural groups with which it worked the Rural Action Project provided a useful bridge to make contact with external agencies and decision making, where previously the latter may have appeared somewhat out of reach.

In seeking to develop the policy agenda and to realize its objective of laying the basis for co-ordination between statutory, voluntary, local authority and community effort, the Rural Action Project set up the mechanism of a statutory co-ordination panel. The idea behind this mechanism was that the panel, which would be composed of representatives from the various government departments, would meet quarterly in order to receive regular reports on the work of the project, and in particular on specific policy issues emerging from the local area work. The Statutory Co-ordination Panel proved to be of only limited effectiveness largely due to the fact that the Department of Agriculture (NI) refused to appoint a representative to the Panel (writing to say that it would prefer bilateral contact with the Project), while many of the other departmental representatives appointed had limited decision-making power. Nevertheless the panel continued to meet - locating these meetings in the various local areas in which RAP was working - and provided a source of interest, informed comment and formal contact with at least sections of the policy-making process. With the benefit of hindsight it is possible that the Statutory Co-ordination Panel could have been more effective if the Rural Action Project itself had defined a clearer remit for it from the outset.

After some two years of operation, agencies and departments were drawn into the work of the Rural Action Project by their involvement in the various community based initiatives. Thus the Department of Agriculture became actively represented at different levels of the Farm Diversification initiative in the South Armagh and West Fermanagh areas, an involvement that was underlined by the establishment of an evaluation panel set up as a prerequisite for the receipt of funding for this work from the International Fund for Ireland. Similarly, the Northern Ireland Tourist Board was to become involved in agritourism proposals in the Glens of Antrim and West Fermanagh, while the planning authorities and the Northern Ireland Housing Executive responded to case studies emerging from the various local areas. The overall issue of deprivation and access to services in remoter rural areas was discussed in the latter years of the Project with the relevant health and social services and education authorities. In the longer term the wide range of such departmental and agency contacts that were to be built up through the diverse RAP initiatives underlined the logic of an integrated rural development strategy, and the need for a policy response along these lines.

Although developed specifically as an anti-poverty initiative as part of the second EC Anti-Poverty Programme, the work undertaken by the Rural Action Project (NI) identified the need to involve a wider section of the rural community than simply those categories defined as 'the poor'. Indeed the Project's emphasis on rural poverty upset many rural communities that could objectively be considered to be deprived. This classification was often viewed by rural dwellers as a slur on their community, and the most that was allowed was for their area to be termed 'disadvantaged'. A lingering sense of self-sufficiency proved to be an obstacle for any stronger description. Given this sense of reluctance the priorities of rural community action often had to be phrased in quite different terms than urban based work, and the EC emphasis on a 'participatory' model of development had to encompass the many elements that made up the rural community, rather than concentrating on those most in need.

Thus the Rural Action Project through its work came to acknowledge the insight of Benno Galjart, who concluded from a study of participatory development projects in rural areas:

> What is important is that a geographically limited target population should understand that normal development leads to gross inequalities to which each may become subject and that this can only be prevented if different 'rules of the game' are accepted. These rules must not be imposed but developed by the target population itself. First and foremost they have to cover the creation of employment, solidarity with other members of the local group in terms of a mutual protection of life chances and awareness of the dangers of creating 'second class citizens' ... (Galjart, 1981).

The development of 'new rules' however, proved to be a slow process and underlined the importance of initiating a process of community development education for rural activists, designed to meet the needs and circumstances of rural areas. On the other side of the coin there was a need to emphasize to government that externally imposed 'solutions' were unlikely to meet rural needs effectively.

Alongside its extensive experience at local level, the Rural Action Project sought to engage government departments in policy discussion in the context of the analyses of rural society then under debate within the European Commission. In a document entitled 'The Future of Rural Society' (1988), the Commission discussed a scenario in which the rural world would no longer be dependent on agriculture, despite the fact that farming and forestry still covers 80 per cent of the land mass of the European Community. Consequent recognition of the urgent need for reform of the Common Agricultural Policy, together with the need for a new perspective on the future of rural societies, resulted in a suggested integrated rural development approach. Of particular importance to rural communities in Northern Ireland was the Commission's emphasis on continued support for areas suffering from natural and structural handicaps, and the recognition that socio-economic development in rural areas must be accompanied by appropriate education and training measures adapted to local projects and action plans.

For a period, however, the concepts being discussed in Brussels seemed far removed from the priorities of policy-making in Stormont. Ironically however, the Commission's views did find a welcome echo in Belcoo, County Fermanagh, and in the Loughshore area of County Tyrone, where local community activists had long been calling for 'an integrated' response to their development problems. Indeed considerable confusion and frustration was experienced at both local authority and local community level during the late eighties as different messages were being passed down from both Brussels and Stormont. The former discussed approaches that seemed appropriate to local demands, while considerably more caution was shown by government in Northern Ireland. The role of the Rural Action Project in this period was to relate the information that it gained as a European Commission sponsored project to the local rural communities and local authorities within which it was working.

Shifting the policy agenda

Government's approach to rural development appeared to change in the brief period between late 1988 and 1990. Apart from the EC debate, there was a new awareness that the approach of leaving rural communities to wither away was not in the overall interests of society as a whole. Social problems connected with urbanization together with a new emphasis on the environmental attractions of the countryside suggested the need to develop policies of countryside management. The potential of tourism based on the scenic value of the landscape and culture of Northern Ireland underlined this approach, which was supplemented by a new openness to ideas about farm diversification and support for dispersed, small scale industry. The Northern Ireland Housing Executive adopted this new direction, and responded to loudly expressed local preferences by introducing a concept of crossroads development in its rural policy statement - a policy shift that owed much to internal lobbying and argument within the Housing Executive itself, and particularly within its West Region.

The other element that influenced government thinking during this period was a new focus within government on issues of equality - particularly as between various sections of society in Northern Ireland. The role of the Central Community Relations Unit (CCRU) in Stormont cannot be underestimated in introducing ideas about the 'differential impact' of policies in various areas. The application of this perspective to rural areas marked quite a new development for departments such as the Department of Agriculture and the Department of the Environment. For rural dwellers in many areas of extreme rurality and disadvantage however, the theoretical concept offered a modern interpretation of a long held sense of historical injustice. In a self-consciously non-sectarian manner voluntary organizations such as NIAPA (the Northern Ireland Agricultural Producers' Association - essentially representing the smaller farmers) came into its own by pointing out how many apparently neutral policies and grant systems had in fact disproportionately benefited the wealthier rural dwellers.

Closely linked to the issue of the equal treatment of the various religious groupings in Northern Ireland was consideration of the overall problem of structural socio-economic deprivation. The then head of the Northern Ireland Civil Service, Sir Kenneth Bloomfield, articulated this concern in policy terms. It was an aspect that featured prominently in the final report of the Rural Action Project - *Rural Development: a Challenge for the 1990s* which heavily underlined the consequences of the lack of an effective rural development policy. In a determined attempt to address the range of issues raised in both the report, and by other organizations concerned with rural development, Sir Kenneth convened a meeting of the various government departments concerned with rural Northern Ireland to meet a delegation from the Project's management committee. Its members emphasized the need for the establishment of a rural community development agency to undertake the support of locally based rural community initiative and the development of a policy for integrated rural planning and development in Northern Ireland.

In a commendably speedy response central government set up the Inter Departmental Committee on Rural Development (IDCRD) in November 1989. Chaired by Bill Hodges, permanent secretary of the Department of Agriculture (NI), its remit was to consider the need for co-ordinated action to address the social and economic problems of the most deprived rural areas. Its terms of reference included the development of an appropriate response to the recommendations made in the Rural Action Project's Final Report. In the meantime it was also agreed to maintain statutory funding for the Rural Action Project, on a temporary basis, until the IDCRD had time to assess the overall situation. The Project's management committee accepted this temporary extension, which continued until July 1991. However the Rural Action Project underlined the temporary nature of this extension, not wishing to pre-empt more long-term developments.

The prospect of involvement in the decision-making processes of central government was approached with a certain degree of trepidation by the Rural Action Project. Apart from a constant voluntary sector fear of incorporation in the statutory process, there were a number of specific concerns:

1. Was the Department of Agriculture the most appropriate and potentially responsive choice for a 'lead' department?

2. Would any rural development initiative be underpinned by adequate additional financial resources?

3. What would be the role of local authorities in the rural development process, particularly given the reservations that many local rural community development groups had about the impartiality and/or effectiveness of their respective district councils?

4. How could the role and contribution of locally based rural groups be safeguarded and supported?

5. What was the most appropriate balance between supporting government in the development of an integrated rural policy, and the encouragement of an independent voice for rural communities - which at times might be critical of government policy?

In the event the Rural Action Project Management Committee and the Inter Departmental Committee on Rural Development agreed to set up a joint working party to consider the views and recommendations made by RAP. The working party undertook this task between January 1990 and June 1991. The then co-ordinator of the Rural Action Project, Jimmy Armstrong, commented on the position taken by the organization:

> The basic objective of rural development was defined by RAP as the creation of viable and self-sustaining rural communities in fragile rural areas. This could best be effected by a bottom-up approach to planning, properly integrated with a top-down allocation of resources. Overall management would come from a body representing all the major rural interest groups (Armstrong, 1991).

The mechanism that was proposed included the three elements of:

(a) a rural development centre which would provide support, assistance and resources to local development groups;

(b) a rural development fund which could offer co-ordinated funding in support of the plans of such groups; and

(c) a rural community network, which would be independent of government and would represent the views of local community initiatives in rural areas.

In the elaboration of these ideas consideration was given to the specific experiences in Scotland and England, as well as further afield. Scotland had seen the establishment of the Highlands and Islands Development Board in 1968, with a certain emphasis on top-down co-ordination. England had a history of support for rural development continuing over many decades, but the work of the more recently established ACRE - a voluntary organization working in support of rural communities - was to provide some interesting ideas. Mechanisms to promote rural development in Belgium and the Republic of Ireland were also studied and commented on while the on-going interest of the EC in supporting integrated rural development, and providing finance through both the Structural Funds and the LEADER programme, offered an additional impetus.

In February 1991, the Secretary of State for Northern Ireland, Peter Brooke, issued a statement indicating that most of the recommendations of the Rural Action Project had been endorsed by the Inter-Departmental Committee on Rural Development and the government. Jeremy Hanley became Minister of Rural Development and the Department of Agriculture was given responsibility for the programme of work. Mr Hanley was later to announce that a rural development council would be set up to provide support for local groups and to advise on issues relating to rural development. Alongside this, a small team of area co-ordinators from the civil service would provide the 'one stop shop' response for the support required for local rural community plans.

A new era for rural community development?

In the euphoria which followed this ready government response to the complex issues of rural development there may be a danger that the difficult economic context, and the long-term nature of the process, will be forgotten. High expectations must be tempered with these realities if local communities are not to experience a sense of frustration in a couple of years time.

Nevertheless, major progress has been achieved, and its results can already be seen in many areas of policy. One recent example of this is in the controversial areas of planning and of rural housing. In co-operation with Community Technical Aid, both the extended Rural Action Project and the more recently established Rural Community Network, have facilitated a consultation process for both the Department of the Environment and the Northern Ireland Housing Executive, with local rural communities (1990-91).

A note of caution sounded by the Rural Action Project before its demise in 1991 concerned its wish that the new rural development initiative should not be seen as the sole answer to all the problems of rural dwellers in Northern Ireland. The role of economic development agencies such as the Industrial Development Board and the Local Enterprise Development Unit would still be important to ensure the generation of employment opportunities in rural areas. Similarly other government policies in relation to transport and the location of public sector jobs were also vital. Furthermore, in relation to Northern Ireland attention had to be paid to the expenditure of the second generation of EC Structural Funds (1994-99). Finally, the need to negotiate between the various rural interests was recognized - with environmentalists, farmers and other rural dwellers all having important contributions to make to the debate on rural development.

Notwithstanding these on-going issues the acceptance of the essential role of local community action in rural areas has been an important achievement in recent years. The need to develop local resources, the persistence of a tradition of dispersed living and the considerable diversity of the Northern Ireland countryside all combine to make a strong argument for managing the pattern of change in such areas through a series of locally related plans. The fact that a crucial aspect of local resources is the imagination, commitment and energy of rural community activists is now acknowledged by the government by the recently established Rural Development Council, and by the Rural Community Network, which was set up as a complementary, but independent, organization to the Council.

What is undeniable is the conclusion that while change in the pattern of rural living has been the inevitable result of economic developments at an international level, both the need and the means to manage that change within the Northern Ireland context, have been deeply influenced by the experiences and recommendations of voluntary and community organizations locally. While the Rural Action Project (NI) may well have articulated many of these recommendations, much credit must be given to those community groups scattered throughout the countryside who maintained both their sense of place and a determination to survive, over the past decades. Without either adequate resources or public recognition such groups ensured that development could be generated 'out of the embers', and that rural development could be forward-looking as well as drawing strength from the past. If evolving rural policies, and the Rural Development Council, continue to use these local groups as a touchstone for progress then it is possible that the next decade will see a new era for community action in rural areas - and particularly in disadvantaged rural areas.

References

Arkleton Trust (1979), *Disadvantaged Rural Europe: Proceedings of a Conference held in Scotland*, Arkleton Trust, Enstone, Oxfordshire.

Armstrong, J. (1990), 'Very Good Regions for Change' in Smyth, D. (ed.), *Opening the Field: Rural Perspectives: Proceedings of a Conference organized by Fortnight Educational Trust at Benburb, County Tyrone*, Fortnight Educational Trust, Belfast.

Armstrong, J. (1991), 'Life after Death: the Rural Action Project's Recommendations to the Inter-Departmental Committee on Rural Development' in McKay, S. (ed.), *Rural Action Project: Project Activities*, Rural Action Project, Londonderry.

Caven, N. (1982), *Evaluation Report of the Community Worker Research Project*, Department of Education for Northern Ireland, Bangor.

Cloke, P. (1988), *Policies and Plans for Rural People: an International Perspective*, Allen & Unwin, London.

European Commission (1988), 'The Future of Rural Society', com (88) 501/2/4, October, Brussels.

Galjart, B. (1981), 'Participatory rural development: some conclusions from research' in *Sociologica Ruralis*, vol. 21, pp. 142-59.

Greer, J. and Kerr, E. (1990), 'Rural Planning and Housing' in Smyth, D. (ed.), *Opening the Field ...*, Fortnight Educational Trust, Belfast.

Gudgin, G. et al. (1989), *Job Generation in Manufacturing Industry*, cited in Morrisey, M. and Gaffikin, F. (1990), *Northern Ireland: the Thatcher Years*, Zed Books, London.

Haughey, M. (1988), *Out of the Embers: a History of Creggan through its People*, Creggan Community Association, Creggan.

Kilmurray, A. (1989), *Rural Development: a Challenge for the 1990s*, Rural Action Project, Londonderry.

Kilmurray, A. (1991), *Rural Action Project: Anti-Poverty Initiative*, Rural Action Project, Londonderry.

Maginnis, K. (1990), 'No Child of New Forestation' in Smyth, D. (ed.), *Opening the Field ...*, Fortnight Educational Trust, Belfast, pp. 2-3.

Matthew, Sir Robert H. (1964), *Belfast Regional Survey and Plan, 1962*, HMSO, Belfast.

Smyth, D. (ed.) (1990), *Opening the Field ... Rural Perspectives: Proceedings of a Conference organized by Fortnight Educational Trust at Benburb, County Tyrone*, Fortnight Educational Trust, Belfast.

Thomas, C. (1986), 'Distance, Time and Rural Communities in Ireland' in Thomas, C. (ed.), *Rural Landscapes and Communities*, Irish Academic Press, Dublin, pp. 145-78.

9 Informal welfare, voluntary action and community care

John Offer

In Northern Ireland, as in Great Britain, much attention has been given in recent years to the overhaul of policy regarding 'community care' and the policy changes, inaugurated in April 1993, have been closely similar, stemming from, in both cases, the Griffiths Report, *Community Care: an Agenda for Action*, of 1987 (DSS, 1988). Thus the importance of informal carers, the need for a mixed economy of welfare, and tailored 'packages of care', including contributions from the voluntary sector, are all emphasized in *A Regional Strategy for the Northern Ireland Health and Personal Social Services 1992-1997*, as is the goal of enhancing individuals' independence enabling them to remain in their own homes where possible. 'Informal carers' are introduced early on in the section on 'the right care in the community' (DHSS, 1991, p. 26).

> Much care in the community is provided by relatives, friends and neighbours - the so-called 'informal carers'. Most informal carers take on their extra responsibilities willingly, but many need help. Boards should ensure that carers have access to a range of services which, as well as providing them with respite on a regular basis, offers them intensive short-term support at times of crisis.

A particular aim is to increase the proportion of people aged seventy-five or over who are cared for in their own homes to 88 per cent by 1997 (up from an estimated 82 per cent in 1992 and the reversion of a trend). These policy objectives, with the focus firmly on informal caring and the need for services 'to respond to individuals' needs and preferences' (DHSS, 1991, p. 27) look like a major break with the past. In many ways this is indeed so but continuities should not be overlooked.

In acknowledging continuities in policy a glance at the Welfare Services Act (NI) of 1949 and Antrim County Welfare Committee's *Initial Proposals for the Performance of Functions under the Welfare Services Act (NI) 1949* is instructive. Section 15 of the act declared:

> a Welfare Authority may make such arrangements as the Ministry may approve for providing Domestic Help (whether whole time or part time) for any person who, being aged or handicapped ..., lives either alone or in circumstances in which proper care and attention would, but for such help, not be available to him.

In response, Antrim's Welfare Committee adopted the view that 'many of the problems of old and infirm people ... can best be met, in the majority of cases, in their own homes' (p. 7) and hoped to establish a domestic help service to help such persons, adding that 'the longer such persons can remain in their own homes the better for them, and the less expense on the county' (p. 15). Moreover, this legislation permitted the welfare authority to employ a voluntary organization as its agent and to contribute to the funds of voluntary organizations. Antrim's response was strongly positive on both fronts.

So here already were commitments to support to enable people to stay in their own homes and to the rudiments of a mixed economy of welfare. And such commitments have their own ancestry in Poor Law provisions. Nevertheless, it seems likely that in practice there was a stronger predisposition to place people in institutions than is now the case. Corroboration comes from a Nuffield Foundation Report of 1947, called *Old People* and chaired by that distinguished veteran of poverty research and the policy lobby, Seebohm Rowntree. According to the report, the provision of an adequate number of suitable homes:

> will lessen the need for extensive plans of home help, home nursing, visiting, and home meals services for old people who would be better off in a Home or Institution. The right sphere for such domiciliary services is in helping able-bodied old people in cases of temporary illness or during convalescence (Nuffield Foundation, p. 96).

More generally, one can suggest a way of thinking in which knowledgeable social scientists and cosmopolitan planners are pitted against vernacular myopics, the potency of intervention by posses drawn from an élite of trained professionals against lay incompetence, and the beneficial discipline of enforced communal living against a burdensome and sapping struggle to maintain solitary independence. In social policy matters such a partiality for state action and aloof bureaucratic hierarchies was in large measure the work of Fabian socialism, Sidney and Beatrice Webb in particular. (The Webbs it was who thought that the proper sphere of work for voluntary organization was the everlasting one of identifying new, emerging needs, so that government could step in and meet them). The hegemony of this way of thinking was seldom effectively challenged until the 1970s. It is no accident that 'informal care' and 'informal carers' are new terms. What they describe had always existed in Northern Ireland and elsewhere. Of course it had had to, but the terms imbue the work, and those that carry it out, with a status reprehensible, if not incomprehensible, from the point of view of the earlier way of ideas.

The idea of informal care

'Informal welfare' today embraces physical care, advice and money which is given to individuals by family members, friends and neighbours. It is a big field, ranging from watchful neighbourliness to round-the-clock tending. By 'informal care' seems to be meant the large enclave of that area where physical care of sick, disabled and elderly people is involved. 'Informal care', 'caring' and 'carers' are thus often taken to refer to activities and individuals which directly shadow the activities and individuals involved in formal, statutory, care. 'Carers', then, run the risk of being viewed as lay equivalents of nurses and social workers, and 'caring' involves activities the absence of which would lead to accommodation in an institution directly provided by government, or now, increasingly the case, provided by private or voluntary bodies more or less accountable to government.

People who give 'informal care' have occasionally been described as forming part of the voluntary sector (Pinker, 1979, p. 46). Certainly self-help groups can grow out of people sharing their experiences; thus 'caring' may lead to the establishment of voluntary organizations. But this scarcely justifies not making a distinction between two different activities. There may be cases of people who undertake 'informal care' who have no previous contact with the person being 'cared for' and who view their work simply as voluntary work. In fact, study after study has shown that care comes from people already in relationships with the person who is 'cared for' (for example, Parker, 1990). Neighbours and friends do figure; the bulk of care, however, comes from family members.

Informal care beguiles social policy

The importance of taking seriously 'carers'' own interpretations and perceptions of their work will be raised again when research into 'informal care' in Northern Ireland is reviewed. First it is desirable to identify some of the factors which have put 'informal care' very high on the agenda of social policy in Northern Ireland. They apply, indeed, to the whole of the UK and can all be traced back to the mid-1970s.

One factor is that political parties, not only the Conservatives, sought to restate the 'proper' sphere of government activity (the Conservatives of course doing this as the party of government from 1979 to the present). This re-think of principle has emphasized the responsibilities of individuals and the rightness of reducing direct intervention by the state in people's lives. A second factor has been a calling into question of the *effectiveness* of public expenditure in some areas of provision. (A classic instance is the Audit Commission's review of expenditure on community care policy in 1986.) A third factor is that expenditure on social provision has been challenged by considerations of economic policy, often related to changing currents in economic theory. A fourth factor was the emphasis placed on community care as an objective rather than institutional care, troublesomely vague as this objective proved. A fifth factor has been the emergence of groups urging more 'consumer' participation in the provision of statutory services and more accountability of services to users.

A sixth and final factor is the development of research giving prominence to informal care. This development owes much to the other factors, although it did have an independent history. What had been forgotten as a 'division' of welfare (it was ignored by Titmuss in his seminal 'social division of welfare' essay in his *Essays on the Welfare State* of 1958) was, during the 1970s, dragged into the sun. The writer of this chapter's interest in the topic as important for research as well as in policy analysis was prompted by Pinker's observation that we lack adequate explanations of 'why individuals define their needs as they do, and why these definitions so often appear to be at variance with those of the social scientists' (1971, p. 106). With this gulf brought into the open it was a natural step to want to study the everyday welfare practices and beliefs of people in ordinary life.

Mayer and Timms' *The Client Speaks* (1970) was a pioneering glimpse into the lives of those using a formal service, but drew attention to how little work had been done. Abrams' research (Bulmer, 1986) at Durham dates from the 1970s but otherwise little research seemed to be happening. The Wolfenden Report of 1978 brought public acknowledgement of the importance of informal care, with the report urging the voluntary sector to relieve, reinforce and where it became necessary replace carers (Offer, 1979). Following the appearance of the Wolfenden Report came the Barclay Report (1982) on social work, which encouraged social work to 'enable, empower, support and encourage, but not usually to take over from' 'networks' of informal care (p. 209). This report was criticised at the time for displaying a shallow understanding of informal care (Allan, 1983 and Offer, 1984). Research expanded rapidly during the 1980s, to the extent that bibliographies and synthesising reports were required (Parker, 1990; Twigg (ed.), 1992 and Glendinning & McLaughlin, 1993). An early research study in this period of expansion, commenced in 1983, was undertaken in Northern Ireland, of which the author of this chapter was co-director.

Fruits of research

It is sensible to begin a section on what we know about informal care in Northern Ireland with some basic figures. According to a Policy and Planning Research Unit report of 1986, 64 per cent of those receiving informal care were female (mainly because elderly women tend to live longer than their husbands). Of the population (aged sixteen or older) 4 per cent of males and 6 per cent of females were said to be carers of someone at home, and 5 per cent of males and 8 per cent of women to be carers outside the home: thus 9 per cent of males and 12 per cent of females were recorded as carers. In terms of the age of carers 10 per cent of the population aged 45-59 were caring for someone at home. Of those receiving care 40 per cent were a parent of the carer, but as many as 10 per cent were friends or neighbours of the carers.

The first detailed research into informal care in Northern Ireland commenced in 1983 and culminated in two main publications (Cecil, Offer & St Leger, 1987 and Offer, St Leger & Cecil, 1988). This study looked at caring in a rural community, Garvagh near Coleraine. A deliberate aim of the research was to look at all aspects of informal care from day-long care to acts of good neighbourliness as they occurred in a community setting. The methods used included participant observation, intensive interviews and the completion of questionnaires. The study explored in detail the circumstances of twenty-two households in which severely disabled and elderly people were being cared for. Five male principal carers were identified in this group. It also explored in detail nine households in which a disabled child was being cared for. In neither of these sets of households was the voluntary sector a significant contributor to assisting carers. Indeed in nearly all cases the bulk of caring was undertaken by one person, usually a family member and mostly a woman, who often experienced isolation, boredom, a restricted life, worry about the future and financial difficulties as well as problems in the actual tasks of caring. Very few had actively chosen to care: care had been expected of them. However, some who were caring, whilst often critical of the support they received from the state and other bodies, did express satisfaction as resulting from their caring work (e.g. Offer, St Leger & Cecil, 1988, p. 39).

In the late 1980s St Leger and Gillespie undertook research in three contrasted communities in Belfast - Ballymacarrett, Ligoniel and Tullycarnet - designed deliberately to complement the earlier rural study of Garvagh. Information was collected using both qualitative and quantitative methods. Particular attention was paid to the differing nature of ordinary life in the three communities and to exploring the implications for informal caring activities. Excluding home helps, fifty-two 'principal carers' were identified, of whom twenty-two were wives caring for husbands, eleven husbands caring for wives (the majority of spouses being cared for were appreciably or severely disabled). Six of the principal carers were daughters; eleven further carers were relatives (including one son) with just one carer being a friend.

Only a few of the findings of the study can be highlighted. Once again women both provide and receive the bulk of care. This is explained by the authors as arising because not only are they more likely than men to survive into late old age but also, age for age, they are more likely to be sick or disabled (1991, p. 59). However, the study does observe that the sex imbalance in the provision of care is rather less than much of the literature suggests.

The authors suggest that the morale of carers was generally good, although they add that (p. 61):

> in a few cases it seemed likely that pressure on carers was likely to increase, possibly to danger-level, as the person cared for became more dependent, possibly more confused and therefore less able to provide any form of reciprocation or response.

On the relationship between the voluntary sector and informal care the authors found that (p. 67):

> the role of the voluntary sector ... in the areas studied is not primarily to provide casework services but to establish social and leisure groups ... and to provide bases for self-help or/and pressure groups.

However, the authors recognize the likelihood of change following the implementation of the government's paper *People First: Community Care in Northern Ireland in the 1990s.*

Finally, it should be noted that, as in Garvagh, the churches have a peripheral role in providing help or guidance on other than specifically religious issues.

A recent pioneering study undertaken by Conliffe (1993) of the impact of the caring task on the lifestyles of aging mothers and other carers with primary responsibility for an adult with learning disability must also be mentioned. Of particular relevance is that, compared with the Republic of Ireland and the United States of America, the Northern Ireland cohort of ageing mothers had the smallest percentage of those in receipt of respite care (9.3 per cent). In the Republic of Ireland the figure was 21.4 per cent and in the USA 11.7 per cent (p. 40). Moreover, these carers identified a significant need for respite care and felt that it should be extended so that the service was adequate to meet the needs of all Northern Ireland carers; that it should be dependable, regular, safe; respond more to the carer's needs than to the exigencies of the service; offer choice; be appropriate to age; and structured to respond flexibly to the changing needs of both carer and caree.

Conliffe found that voluntary organizations did furnish some help in the form of respite care or support groups, and that many carers were indeed active in these organizations. An expansion of respite care in the current context of policy would involve an expansion of voluntary activity in this field. (It is worthwhile noting here the supportive discussion of the scope and need for respite care in the House of Commons Social Services Committee Report on services for people with a mental handicap and people with a mental illness (1990, pp. xxx-xxxi).

Reference should also be made to a short study undertaken for the Equal Opportunities Commission by Evason, Whittington and Knowles (1993). This is a largely quantitative study of seventy-seven women and sixteen males undertaking care. They were selected from those carers known to voluntary bodies. The carers' own community and social rather than personal backgrounds are not much discussed: the focus is on the physical, mental and social costs of caring. Perhaps the most unusual finding of this brief survey is that 66 per cent of carers felt that the state should be doing more to help them.

Conclusion

The discussion of the research studies reveals that, at least until recently, the voluntary sector in Northern Ireland was of little significance for informal carers. This may be misleading as an indicator of present and future trends. In the context of current community care policy as discussed at the beginning of the chapter, the voluntary sector is exhorted to supply care on a contractual basis alongside other providers to make up packages of care framed to take account of carers and those they care for. (For a discussion of the voluntary sector in this context as viewed by a senior civil servant see Hayes, 1986.) Moreover, since at least some of the research was carried out, Crossroads Care, which began in Belfast in 1982, has been able to enlarge its work in giving respite to carers. Extra Care too is active in providing respite for the carers of elderly people. And Carers National Association is active across the province. There are branches in Belfast (two), Antrim, Lisburn and

Portadown, affiliated organizations in Banbridge, Derry, Newry and Strabane, and eight carers' groups mostly located in other towns. Carers National acts as a pressure group for carers, provides advice and information and is currently campaigning, in connection with assessments for community care assistance, to improve the position of carers and those they care for, in particular in respect of requesting and obtaining an assessment and securing adequate services following assessment. Hospice care for the terminally ill, which can have a much-needed respite care function, has also been expanding since its launch in Northern Ireland in Belfast in April 1985 (Acheson, 1986). Recent trends thus suggest that the voluntary sector is set to play a more substantial part in the lives of informal carers.

References

Acheson, Nick (1986), 'Successful start for Northern Ireland's first hospice', *Scope*, no. 90, Feb., pp. 10-11.

Allan, Graham (1983), 'Informal networks of care: issues raised by Barclay', *British Journal of Social Work*, vol. 13, pp. 417-33.

Antrim County Welfare Committee (1949), *Initial Proposals for the Performance of Functions under the Welfare Services Act (NI)*, Belfast.

Audit Commission (1986), *Making a Reality of Community Care*, HMSO, London.

Barclay, Peter M. (1981), *Social Workers: their Role and Tasks: the Report of a Working Party ...*, Bedford Square Press for the National Institute for Social Work, London.

Bulmer, Martin (1986), *Neighbours: the Work of Philip Abrams*, Cambridge University Press, Cambridge.

Cecil, Rosanne, Offer, John & St Leger, Fred (1987), *Informal Welfare: a Sociological Study of Care in Northern Ireland*, Gower, Aldershot.

Conliffe, Chris (1993), *The Burden of Care*, Institute for Counselling and Personal Development, Belfast.

Department of Health and Social Services (1990), *People First: Community Care in Northern Ireland in the 1990s*, HMSO, Belfast.

Department of Health and Social Services (1991), *A Regional Strategy for the Northern Ireland Health and Personal Social Services, 1992-1997*, HMSO, Belfast.

Department of Social Security (1988), *Community Care: an Agenda for Action*, (Griffiths Report), HMSO, London.

Evason, Eileen, Whittington, Dorothy & Knowles, Leslie (1993), *The Cost of Caring*, Equal Opportunities Commission for Northern Ireland, Belfast.

Glendinning, Caroline & McLaughlin, Eithne (1993), *Paying for Care: Lessons from Europe*, HMSO, London.

Hayes, Maurice (1986), 'Voluntary action: retrospect and prospect', *Scope* No. 90, Feb., pp. 6-8.

House of Commons Social Services Committee (1990), *Eleventh Report, 1990-1991, Community Care: Services for People with a Mental Handicap and People with a Mental Illness*, HMSO, London.

Mayer, J. E. & Timms, N. (1970), *The Client Speaks*, Routledge & Kegan Paul, London.

Nuffield Foundation (1947), *Old People: Report of a Survey Committee on the Problems of Ageing and the Care of Old People under the Chairmanship of B. Seebohm Rowntree*, Oxford University Press, London.

Offer, John (1979), 'The informal system of social welfare', *Social Service Quarterly*, Spring.

Offer, John (1984), 'Informal welfare, social work and the sociology of welfare', *British Journal of Social Work*, vol. 14, pp. 545-55.

Offer, John, St Leger, Fred & Cecil, Rosanne (1988), *Aspects of Informal Caring*, DHSS, Belfast.

Parker, Gillian (1990), *With Due Care and Attention*, Family Policy Studies Centre, London.

Pinker, Robert (1971), *Social Theory and Social Policy*, Heinemann, London.

Pinker, Robert (1979), *The Idea of Welfare*, Heinemann, London.

St Leger, Fred & Gillespie, Norman (1991), *Informal Welfare in Three Belfast Communities*, DHSS, Belfast.

Titmuss, Richard (1958), *Essays on the Welfare State*, Allen & Unwin, London.

Twigg, Julia (1989), 'Models of carers', *Journal of Social Policy*, vol. 18, pp. 53-66.

Twigg, Julia (ed.)(1992), *Carers: Research and Practice*, HMSO, London.

Wolfenden, John, Baron (1978), *The Future of Voluntary Organisations: the Report of the Wolfenden Committee*, Croom Helm, London.

10   Women, peace, community relations and voluntary action

Marie Smyth

When discussing the role of women in organized forms of social action one must consider both women's organizations and general voluntary organizations. The majority of voluntary organizations include women. The existence of women's organizations masks the reality at the practical, operational level, namely that voluntary organizations are often predominantly female arenas. Women are involved in the voluntary sector in a number of ways. First, they are involved in voluntary organizations both with large organizations such as Relate, or with small local organizations such as tenants' associations or neighbourhood groups whose remit is to provide a service or represent views of both men and women. In these organizations, women generally work co-operatively alongside men in order to achieve the goals of the organization.

Second, women are involved in organizations composed predominantly of women, either because they provide a service mainly used by women, or because of gender segregation. This kind of voluntary sector involvement may be thought of as 'participation in groups or organizations *of* women'.

Third, women are involved in a relatively new growing field in the voluntary sector. This is 'participation in groups or organizations *for* women'. Here, the group recognizes the contribution of women and its value and aims to build women's consciousness and to redress imbalances or to correct damage done, for example, to women's self esteem.

Abbott and McDonough (1989) state:

> Women form the backbone of community activity - indeed many workers recognize women as the mainstay of community action in Northern Ireland.

The role of women in the formation and continuing functioning of voluntary organizations has rarely been studied. (An exception is Wilson, 1977). That the contribution of women is often unacknowledged or 'hidden from history' is predictable. Murphy (1992), among others, has pointed out about the inclusion of women in Irish history that:

> History from the perspective of those previously left out (in this case a majority) takes on entirely new dimensions and emphases (p. 22).

Women, through the intervention of religious orders such as the Sisters of the Good Shepherd, the Sisters of Mercy, the Sisters of Nazareth and lay organizations such as the Belfast Women's Temperance Association, were responsible for setting up various residential homes for children, the poor and other deprived sections of the community from the mid 1880s onward. Wilson (1977) notes the irony of single women, with no experience of motherhood and marriage, instructing their working-class sisters in the skills of both.

Concerning contemporary women in Northern Ireland Edgerton (1986) writes that they:

> Tend to marry young, start their families soon afterwards and remain restricted by strong family networks. They are not helped to examine in any critical way their domestic role in the home, or indeed their relationships to their husbands and families: rather they are socialised into a strong maternal role directed to 'keeping the family together', 'making ends meet' and servicing political campaigns largely determined by men. The situation has changed little in recent years despite the shattering of many old molds in Northern Ireland (p. 61).

Edgerton argues that women's participation in the 'public protest' of the late sixties onward in Northern Ireland coexisted, and continues to coexist, with 'domestic acquiescence'. Dealing mainly with Catholic women in urban areas she charts the involvement of women in street protests and the rent and rates strike. She explains the militancy of the women paradoxically by their inherent conservatism.

> ... The 'security forces' were seen as a threat to working class homes; beside the arrests and internment, there was the constant annoyance of army raids, housing being ransacked and children harassed ... the traditional maternal role as guardian of the family was being confronted by external, alien elements. Little wonder that working class women in besieged Nationalist areas were spurred to action (p. 67).

Shannon (1992) argues that:

> There is substantial evidence [she does not say where it is] that more women are challenging these structures (the churches, schools and the economic system) as a consequence of the self-confidence and empowerment gained from their earlier participation in the politics of community defence, and, more recently, from the widening network of women's support groups and adult education courses. For instance, women have been at the forefront in compiling data for various published studies on the impact of poverty, unemployment, poor housing and health conditions that continue to afflict their respective communities (p. 31).

She continues:

> A ... significant development documented through oral interviews has been the extent of volunteer work that women do for those deeply affected by the Troubles, ranging from teaching prisoners and helping their families to cope, to organizing programmes for city teenage males that lessen the opportunities for potential recruitment by paramilitaries, to assisting at day care centres for handicapped and emotionally disturbed children, to counselling widows of policemen. Women volunteers continue to have a high profile in organizations involved in reconciliation work. These activities, as well as the cross community cooperative efforts of women's groups, have been especially important in breaking down the ideological prisons constructed by republicanism and loyalism and have enabled women to pool their energy and talents. It is significant that the historic visit of President Mary Robinson to Belfast, the first ever by an Irish President, came at the joint invitation of women's groups situated in the Protestant Shankill and the Nationalist Falls Road areas ... Perhaps the pragmatic and non hierarchical methods employed in women's collaborative work can provide useful lessons for all who wish to move beyond the 'them and us' character of current politics to the more open and inclusive attitudes that precede a just and permanent resolution of the current conflict (pp. 31-32).

Rooney and Woods (1992) conducted a one-year study of the political and community participation of women in Northern Ireland. Their study interviewed male and female local councillors in three wards, and a postal questionnaire was sent to women members of women's groups. They did not examine women's participation in gender mixed community organizations. They found that, although most political parties claimed 50 per cent female membership, this was not reflected in the party hierarchies. Furthermore it appeared that cross-community work was easier for women. Rooney and

147

Woods reported attitudes to women among male politicians which they categorized into three types: admiring condescension: marginalization, and tactical acceptance.

Women, peace and community relations

Morgan (1992) found evidence to suggest that differences exist as between men and women in Northern Ireland in their attitudes to community relations, although these differences were less great than the differences between the attitudes of Protestants and Catholics. She tentatively suggested that these male-female differences could be due to differences in breadth of social contact and religious commitment between men and women.

Mitchison (1988) asserted that, with regard to differences in patterns of participation of Catholic and Protestant women:

> In Northern Ireland Catholic women have marginally more freedom than Protestants. Catholic culture has a tradition of voluntary work in the community and, within a disenfranchised society, rebellion comes more naturally. And, while the role of women in the loyalist movement appears to have remained subsidiary and relatively unchanged, Republicans have responded to pressure from women in the movement and from the British left wing.

Voluntary organizations in Northern Ireland are affected by sectarian division and its symptoms such as residential segregation. It has frequently been noted that there is a lower level of community organization within the Protestant community and a lower participation of Protestant than of Catholic women in women's organizations.

There is some evidence to suggest that women may have slightly more moderate political attitudes than men in Northern Ireland (Hamilton et al. 1990), but once again the differences between men and women are less significant than those between Catholics and Protestants. Morgan (1992) pointed out that research evidence does not support the often made assumption that women are more conciliatory and more positive in their attitudes to the 'other' community. Morgan also found that women were more pessimistic, or realistic, about the state of community relations in Northern Ireland and its future, than were men. On social attitudes, women did not give significantly more priority to social issues related to the family and children.

Women's participation in voluntary organizations

Women's contributions to voluntary organizations are often taken for granted and are therefore not credited specifically to women. Nor is the impact of largely female labour on the culture of such organizations acknowledged or studied. One of the large voluntary organizations in Northern Ireland is Relate, formerly the Northern Ireland Marriage Guidance Council. Relate is not seen as a women's organization, yet of the sixty-four people who worked with Relate, six were men. In the associated Family Mediation Service in Northern Ireland, of fifteen volunteers, one was a man. Relate is not seen, nor should it be seen, as a women's organization, yet the reality is that it survives very largely on women's voluntary work, as, one suspects do many other voluntary organizations. Abbott and Frazer (1985) and Abbott and McDonough (1989) assert that women are active initiators in voluntary organizations, yet tend not to perform leading roles and are restricted to certain roles with limits on the amount of power they exercise.

Abbott and Frazer (1985, p. 11) suggest:

> Because of the importance of local conditions and facilities to women, they usually form the consistent attenders at public meetings, tenants' associations, parent-teachers' groups and local action campaigns. However, while forming the backbone of such groups, they are rarely found in positions of power and often will not be adequately represented on delegations that go to negotiate with public authorities. On occasions where women initiate work ... they rarely retain their influence. The campaigns which women are allowed to control are those which are considered as of little importance.

O'Connor's (1992) study of the participation of rural women in the establishment of a community-led local development initiative in the Fermanagh/Cavan/Leitrim area showed that women comprised one third of the participants at the public meetings held to establish the project. When twelve women were proposed for election to the executive committee, only two accepted.

> The women all cited a combination of family and work commitments as reasons for declining the invitation to be part of the management team ... none of the men proposed ... including those who accepted or rejected, ever mentioned family commitments. The assumption is that it did not occur to them to equate possible involvement in Community Connections with the impact of this on home and family situations.

Two women were elected to the executive committee. In O'Connor's view, they are 'exceptional women'; both with professional qualifications, they have jobs outside the home, together with home duties and responsibilities.

Mina Wardle of Shankill Street, Agoraphobia and Prescribed Drugs Abuse Group points out (1992):

> The family life situation ... is maybe peculiar to working class areas: but women are still fighting their way out of a system where the husband is the boss of the house, and the woman is the mother, the parent, and the wife and whatever else she has to be. We still have women in the group, believe it or not, who have to ask can they have a night out to go to a meeting, who have to say what time they will be home at - and very often they have to leave a number they can be phoned at, in case one of the children wakens during that time (p. 53).

Donnison (1988) argues that community projects:

> Tend to follow a pattern to be seen in many other movements - religious, political, industrial and military. During the early, heroic years they operate in open, informal, highly participative ways. Women often play leading parts. But hierarchies reassert themselves, formality and secrecy creep back, men take over, the organization comes to exist increasingly for its own sake and for the benefit of the dominant group within it.

Abbott and McDonough (1989) question the inevitability of this process.

> The processes of support and encouragement are slow and painstakingly shared. The women's movement has always tried to organize alternative models to notions of male leadership based on the cult of the personality. Whilst nobody could deny that individuals have particular qualities and talents, the women's movement asserts the thesis that skills and talents are not simply innate features but can be learnt and are hence shareable.

As elsewhere, the application of a critique of the position of women to the practice of community organizing and community work points to the need for change in the fundamental ways in which things have been done and are continuing to be done. The very structures in which community and voluntary organizing are conducted and the processes of community development are gendered in ways which maintain inequity between men and women, undervalue and render invisible women's contribution, and reproduce the ideology of sexism.

150

Women and caring

Any discussion of the involvement of women in the voluntary sector must acknowledge the vast contribution made by women to the well-being of the community. Women work long hours delivering childcare and other domestic services within the home whether they are in employment or not. As a consequence they are often unable to develop their roles outside of the home. This also influences the way women are perceived within the voluntary sector as a whole. The identity and space available to women, has often tended to become confined to the plethora of women's organizations which provide a range of services for women and children, and/or which campaign for changes in women's lot. Within the remainder of the voluntary sector, a gender blindness often operates and a fear of feminism reduces to silence discussions on the role women play.

Within this silence, assumptions about 'appropriate' roles for women and about cultural norms have ensured that the women's contributions have been ghettoised and assumptions about the 'natural' abilities or predispositions of women towards caring roles operate. Nor is it simply a 'male conspiracy'. The social identity of women, cultural norms and the socialization process have ensured that women perceive of themselves as carers and assume that if there is caring to do, they will do it. This is a powerful process - and since, for some women the loss of a caring role would threaten that caring identity, it is resisted.

None of this would be problematic were it not for the fact that the role of carers is socially, economically and politically marginalized and undervalued, and the occupants of those roles are often isolated and poorly supported.

Health and Social Services Boards are implementing new government policies on community care contained in the Griffiths Report (1988), the policy paper *Caring for People* (1989) and the white paper *People First* (1990). These papers collectively indicate a shift away from institutional care to care in the community, and to a 'mixed economy of care' with services being provided by the statutory bodies, by voluntary and private bodies and by 'informal care networks' - families and communities. Implicit in this is an understanding that the lion's share of informal care is provided by women. McShane (1991) points out that:

> In Northern Ireland there are still many stable communities with relatively strong family ties, a tradition of helping and a system of informal welfare based on these. But there are others, such as depopulated rural areas, peripheral estates with few community facilities, or inner city areas disrupted by redevelopment and the troubles where there may be little support available ... it is important to recognize the

whole picture of a local culture and its values and that it is also characterized by conflicts, disagreements and the ostracism of some groups and individuals. The support that projects offer to some people may be flying in the face of the 'community' response to them ... some people want to keep a social distance, and may prefer to seek help from more formal and impersonal sources (p. 12).

St Leger and Gillespie (1991) point out that:

As in most societies, women in Northern Ireland are effectively the main sustainers of the kinship structure. It is they who maintain contact with kin, face to face, by telephone or letter ... (p. 67).

In spite of women's increased role in the labour market a number of studies (Evason, 1980; Watson, 1985; Donnan and McFarlane, 1985; McCorry, 1988; Kilmurray and Bradley, 1989; Cromie, 1987a, 1987b; McEwen et al., 1987) confirm that women in all occupational groups still retain primary responsibility for childcare and domestic work. Cecil (1987, 1989) found, in her examination of informal care of elderly and disabled people in a rural community in Northern Ireland, that care was provided by women, whether on an unpaid basis, or as paid home helps, confirming the view that informal care is seen as women's work.

St Leger and Gillespie (1991) found:

... the great majority of those rendering practical help to people outside the house were in fact women ... These data understate women's input ... care given to a disabled person within the household was given appreciably less often by men than by women ... those caring for female heads of household (i.e. mainly husbands) predominantly spent under ten hours per week on this, while those caring for the male head of household in the great majority of cases spent more than ten hours. Men are slightly less likely to undertake the more onerous, or personal kinds of caring (p. 68).

Women's 'careers' as carers mean that women not only look after children, but also look after dependent adults (Finch and Groves, 1983). Nor is caring the prerogative of married women: single women also care. Women in general are more likely to experience the role of carer, and, when the carer is in employment, the tension between the roles of carer and employee can be very great.

Childcare is predominantly done by women, whether or not there is a man in the household, irrespective of whether the woman is in or out of employment, and irrespective of the employment situation of men in the household. Eighty per cent of women become mothers and women will normally see themselves as responsible for childcare whether or not there is a man in the household. Having a disabled child multiplies the work and the stress involved in parenting. Childcare legislation is based on the assumption that parenting is entirely a private personal responsibility, with the assumption that the social and economic resources for good enough parenting lie within the grasp of all parents (Campbell, 1987; David, 1983, 1985, 1986; Dworkin, 1983).

Evason, Whittington and Knowles (1993), in the first report on a longitudinal study of carers in Belfast for the Equal Opportunities Commission, conclude:

> It is evident that, far from those needing care having access to a range of possible sources of informal assistance, one person, normally a close relative, provides the larger part of the aid required.

They describe the cost of caring to carers:

> The costs include poorer health, loss of social contacts, and in some cases, social isolation. In particular, caring clearly affects employment. ... these costs bear more heavily on women than men ... Given current demographic and other trends a growing number of women will have caring responsibilities which extend across the larger part of their adult lives as they move, for example, from child care to parent care to spouse care ... In times of severe financial constraint there will be a strong temptation to view carers as a cheap resource to be utilised in the construction of low-cost solutions to the need for care. For those concerned with gender equality the challenge over the next decade must be to ensure that this temptation is resisted.

Mina Wardle, Belfast, states:

> We are particularly worried about carers, and there is definitely discrimination against women carers. Someone who's had to give up a career to look after a mother or a father, for example, and is out for a long time, can't get back into that career again. They suffer great financial loss. They suffer loss of identity. They suffer everything but most of it is financial. And there is no help available for these women at all, there's no-one to advise them. Nobody seems to care and nobody seems to want to do anything about it. You're a woman and it's your responsibility to look after your parent (1992, pp. 52-3).

153

Groups for women: the women's movement in Northern Ireland

In recent years there has been a rapid growth of groups organized by women which provide specific services for women. The main providers of many of the key services for women are groups such as Women's Aid, Rape Crisis, Rape and Incest Line, Derry Wellwoman, Women's Education Project. Statutory services often refer women to these voluntary services, but to date have themselves shown little inclination to develop services to meet needs specific to women. The organization and structure of many of these women's organizations differ from those in other parts of the voluntary sector. There is often considerable consumer involvement in management and decision making, and attempts are made to avoid hierarchical structures within the organization. There is also a tendency for women who have been recipients of the service to become involved at a later date in the provision of service for other women.

Roulston (1989) charts the emergence of feminist and women's groups in Northern Ireland in the 1970s:

> The introduction of internment brought women in Catholic areas into the foreground for a time. Women in both Catholic and Protestant areas also mobilized against paramilitary violence on occasions. Poverty and poor housing provoked campaigns in which women took initiatives. In such campaigns, women became involved as the guardians of family life and of the interests of the community rather than as fighters for women's benefits alone. Women, especially mothers, were seen as having a unique insight into the needs of the community and a special role to play in protecting or promoting the interests of the community [see Buckley and Lonergan, 1984]. In spite of the fact that movements based on such ideologies have often been short lived, or have been transformed into something alien to the ideas of their founders, such ideologies persist and resurface periodically. The mobilization of women is often achieved by reference to their responsibilities in and for the family rather than by appealing to their interests as individuals.

Roulston describes the division between the various women's groups in the North. She was a participant in the disputes as a member of the Northern Ireland Women's Rights Movement and outlines the major differences between them and how those differences relate to the politics of Northern Ireland. She concludes:

> The attempt to create a broad women's movement in Northern Ireland has proved, inevitably, to be extremely difficult.

Some of the groups in the broad women's movement began by concentrating on lobbying and campaigning. Coleraine Women's Group (1974-78) concentrated on lobbying for legal reform particularly on divorce. Some members of Coleraine Women's Group went on to form Coleraine Women's Aid, which concentrated on providing refuges and other support for women who are victims of domestic violence. Women's Aid, which was established in 1975, participated in, and continues to participate in, campaigns and lobbies as well as providing services for women with specific needs. Women's Aid was active in the campaign to release Noreen Winchester who had been sentenced to seven years in prison for the manslaughter of her father, who had physically and sexually assaulted her for the previous five years.

Some groups focused almost exclusively on a political agenda, such as Women Against Imperialism (1978-80), formed as a result of a split within the Belfast Women's Collective (1977-80). Women Against Imperialism focused much of their energy on highlighting the conditions for women prisoners in Armagh jail. Eight members of Women Against Imperialism served jail sentences for non-payment of fines as a result of arrests made at a protest outside the jail. Members of Women Against Imperialism became active in working in the Falls Women's Centre.

Some groups, such as the Craigavon group, were engaged both in campaigning and providing services (Morgan & Ruddy, 1985). Their campaigns concentrated on day care and equal pay, but they also ran courses for women and provided an advice service for women, and ran a women's centre. Other groups began with a strategy of providing services for women where none had existed and, sequentially or simultaneously, campaigned and educated about the situation of women, often making demands for legal and political change.

In the early days of the women's movement, women worked to produce newspapers and in lobbying, writing, running conferences often with few resources other than what they could raise at fundraising events. The development of various government schemes for the employment of unemployed people meant that women's groups (and indeed one local authority, Belfast City Council), began to employ women to work specifically with women. Women began to receive resources from local and central government to run women's centres and refuges for battered women. The range of concerns of the groups broadened to include education, employment, and health.

Belfast Women's Aid began in 1974 when social workers and staff at the National Society for the Prevention of Cruelty to Children formed a committee and rented a house from Queen's University. The house was closed in 1976 as a result of a fire; a women's group was formed by some of the volunteers of the first house and a refuge was opened in 1978. By the mid 1990s there were refuges and support groups in Derry, Coleraine, Omagh, Newry and North Down. A fourth house in Belfast, with an emphasis on work with survivors of incest and sexual abuse, was opened in October 1991.

Women's Aid acts as a pressure group for social change, not just as a service provider. It sees itself as an organization which campaigns to change attitudes to women and to violence against women in the wider society. The philosophy of Women's Aid has been overtly feminist and a community development approach is used. This means that women using its refuges are involved in decision making.

Funding of women's organizations

A review of funding and support for community groups in Northern Ireland (Mulrine et al., 1991) shows that with the exception of the Northern Ireland Women's Aid Federation, women's groups have tended to appear in the lists of organizations receiving smaller grants.

In 1985 Abbott and Frazer pointed out that:

> ... The major factor which restricts the development [of women's groups] is the lack of resources. Almost all the projects ... have been developed ... on very limited resources and ... could immediately expand their work dramatically if more resources were available. While the North's main charitable trust, the Northern Ireland Voluntary Trust, has made the support of women's groups one of its main priorities in the last three years ... the need for statutory agencies to make it a priority to support work with women in the community should by now be recognised as overwhelming. The evidence has come from two directions. In the first place, many feminists have ... pointed out the inequalities and injustices ... that women face and this is especially true in Northern Ireland ... Secondly, the many community workers ... who, for the past decade and more, have been concerned with the problems of deprivation and poverty in run-down, working-class communities ... have been confronted on a daily basis with the fact that ... it is women who have to cope with the worst effects of inadequate living conditions and the additional pressures resulting from the Troubles.

Ruth Taillon (1992) carried out a study of the funding of women's organizations. She surveyed more than 190 women's groups, 81 charitable trusts, and all statutory funders and found that, while six central government departments grant aided women's organizations directly or indirectly through semi-independent bodies, there was little consistency in their approach. She

156

recommended the introduction of a separate budget for the voluntary sector and the introduction of guidelines and criteria of eligibility. She also argued for the adoption of an 'equality strategy' which would 'recognize women as a disadvantaged group and would provide for positive action measures'.

Taillon illustrates the lack of consistency among Health and Social Services Boards by pointing out that each of the four boards has interpreted its identical statutory remit differently with the result that there are four different policies and practices on grant aid to women's and childcare groups. The Department of Education no longer funds women's voluntary groups and has transferred funding responsibility to the five Education and Library Boards, none of whom seemed, in 1991, to be funding any women's groups. Of the twenty-six district councils, Taillon found that 'only a minority were funding any women's groups at all', but she pointed out that some councils offered non-monetary support to women's groups.

The Community Relations Council gave an unspecified amount of grant to ten women's organizations in 1990-91. Government's Central Community Relations Unit awarded a total of £51,000 to three women's organizations. Taillon identified community relations funding as the only apparent growth area in statutory funding, and reported that groups felt that their priorities for work were being controlled by the need to include some aspect of 'reconciliation' between Catholics and Protestants before the work could meet the criteria for funding. Taillon reported that groups felt that this was 'to the detriment of important issue-based activity for women, including valuable cross-community work'.

In relation to European funding, Taillon pointed out that the European Commission's 'positive recognition of women as a disadvantaged group does not appear to be reflected in departmental (local) administration of European money ...'; 'the region's [Northern Ireland's] Objective One status may not be being used to maximum advantage; only a small fraction of European money is reaching the voluntary sector'. She points to the need for women's groups to obtain information about sources of European and matching funding.

In 1991-92 the Department of Health and Social Services awarded a total of £332,280 in revenue grants to eight women's organizations, and a further £34,328 to groups which contained a specific women's element. The Department of Education for Northern Ireland awarded £194,800 to the Workers Educational Association, an unspecified portion of which went to the Women's Studies Branch.

Taillon indicated that women provide a range of services to meet needs not being met by the statutory services. Women in her study reported that they were 'increasingly being called on to replace services which should be provided by statutory agencies, or to "pick up the pieces" as a result of social cutbacks'. Taillon also drew attention to the fact that the level of skill and expertise used by women in doing this work is often unrecognized, and reported a 'strong consensus among groups involved in service provision that the commitment and talents of staff and volunteers are being exploited ... being expected to provide full-time work for part-time funding'.

Many groups, she reported, were run on very tight budgets and were often dependent on statutory funding. Government policy of encouraging groups to seek independent funding from private sources was perceived as not realistic. These groups were often located in areas of high need, and users were unlikely to be able to contribute. Resources devoted to fund raising were often resources diverted from service provision. Furthermore, the so-called enterprise culture was felt to run counter to the ethos of many of the groups. Difficulties were also reported with making applications, with the discretionary nature of trust funding, and with raising capital costs.

Lack of facilities for disabled women and the necessity of having childcare provided in order to ensure that women can participate in activities was also highlighted by Taillon. She points to the high demand for educational provision for women, and the need for more flexibility in accrediting women's learning. Taillon believed that women suffer disproportionately from a lack of social amenities, are more likely to be responsible for shopping and household tasks, but are less likely to have access to transport. Social and recreational facilities tend to be geared towards the needs of males rather than women or young people. Rural women especially suffer from isolation, lack of amenities, lack of mobility and restricted access to facilities that do exist.

References

Abbott, M. & Frazer, H. (eds) (1985), *Women and Community Work in Northern Ireland*, Farset, Belfast.

Abbott, M. & McDonough, R. (1989), 'Changing Women: Women's Action in Northern Ireland' in Deane, E. (ed.), *Lost Horizons, New Horizons: Community Development in Northern Ireland*, Workers Educational Association/Community Development Review Group, Belfast.

Buckley, S. & Lonergan, P. (1984), 'Women and the Troubles, 1969-1980' in Alexander, Y. & O'Day, A. (1984), *Terrorism in Ireland*, Croom Helm, London.

Campbell, B. (1987), *The Iron Ladies: Why Do Women Vote Tory?*, Virago, London.

Cecil, R., Offer, J. & St Leger, F. (1987), *Informal Welfare: a Sociological Study of Care in Northern Ireland*, Gower, London.

Cecil, R. (1989), 'Care in the Community in a Northern Ireland Town' in Donnan, H. & McFarlane, G. (eds), *Social Anthropology and Public Policy in Northern Ireland*, Avebury, England.

Cromie, S. (1987a), 'Men and women who choose business proprietorship as a career', *International Small Business Journal*, 5, pp. 43-60.

Cromie, S. (1987b), 'Motivations of aspiring male and female entrepreneurs', *Journal of Occupational Behaviour*, 8.

David, M. (1983), 'The New Right in the USA and Britain: a new anti-feminist moral economy', *Critical Social Policy*, vol. 12, no. 3, Spring, pp. 31-46.

David, M. (1985), 'Motherhood, Childcare and the New Right', lecture to the British Association for the Advancement of Science, Annual Meeting, 20-30 August.

David, M. (1986), 'Moral and Maternal: the Family in the Right' in Levitas, R. (ed.), *The Ideology of the New Right*, Polity Press, Cambridge.

Donnan, H. & McFarlane, G. (1985), 'Social life in rural Ireland', *Studies*, Autumn, pp. 281-98.

Donnison, D. (1988), 'Secrets of success', *New Society*, January 29.

Dworkin, A. (1983), *Right Wing Women: the Politics of Domesticated Females*, The Women's Press, London.

Edgerton, L. (1986), 'Public Protest, Domestic Acquiescence: Women in Northern Ireland' in Ridd, R. & Calloway, H., *Caught up in Conflict: Women's Responses to Political Strife*, Macmillan, London.

Evason, E. (1980), *Just me and the Kids: a Study of Single Parent Families in Northern Ireland*, Equal Opportunities Commission for Northern Ireland, Belfast.

Evason, E., Whittington, D. & Knowles, L. (1993), *The Cost of Caring*, Equal Opportunities Commission for Northern Ireland, Belfast.

Finch, J. & Groves, D. (eds) (1983), *A Labour of Love: Women, Work and Caring*, Routledge & Kegan Paul, London.

Hamilton, A., McCartney, C., Anderson, T. & Finn, A. (1990), *Violence and Communities*, Centre for the Study of Conflict, University of Ulster, Coleraine.

Kilmurray, A. & Bradley, C. (1989), *The Needs and Aspirations of Women in South Armagh*, Rural Action Project, Derry.

McCorry, M. (1988), *Women and the Need for Training*, Women's Education Project/Equal Opportunities Commission for Northern Ireland, Belfast.

McEwen, A., Agnew, U., Fulton, J. & Malcolm, S. (1987), *Women in the Professions*, Equal Opportunities Commission for Northern Ireland, Belfast.

McShane, L. (1991), *The Community Support Programme: Interim Report*, Northern Ireland Voluntary Trust, Belfast.

Mitchison, A. (1988), 'Ulster's family feminists', *New Society*, February 19, pp. 17-19.

Morgan, P. & Ruddy, B. (1985), 'Working with Women in a New City Setting' in Abbott, M. & Frazer, H. (eds), *Women and Community Work in Northern Ireland*, Farset, Belfast.

Morgan, V. (1992), 'Bridging the Divide: Women and Political and Community Issues' in Stringer, P. & Robinson, G. (eds), *Social Attitudes in Northern Ireland; the Second Report, 1991-1992*, Blackstaff, Belfast.

Mulrine, C., O'Neill, J., Rolston, B. & Kilmurray, A. (1991), *A Report into Funding and Support for Community Development in Northern Ireland*, Community Development Review Group, Belfast.

Murphy, C. (1992), 'Women's history, feminist history or gender history?', *The Irish Review*, 12, pp. 21-26.

O'Connor, E. (1992), *Community Connections: the Role of Women in the Formation and Operation of a Cross-border Community Development Initiative*, Northern Ireland European Women's Platform, Belfast.

Rooney, E. & Woods, M. (1992), *Women, Community and Politics in Northern Ireland: a Research Project with an Action Outcome*, Centre for Research on Women, Community Education Research and Development Centre, University of Ulster, Coleraine.

Roulston, C. (1989), 'Women on the margin: the women's movement in Northern Ireland, 1973-1988', *Science and Society*, vol. 53, Summer, pp. 219-36.

Shannon, C. (1992), 'The hidden heroines: reflections on the women of Northern Ireland', Institute of Irish Studies, Queen's University, Belfast (unpublished Institute seminar).

St Leger, F. & Gillespie, N. (1991), *Informal Welfare in Three Belfast Communities*, DHSS, Belfast.

Taillon, R. (1992), *Grant-aided or Taken for Granted: a Study of Women's Voluntary Organisations in Northern Ireland*, Women's Support Network, Belfast.

Wardle, M. (1992), 'Discrimination against Women: Workshop Discussion', in Cullen, B. (ed.), *Discriminations Old and New: Aspects of Northern Ireland Today*, Institute of Irish Studies, Queen's University, Belfast.

Watson, T. (1985), *Cleaning Up: Women and the Contract Cleaning Industry in Northern Ireland*, Northern Ireland Women's Rights Movement, Belfast.

Wilson, E. (1977), *Women and the Welfare State*, Tavistock, London.

11   The origins of voluntary action in Belfast

Arthur Williamson

This chapter discusses the origins of voluntary activity in Belfast. It draws attention to the remarkable upsurge of voluntary action in the final years of the eighteenth century. It discusses the contribution of a number of remarkable men and women who were outstanding voluntary activists and who made a major contribution to the relief of poverty and to the development of medical care and care for disabled people in Belfast. It considers the onset and growth of sectarianism in Belfast and the different approaches of the Protestant social activists and philanthropists and of the authorities of the Catholic Church to the organization of social relief and philanthropy.

In Ireland, as in virtually every country with a developed system of social services, the origins of those services are rooted in a combination of voluntary and governmental action. R. B. McDowell (1964, 169f.) has shown that, before it was dissolved in 1801, the Irish Parliament made substantial contributions to some of Dublin's voluntary hospitals. Guided by stringent rules about value for money, support for Dublin hospitals continued through the nineteenth century despite attempts to curb it and notwithstanding the allegation that no state support was given to similar institutions in other parts of the empire (McDowell, p. 171).

In Belfast, as in Dublin, voluntary institutions played the major role in the provision of poor relief and health care throughout the nineteenth century and well into the twentieth. Indeed voluntary action was such an integral part of the fabric of Belfast's emerging industrial and urban society that the social relations and social processes of that society, to say nothing of its emerging concepts and values, cannot be understood without an awareness of the development of voluntary action.

For the last fifty years in Northern Ireland statutory social services have predominated over the voluntary sector. It is now increasingly being acknowledged that a history of social policy which does not take account of the voluntary origins of most of our social and health services is partial and inadequate. Sources for the study of statutory social welfare services are comparatively recent and are relatively accessible to students. By contrast, the origins of the voluntary services are diffuse and opaque and are therefore overlooked both by teachers and by their students. An awareness of the voluntary origins of our services is particularly topical and important in the 1990s when the dominance of the statutory sector in welfare and health provision is being replaced by new relationships between purchasers and providers of care.

The origins of voluntary action: the Poores Money (1631) and the Belfast Charitable Society, (1771)

The first organized voluntary activity intended to help the poor of Belfast was the Poores Money to which the first recorded donation was that of a certain Edward Holmes, burgess of the borough of Belfast who 'dyed in June 1631 and left the poor decayed inhabitants of Belfast £40.' A panel inscribed with the names of early contributors to the Poores Money is displayed in the boardroom of the Belfast Charitable Society, established more than a century later in 1771 when the foundation stone of the present building in Clifton Street was laid. It was opened in 1774 and received visits from John Wesley in 1778 and from John Howard, the prison reformer, a few years later. The origins and development of the Society are chronicled in exhaustive detail in R. W. M. Strain's *Belfast and its Charitable Society* (1961).

By contrast with Dublin, Belfast at the end of the eighteenth century had few charitable institutions. In Dublin the early part of the century had seen the foundation of a number of voluntary hospitals including the Charitable Infirmary at Jervis Street, (1718), Dr Steevens' Hospital (1720), Mercer's Hospital (1734), the Foundling Hospital (1750) and of several specialist hospitals of which the Rotunda (1745), an obstetric hospital and St Patrick's Hospital, established with the aid of a legacy from Jonathan Swift are the most celebrated (Gatenby, 1992).

In 1800 Dublin was a large and prestigious city of 180,000. Belfast, however, was little more than a market town of some 19,000 though its position on the Lagan gave it natural advantages for the development of the linen industry. The period 1790-1815 was a remarkable time in Belfast's history. The French and American Revolutions had shaken the foundations of the established order. The young town was growing and the linen trade was bringing new prosperity. Its cultural life was strongly linked with Scotland and the stream of Presbyterian students who went to study medicine or theology at Glasgow or Edinburgh brought back with them new liberal political and philosophical ideas current in Scotland at the time. Sectarianism was unknown. In 1782 the Catholic population was only 8 per cent and its rise was gradual. Territoriality did not become a feature of life in Belfast until the middle of the next century. When state involvement in social welfare and education was virtually non-existent the intelligentsia of Belfast responded to the social and intellectual needs of their growing and rapidly industrialising town.

The Charitable Society remains the oldest voluntary organization still functioning in Belfast. From it sprang a number of medical charities and other bodies for the poor of Belfast. The Society was notable for its role in the development of Belfast, and in particular for its work in public health, where it pioneered both the installation of pure water throughout the city, and proper arrangements for sanitary burials. The Society was established 'for the support of vast numbers of real objects of charity ... for the employment of idle beggars that crowd to it ... and for the reception of infirm and diseased poor.' In the 1990s it continues to provide a home for about 150 elderly men and women mainly from Belfast and the counties of Antrim and Down.

It is not necessary here to dwell on the details of its history. It is of interest, however, to note some of those who were active in the establishment of the Society. The second half of the eighteenth century had seen a decline in the influence of Belfast's titled aristocracy and the emergence of wealthy families of manufacturers and mill owners. These formed what McDowell (1960) has called, 'that vigorous, industrious, intellectually alert middle class which played such a decisive part in moulding British and Ulster life'. Wealth was becoming decentralized and a new merchant aristocracy was emerging with a strong civic spirit and with energy and idealism. At the turn of the century voluntary action was becoming a significant force for change and was closely associated with the radicalism which had characterised Belfast during the previous two decades. Henry and Robert Joy, sons of Francis Joy, owner of the *Belfast News Letter* were among the leaders of the Charitable Society and were active both in fundraising and in the administrative arrangements which led to its incorporation in 1774, two years before it received its first grant from the Belfast Corporation. In addition to the Joy brothers, Valentine Jones, Dr James Ross and Samuel McTier formed the core of the group which established the Charitable Society.

Less well known than its social relief work is the contribution of the Charitable Society to industrial innovation in the form of the introduction of cotton spinning to Belfast. In 1778 Nicholas Grimshaw, a member of the committee, provided a carding machine and spinning wheel and by 1780

163

ninety poor children were working in Belfast's first cotton spinning mill on equipment supplied by Robert Joy and Thomas McCabe (Boyle, p. 43).

Social radicalism and voluntary action: Mary Ann McCracken and Dr James Macdonnell

The association between social radicalism and the Society continued into the next generation when a number of prominent Belfast radicals were active in its leadership including Mary Ann McCracken, 1770-1866, and Dr James Macdonnell, 1763-1845. A member of a family with Scottish Covenanting roots, Mary Ann was the niece of the Joy brothers and the sister of the United Irishman, Henry Joy McCracken, who was hanged in 1798 for his part in a rising of United Irishmen. Mary Ann McCracken remained deeply involved with the work of the Charitable Society for most of her long and industrious life. A remarkable woman, she was a contemporary of Elizabeth Fry, the Quaker social reformer and of Mary Wollstonecraft, author of *The Vindication of the Rights of Women*, published in 1792. She grew up with the Charitable Society. For many years she was particularly concerned with the welfare of the poor children of Belfast (McNeill, 1960, 1988). Strain documents her energetic concern for children and young people including her interest in their nutrition, education and personal development. Her notebooks show that, even when she was more than eighty years of age, in 1851, she continued to be active in the work of the Ladies' Committee and to take a keen interest in the children (Strain, 116f).

Dr James Macdonnell, MD, who was born in Cushendall, was one of the most notable figures in this first phase of voluntary action in Belfast. Macdonnell was the son of a Catholic father and a Protestant mother and was brought up a Presbyterian. Like many of his contemporaries in Belfast his sympathies seem to have lain in the direction of the Non-Subscribing Presbyterians. Macdonnell's contribution to the intellectual, political and medical life of Belfast has been chronicled by Sir Peter Froggatt, (Froggatt, 1981; McNeill, 1988, pp. 78-82). A graduate of the medical school of Edinburgh University, Macdonnell practiced medicine in Belfast and was prominent for his sponsorship of free medical care for the poor as well as for his literary and scientific work and for his support for the Irish language and Irish music, particularly that of the harp. He was also influential among the United Irishmen, was one of the founders of the Belfast Society for Promoting Knowledge, later the Linenhall Library, and was a board member of the new Belfast Academical Institution when it was established in 1810. Macdonnell was one of the founders of the Belfast Medical Society, (1822). He also encouraged the establishment of the Female Society for the Clothing of the

164

Poor (1820) perhaps the first non-medical Belfast charity run by women, and the Society for the Relief of the Destitute Sick, (1826) also run by women, a voluntary organization which continued to function into the twentieth century.

Macdonnell's pioneering work for Belfast in the field of medical charities deserves to be more widely known. He believed that the growing borough of Belfast needed a free dispensary from which charitable doctors would carry out domiciliary visits to sick poor. He first tried to open a dispensary in 1792 and, when that failed, he tried again five years later. That attempt also failed but Macdonnell tried yet again in 1799 with support from many of Belfast's leading citizens. This time the initiative was successful and in 1817 his dispensary moved to Frederick Street and became established as the Belfast Fever Hospital and Dispensary. At its commencement all the income of the dispensary was from charitable sources but soon, because it cared for fever patients, it received a subvention of some £400 per year from the government under an act of 1807 (47 Geo. III).

Macdonnell's foundation has continued to serve the people of Belfast and Northern Ireland for nearly two centuries. Toward the end of the nineteenth century it became known as the Belfast General Hospital and Dispensary, then the Royal Hospital. In 1903 a 300 bed hospital was opened on the Grosvenor Road and became known as the Royal Victoria Hospital (See Malcolm, 1851; Allison, 1972).

During the whole of the nineteenth century Belfast was characterised by runaway growth and by endemic disease. Whereas the population of the city in 1801 had been only 19,000 by 1851 it had risen to 87,000. Fifty years later it had grown almost fourfold to 350,000 and, in area, sevenfold (Budge & O'Leary, 1973, p. 28). Throughout most of the century public health standards were, by late twentieth century standards, unimaginable. Poverty was often dire, particularly during periods of economic stagnation, and street begging and homelessness were common. Many of the poor lacked not only food and shelter but clothing and bedding. Infectious disease was endemic and there were horrific epidemics of cholera, typhoid and typhus. The city experienced a devastating epidemic of Asiatic cholera in 1832 when 500 people died. There were further epidemics in 1836 and in 1847 when accommodation for fever victims was provided in hastily erected sheds at the General Hospital at Frederick Street because the workhouse refused to accommodate them.

The Fever Hospital and Dispensary, however, was not the first voluntary hospital in Belfast. In December 1793 a meeting of Belfast women was called to establish a new charity to be called the Humane Female Society for the Relief of Lying-In Women. The following year a house was rented in Donegall Street and a six bedded hospital was established. This is the origin of the Royal Maternity Hospital which moved to its present site beside the

Royal Victoria Hospital in 1933. Much of the initiative for this seems to have come from Mrs Martha McTier who was voted to be the first honorary secretary of the committee. It will be remembered that her husband, Samuel, was one of the founders of the Belfast Charitable Society. He was also president of the first Belfast Society of the United Irishmen. Mrs McTier was the sister of Dr William Drennan, 1754-1820, a literary as well as a medical man, one of the founders of the United Irishmen in 1791 and later of the Belfast Academical Institution (Drennan Letters, PRONI).

Another institution for the poor which commenced in the early nineteenth century was the Belfast House of Industry established in 1809 with considerable voluntary support. This was the first society in Ireland to respond to the needs of poor people by offering them both accommodation and an opportunity to work. It appears to have been prompted as much by a desire to provide work as by the wish to reduce the prevalence of begging. Following a public meeting to discuss the matter a voluntary committee of twenty-one people was established with Henry Joy of the *Belfast News Letter* taking a leading role. Visitors were appointed to interview people wishing to benefit from the facilities of the society. Money was subscribed; work, food and accommodation was provided for men and women. Disabled people were a particular priority. The committee raised money to provide spinning wheels, reels and flax for weaving. People worked both in the House of Industry itself and in their own homes on equipment provided by the committee. Men had work breaking stones. Up to 500 people were fed with soup each day at the rate of one quart per adult. In 1817, during the fever epidemic, the House of Industry spent £5,000 on the relief of some 1,200 poor families (Strain, p. 158, 169f.). There was close co-operation between the House of Industry and the Charitable Society. The House of Industry became redundant when the Irish Poor Law was passed in 1838. Members of the public, who had willingly made voluntary contributions, were no longer willing to do so when the poor rate was levied under the new legislation.

A number of religious voluntary societies were established to respond to the social needs of the expanding city. Indeed much voluntary action at that time appears to have been associated with the churches or to have been interdenominational. Two Presbyterian societies, one orthodox and one Non-Subscribing, reflected the theological tensions which dominated Presbyterianism in Ulster. These were the Belfast Domestic Mission and the Belfast Town Mission. The Town Mission was established in 1827 by several clergy together with Mr Bryce, principal of the Belfast Academy. It employed visitors to call at the homes of needy people and to bring aid to them. An extract from the diary of one of these visitors, vividly evokes the scene in one home:

166

In a house I found a poor woman sitting picking among cinders. That was her daily employment. She said 'I go out in the morning to gather them. Then I come home and clean them and sell them and that is the way I get a morsel of bread.' (Murray, 1977, p. 101).

Dr Andrew Malcolm: physician, social activist and social statistician

The Belfast Domestic Mission to the Poor was established by members of the Non-Subscribing Presbyterian Church at an annual meeting of the Unitarian Society where a letter from Dr A. G. Malcolm had been considered.

Malcolm had written to the Unitarian Society to draw the attention of its members to the need for a domestic mission to visit the poor in their homes. The Domestic Mission continued under the aegis of the Non-Subscribing Presbyterian Church for nearly a century until in 1944 a new initiative, the Malcolm Youth Club, was opened (McCafferty, 1953). Malcolm, 1818-57, was an influential and important figure in Belfast in mid century. As a voluntary activist he had few equals either for energy or for social commitment. Born in Newry and educated at the Royal Belfast Academical Institution he took his MD at Edinburgh in 1842 with a dissertation on fever, having a short time before been himself a fever victim. In the same year he returned to Belfast, set up in private practice and was appointed as dispensary doctor, a voluntary position. In 1846 he took up a position at the Belfast General Hospital. He was later to be the moving force in establishing two influential societies which have often been confused. The first of these was the Belfast Working Classes Association for the Promotion of General Improvement, established in 1846 with the aid of some of Belfast's leading mill owners, of which Malcolm was the founder and first president. This society promoted working class education, established the *People's Magazine*, opened the People's Circulating Library and the People's Newsroom, a reading room which subscribed to 96 papers and periodicals (Calwell, 1977, p. 63f.). The Belfast Society for the Amelioration of the Conditions of the Working Classes (Calwell, 1977, p. 79f.) had as its primary purpose the provision of public baths and wash-houses (Malcolm, 1848). Malcolm served as its first secretary. In addition he was the president of the Belfast Clinical and Pathological Society. He was also active in the wider field of social and health policy and read a paper 'The sanitary state of Belfast with suggestions for its improvement' at the Statistical Meeting of the Belfast Social Inquiry Society in 1852 (Malcolm, 1852).

Malcolm was concerned about the need to develop a sense of citizenship and civic responsibility in the new industrial classes. He was tireless in his efforts on behalf of the sick poor of Belfast. In addition to his professional work and his committee activities he found time to write a history of the General Hospital and the other medical establishments of Belfast at the time (Malcolm, 1851). Malcolm was also an influential figure in the Day Asylum which was set up in March 1847 and where he served as secretary. (For a biography of Malcolm see Calwell, 1977). 1847 was a year of unparalleled disaster. Cholera was at its height; many of the poor were virtually without clothes and the non-sectarian Society for Clothing the Poor distributed clothes received from the United States and gave a large number of blankets to the Society for the Relief of the Destitute Sick. The Day Asylum operated under the wing of the Belfast Night Asylum which had been established in 1841. This was primarily a hostel for homeless women and young people. Eighty persons were accommodated in two dormitories, one for each sex. No food was provided but fires heating each of the rooms were also used to roast potatoes. The Day Asylum was maintained by public subscriptions and by the proceeds from fundraising events.

The Night Asylum was shortlived and closed at the end of 1847 when government regulations concerning outdoor relief changed. Before it closed, however, it provided a base for the Day Asylum and Free Industrial School which operated from a converted weaving factory at May's Dock on the River Lagan. The Asylum and School attracted considerable public interest particularly because it provided work for women in oakum picking and in mending and patching. The American consul in Belfast, T. W. Gilpin, gave as a gift to the Asylum forty barrels of maize or Indian meal as it was known. Its clients were classified as: persons discharged from gaol or hospital; persons reduced to the state of begging; strangers looking for work; destitute children. It is of interest for another reason. Its committee consisted of fifty-four members who included some of the leading churchmen of Belfast and, unusually, the Roman Catholic bishop of the time, Bishop Cornelius Denvir. This was possibly the first example of co-operation between the authorities of the Catholic Church and leading Presbyterian churchmen and members of other denominations.

Voluntary social action at midcentury: the context of religious polarization

Leslie Clarkson has traced the links between Belfast and the rest of Ulster (Clarkson, 1983) and draws attention to immigration from the countryside. Whereas in 1801 Catholics comprised less than one tenth of the population of the city, by 1861 they numbered one third and by 1901, one quarter. Belfast's growing industries attracted workers from the countryside, Episcopalians from south Ulster, Catholics from the north and west and

Presbyterians from the north. The influx led to pressure on jobs and housing. Thus developed the segregated pattern of housing and the sectarian conflict which has characterized Belfast's history for more than a century. Thus the foundations of Belfast's unhappy history of community relations were laid in the mid nineteenth century.

The subject of community relations in Belfast is discussed by Heatley (1983, p. 135) who draws attention to what he calls the 'swift decay in relations' between Belfast's Presbyterian majority and its Catholic minority from the 1830s onwards. In 1842 there was rioting in Belfast owing to a shortage of food. The military were called to deal with the rioting but were so appalled at what they saw that they took up a subscription to buy bread for the starving rioters. Later in the 1840s Belfast was to feel the effects of the Famine as impoverished small farmers from Cavan, Monaghan, and from parts of Tyrone and Armagh fled to Belfast in the hope of finding work in the mills of the lower Falls.

Sectarian rioting occurred in 1845, 1857 and 1863 and 1886. Catholics, because of their rural origins, were often unskilled and nearly one third were illiterate (Heatley, p. 140). Although Belfast's charitable societies were overwhelmingly Protestant the Catholic hierarchy did participate in some charities such as the committees for relief which were set up to cope with the distress of 1847 and 1857 where Bishop Denvir was a member. Later Bishop Dorrian and Bishop Henry were on the committee of the Coal Relief Fund.

Belfast's growth from 1850-1900 was more rapid than that of any other city in Britain or Ireland (Clarkson, 1983, p. 159). As the last of the cities of the Industrial Revolution it grew on the basis of textiles, engineering and shipbuilding. In the second part of the century its middle class enlarged and increased its prosperity. Working-class employees of the shipyards, the ropeworks, of Gallagher's tobacco works and of many developing industries participated in the new affluence. Highly paid craftsmen created a large skilled labour force, reckoned to be about 25 per cent of the workforce (Baker, 1970). Moore, in his study of housing in nineteenth century Ireland, discusses the development of housing in Belfast and Dublin and contrasts the favourable conditions of the skilled working class with those of the poor (Moore, 1986). By 1851 the religiously segregated pattern of housing was becoming established. There had also been an expansion of the city in the direction of Ballymacarrett, soon to be served by two new bridges.

The work of Catholic religious orders and of St Vincent de Paul

Bishop Denvir continued to lead Belfast's Catholics until the mid sixties in an atmosphere of increasingly disturbed community relations. In an attempt to respond to the educational needs of the Catholic poor Bishop Denvir invited the Sisters of Mercy to Belfast and his successor, Bishop Patrick Dorrian, brought the Christian Brothers. Each order contributed a great deal to raising educational standards among the poor thus helping them to improve their employment opportunities. Although originally an order of teachers, later in the century the Sisters of Mercy became well-known for their nursing services to the poor. In 1883 Bishop Dorrian purchased a private dwelling on the Crumlin Road and shortly afterwards the Mater Hospital commenced with thirty-four beds under the auspices of the Sisters of Mercy. During his last illness the Bishop passed the responsibility of the hospital to trustees and instructed them that it should be enlarged and should provide facilities for medical education. The hospital was subsequently recognised, on 28 July 1899, by the Royal University of Ireland as a teaching hospital. Towards the end of the century there was considerable support for extending the hospital but little support was received from the hierarchy which, no doubt, had other claims on its resources. The foundation stone of a new hospital was laid in December 1898 and a 150 bed hospital was opened in April 1900 (Casement, 1969; Verzin, 1987).

The needs of Catholic orphan children were met by the St Patrick's Orphan Society in May Street, founded in 1839 with the encouragement of Bishop Denvir. This was later taken over by the Sisters of Mercy who opened an orphanage on the Crumlin Road. The Sisters of Charity and the Presentation nuns, together with the Sisters of Mercy, were considered to be very successful in raising Catholic children. The Good Shepherd Sisters (1867) opened the first steam laundry in Ireland which continued to function until the 1970s. The primary focus of the work of the Good Shepherd Sisters was with unmarried mothers. Today there are two houses in the grounds of their convent, 'Marianville' for homeless women and 'Roseville' for battered wives. Other orders of sisters who came to Belfast to work among the Catholic poor were the Irish Dominican Sisters (1870), the Bon Secour Sisters, (1872) and, in 1900, the Sisters of Charity (Clear, 1987). The Catholic authorities favoured an institutional approach to the care of children whereas Episcopalians and Presbyterians established the Protestant Orphan Society and the Presbyterian Orphan Society which formed networks of foster families with whom children were boarded out (Barkley, 1966). Under the Industrial Schools, (Ireland) Act of 1866 children found begging were allowed to be committed to industrial schools. Archbishop Cullen insisted that Catholic children should only be cared for by Catholic authorities. The subject of boarding out pauper children in Belfast was discussed in an article of that title by Isabella Tod, the feminist campaigner and vice-president of the Belfast Health Society (Tod, 1878).

In mid-century the growth of the Catholic population in Belfast and the crises which resulted from crop failures and from economic circumstances coincided with the introduction to Ireland of the Society of St Vincent de Paul in 1845. The order had been established twelve years earlier in Paris by Frederic Ozanam, a twenty year old student at the Sorbonne. Little has been written about the work of the society in Ireland (Dallat, 1983). Its members combined social and spiritual goals, operated at a parish level with the leadership of the parish priest, and directed their work mainly at their fellow Catholics. They engaged in a wide range of social and spiritual work including visiting the poor, visiting in prison, helping homeless men and boys, running boy's clubs, and encouraging savings. In times of particular distress they ran soup kitchens. By 1889 the Society had opened a home for boys and a night refuge in Academy Street. A women's auxiliary, the Belfast Catholic Ladies' Association and the Ladies' Society of St Vincent de Paul did work similar to that of the men.

Of the voluntary social welfare societies of Belfast few were non-sectarian. In theory the main voluntary associations were open to all but Catholics may well have been deterred by the number of clergymen on their committees and by their puritan ethos. Jordan (1989, p. 632) has observed that only 2 per cent of the men working in Belfast's charities in the second part of the nineteenth century were Catholics. Sectarian feeling heightened during the Home Rule agitation in the later part of the century. Protestants were suspicious of the Catholic religious orders and regarded them as threatening. Catholics were acutely aware of their minority status in Belfast and the Catholic middle class was small in numbers, lacking in confidence and, comparatively speaking, in resources and in lay leadership. The Hamills of Trench House were the leading family in the field of voluntary action in Belfast at the time but little is now known of them. For whatever reason few, if any, voluntary social welfare organizations under lay leadership are to be found in Belfast's Catholic communities in the late nineteenth century.

Because Catholic charity was in the hands of the parish clergy and of the religious orders it would have been virtually unthinkable for a Protestant man or woman to have become a member of a Catholic voluntary social service organization. Jordan has written (1989, p. 582) that 'by the end of the nineteenth century the division between Catholic and Protestant benevolence was almost complete'. As in so many areas of northern Ireland society, parallel structures emerged with little collaboration between the two communities apart from during times of extraordinary distress in 1847, in the late 1850s, and in 1879.

Protestant philanthropy: care for disabled people and the establishment of specialist hospitals

Among the Protestant middle class voluntary activity continued to flourish as it had done from the beginning of century. Working men supported the General Hospital on a regular basis with deductions from their wages and had a representative on the hospital's board. It became necessary to formalise arrangements following the passing of the Truck Amendment Act of 1887. In the following year the Working Men's Committee was established. Representing workmen in many of Belfast's largest industrial enterprises, this committee became an influential pressure group at a time when the hospital was beset by chronic indebtedness. In 1891 the committee pledged £2,000 towards the expenses of the hospital. Members 'and their ladies' made an annual visitation to the hospital from 1893 onwards to see how the contributions of their members had been spent (Archives, 1888).

The most active voluntary organizations were those for sick and disabled people. The Society for Promoting the Education of the Deaf, Dumb and Blind, the Belfast Association for the Employment of the Industrious Blind, and the Cripples' Institute were the leading organizations in this field (Cripples' Institute, 1912). The Institute was a remarkable organization founded in 1878 by Mr and Mrs Lawson Browne, members of a family well-known in business and philanthropic circles in Belfast and associated with the Cripples' Institute for several generations. Each summer more than 3,000 disabled people benefited from holidays in its three holiday homes at Bangor and elsewhere.

Disablement and poverty were often closely linked; the Institute developed programmes of residential accommodation, training and employment. Whereas most of the other societies serving disabled people disappeared many years ago, the work commenced by the Cripples' Institute continues today as the Northern Ireland Institute for Disability. The Institute brought together a number of separate charitable activities under one organizational umbrella which it proceeded to incorporate, an unusual step for a voluntary body at the time. Having surveyed the wide field of literature on charities in the nineteenth century, Jordan remarks (1989, p. 466) that she had found ' ... no record in any major study of Victorian and Edwardian charitable effort of such a body'. A century later its main activities comprise residential care and respite care for disabled people together with a hostel for homeless men in Utility Street, near to the location of the Institute's early workshops. It is an indication of the Institute's strength of that it has been able to maintain and develop its role alongside the welfare state of the late twentieth century.

Among Protestants the clergy and the business community provided leadership in recognising and responding to social questions. Presbyterian clergy were the most prominent, as might be expected in a Presbyterian town. The Rev. Dr John Edgar and Rev. W. Johnston were involved in establishing and guiding the development of several charities. Both were active in the temperance movement. Edgar was one of the founders of the Belfast Social Enquiry Society and was active in famine relief in Connaught in 1846. Jordan's analysis (1989) of the occupational origins of men and women in charity work shows that one quarter of the men active in voluntary action between 1840 and 1910 were drawn from the textile industry and some 13 per cent were clergy. Notable by their absence were shipbuilders and engineers who, she remarks, 'were not so interested in religious observance as the linen merchants' and who might therefore, she suggests, have had a different attitude to charity.

Among the business leaders of Belfast who were active in voluntary action were the Ewart family, J. P. Corry, the timber merchant, J. A. Henderson, owner of the *Belfast News Letter* (continuing the tradition of the Joy family a century earlier), the Mulholland family of the York Street Flax mill, Sir Otto Jaffe, a linen merchant of German Jewish background who raised large sums for the Royal Hospital, and Vere Foster best known for his work in the field of education, of whom it was said that he was 'prominent in every Belfast movement that had the welfare of man as its object, provided that the charity was sufficiently all-embracing as to exclude none on grounds of religious belief' (McNeill, 1971, p.16). During the disastrous slump of 1879 he had responsibility for Belfast's main soup kitchen.

Belfast's most outstanding philanthropist in the nineteenth century was Forster Green, a devout Quaker and tea merchant who was a major benefactor of many charities including the Prison Gate Mission for Women, the Midnight Mission and the Homes of Rest associated with the Cripples' Institute in Bangor. He founded the Forster Green Hospital for Tuberculosis in 1890. It is estimated that during his lifetime he gave some £200,000 to charity.

As Belfast's population expanded and its middle class developed during the last part of the nineteenth century charitable hospitals were established to meet particular medical needs. The period between 1865 and 1873 saw the establishment of seven hospitals including the Belfast Hospital for Skin Diseases (1865), the Belfast Ophthalmic Hospital (1867), the Ulster (Benn) Eye, Ear and Throat Hospital (1871), three children's hospitals, the Samaritan Hospital for Women and Children (1873). In 1873, apparently unknown to each other, two committees came into being in Belfast to consider the need for a hospital for children. The first, to establish the Belfast Hospital for Sick Children, was composed of 'men of intelligence and earnestness' who had been inspired by the example of the children's hospital in London at Great Ormond Street (Calwell, 1973). This committee was a secular venture in that the initiative appears to have come from industrialists including linen merchants and manufacturers, bankers and shipowners and included both Catholic and Protestant businessmen. No clergy were present at the initial meeting.

The second group which was interested in the needs of sick children was presided over by J. P. Corry and included a number of clergy. That the proposed hospital should have a religious ethos was important to the members of this committee and this proved to be the stumbling block in a series of unsuccessful discussions about a merger between the two committees with a view to establishing a single hospital. Both projects proceeded separately and the Ulster Hospital for Children was established, later adding the words 'for Women' to its title. Subsequently the hospital's title was once again changed to become simply the Ulster Hospital which is now located at Dundonald (Marshall and Kelly, 1973).

Women and voluntary action: Miss Hobson, Mrs Byers and Miss Isabella Tod

In the later part of the century, as earlier, women continued to work in voluntary social welfare activity. In 1847 a committee of 100 women had led a campaign to collect money for famine relief in Connaught and founded the Belfast Ladies' Society for the Relief of Irish Destitution. Some women took a prominent position in voluntary societies; most served as volunteers in organizations led by their husbands. Toward the end of the century some women emerged in positions of leadership. Among these were Miss Hobson, the founder of the Belfast Association for the Employment of the Industrious Blind, Mrs Margaret Byers (Jordan, 1992), headmistress of Victoria College for the education of girls, who was active in the Prison Gate Mission, the Cripples' Institute and the Victoria Homes and Miss Isabella Tod. Miss Tod, an early suffragette, and, like Mary McCracken, of Scottish Covenanting background, was an outstanding activist, a vigorous campaigner and a powerful speaker on many issues with addresses which were 'full of reason and bristling with arguments'. In 1871 she founded the Northern Ireland Society for Woman's Suffrage and she also served in the Ladies' National Association. She read carefully argued papers on matters of social concern such as the treatment of alcoholics and arrangements for boarding out pauper children (Tod, 1874, 1878, 1897). As secretary of the Belfast Ladies' Institute she campaigned for education for girls and she succeeded in having the terms of the Intermediate Education Bill of 1878 extended to include girls. A leader writer for the *Northern Whig* newspaper for many years, she worked tirelessly for charitable and philanthropic causes.

As in many countries participation in voluntary organizations paved the way for women to enter the wider political arena (McCarthy, 1994). Following the passing of the Local Government (Ireland) Act of 1898, which instituted a system of county councils, women were permitted to stand as candidates in elections as Poor Law Guardians and to vote for local councils. Some of those who had been active in voluntary societies were the first to enter local government.

The complex question of motivation for voluntary action in nineteenth century Belfast lies outside the scope of the present chapter. Nevertheless it is impossible not to reflect on the reasons and purposes which led not only prominent citizens, but the ordinary men and women of Belfast, to contribute a massive volume of time and money to voluntary action. Until more is known about the intellectual and moral ethos of Belfast at the time one can only speculate about the range of motivations which inspired voluntary action. Certainly religion played a large part in inspiring compassion. But it should also be remembered that in many quarters philanthropy was unpopular for doctrinaire reasons. There was plenty, apart from personal inertia, to discourage philanthropy and voluntarism. The Utilitarians had gone out of their way to discourage indiscriminate giving by asserting that it encouraged begging and undermined energy and enterprise (Mill, 1881). The need for hospitals, however, was obvious and uncontentious and it is likely that giving for this purpose was popular because of this and also because of possible future benefit to the donor or to his family. In addition to compassion and, perhaps, to future self interest, sometimes there was guilt. Thomas Sinclair, a prominent grocer and bacon exporter, made a dramatic call for contributions to the Nurses for the Sick Poor Society by appealing to the consciences of Belfast's industrialists and mill owners. Writing in its first annual report he asked: 'What! Have these poor girls coughed out their lives in earning our dividends and shall we refuse them what will help to soothe their dying pillows?' (PRONI, D 3480). Founded in the 1870s and supported by voluntary subscriptions, the Nurses for the Sick Poor Society employed both professional nurses and lay lady visitors to visit chronic sick patients. By the last quarter of the century, hospitals and dispensaries provided care for emergency illness and curable disease. The society, forgotten today, continued to serve Belfast's sick for the next forty years. Its report for 1909 shows that in that year 38,884 visits were made to 1,521 patients.

Conclusion

Belfast in 1899 could scarcely have made a more vivid contrast with the city of a century earlier in the days of Macdonnell, the Joy brothers and the

United Irishmen. Bustling, sprawling and prosperous, the city was in its heyday. At the end of the century, as at the beginning, the Charitable Society, now joined by many voluntary associations, large and small, continued to respond to social need. The foundations of its medical services had been laid by voluntary effort and funding. As yet, statutory social services, with one or two exceptions, were poorly developed. Since 1829 the so-called 'lunatic poor' had had the refuge of the Belfast Lunatic Asylum. A network of lunatic asylums, begun in 1817, was Ireland's first statutory social service (Williamson, 1970, 1992). Since 1841, and the establishment of the Poor Law Union Workhouse, the destitute had received its cold and cruel comfort. Fifty years later it was a huge institution accommodating some 3,000 residents. Disabled residents numbered 1,500; a further 1,000 were over sixty years of age and unable to work. Apart from these statutory institutions, charity and philanthropy, with precarious and occasional support from the public purse, provided the only safety net there was for the unfortunate, the sick, the disabled and the indigent. But charity and philanthropy could not meet the complex needs of industrial society, particularly in times of recession. It was to be a further half century, and after two world wars, until the state would assume responsibility for a comprehensive range of personal social and health services. During that period the first line of support for Belfast's needy continued to be voluntary social action.

Acknowledgement and note on sources

The writer wishes to express his thanks for guidance on sources to Sir Peter Froggatt, Dr Maria Luddy, Dr John Offer and to the staff of the Linenhall Library, Belfast.

Students of the origins and development of voluntary organizations in Northern Ireland are fortunate to be able to benefit from the scholarly legacy of the late Alison Jordan of Victoria College, Belfast. Her monumental thesis, 'Voluntary societies in Victorian and Edwardian Belfast', (PhD thesis, Queen's University, Belfast, Jordan, 1989), is an essential starting point for anyone wishing to study the development of philanthropy in Belfast. See also her book, (1992) *Who Cared?: Charity in Victorian and Edwardian Belfast*. The writer gratefully acknowledges his debt to her work. In relation to the development of public administration in Ireland and the matter of state support for voluntary action in the nineteenth century the reader is referred to McDowell, (1964). A review of legal aspects of charity in nineteenth century Ireland has not been possible within the confines of this chapter. For a discussion of the complex legal questions concerned with religion and the law of charity, Brady's *Religion and the Law of Charities in Ireland*, (1975), should be consulted. His table of statutes, beginning with Magna Carta (1215), of the English Parliament prior to 1800, of the Irish Parliament prior to 1800, of the Imperial Parliament from 1801, of the Oireachtas and of the Parliament of Northern Ireland is particularly useful as is his table of Irish cases beginning in 1602. Readers interested in the development of voluntary care for children in Ireland should refer to the exhaustive study by Joseph Robins (1980), *The Lost Children: a Study of Charity Children in Ireland, 1700-1900*. There is a diffuse literature about medical charities in Ireland. The accounts by Denis Phelan, *Medical Charities of Ireland* (1835) and K. H. Connell (1950), *The Population of Ireland* provide a comprehensive overview.

References

Allison, R.S. (1972), *The Seeds of Time: a Short History of the Belfast General and Royal Hospital, 1850-1903*, Brough, Cox & Dunn, Belfast.

Archives of the Royal Victoria Hospital, Scrapbook, 1887-1901.

Baker, S. (1970), 'Edwardian Belfast', *Belfast Telegraph*, Centenary Edition, September, pp. 6 & 26.

Barkley, J.M. (1966), *The Presbyterian Orphan Society, 1866-1966*, [Presbyterian Orphan Society], Belfast.

Boyle, E. (1983), '"Linenopolis": The Rise of the Textile Industry' in Beckett, J.C. et al., *Belfast: the Making of the City, 1800-1914*, Appletree Press, Belfast.

Brady, James C. (1975), *Religion and the Law of Charities in Ireland*, Northern Ireland Legal Quarterly, Belfast.

Budge, I. & O'Leary, C. (1973), *Belfast: Approach to Crisis: a Study of Belfast Politics, 1613-1970*, Macmillan, London.

Calwell, H.G. (1973), *The Life and Times of a Voluntary Hospital: the Royal Belfast Hospital for Sick Children, 1873-1948*, Brough, Cox & Dunn, Belfast.

Calwell, H.G. (1977), *Andrew Malcolm of Belfast, 1818-1856, Physician and Historian*, Brough, Cox & Dunn, Belfast.

Casement, R.S. (1969), 'History of the Mater Infirmorum Hospital', *Ulster Medical Journal*, xxx, pt.viii, 2, pp. 62-75.

Caul, Brian and Herron, Stanley (1992), *A Service for People: Origins and Development of the Personal Social Services of Northern Ireland*, (2nd edition), December Publications, Belfast.

Clarkson, L. (1983), 'The City and the Country' in Beckett, J.C. et al., *Belfast: the Making of the City, 1800-1914*, Appletree Press, Belfast.

Clear, C. (1987), *Nuns in Nineteenth Century Ireland*, Gill and Macmillan, Dublin.

Connell, K.H. (1950), *The Population of Ireland, 1750-1850*, Oxford University Press, London.

Cripples' Institute (1912), *Illustrated interviews: the story of the Cripples' Institute, the People's Palace and the Homes of Rest at Belfast, Bangor and Ballygowan*, Cripples' Institute, Belfast.

Dallat, Very Rev. Canon Michael (1983), 'The Society in the North: the Early Years' in 150th Anniversary Booklet of the Society of St Vincent de Paul, Northern Ireland Region of St Vincent de Paul, Belfast.

Did Your Granny have a Hammer?: a History of the Irish Suffrage Movement, 1876-1922, (1985), Attic Press, Dublin.

Drennan Letters: correspondence between Dr William Drennan of Dublin and his sister, Mrs Martha McTier of Belfast, Public Record Office for Northern Ireland, Belfast.

Froggatt, Sir Peter (1981), 'Dr James Macdonnell, MD, 1763-1845', *The Glynns*, 9, pp. 17-31.

Gatenby, P. (1992), 'The Voluntary Hospital movement: the end of an era', *Journal of the Irish Colleges of Physicians and Surgeons*, vol. 21, no. 4, pp. 258-60.

Heatley, F. (1983), 'Community Relations and the Religious Geography, 1800-1886' in Beckett, J.C. et al., *Belfast: the Making of the City, 1800-1914*, Appletree Press, Belfast.

Jordan, Alison (1989), 'Voluntary societies in Victorian and Edwardian Belfast' (PhD thesis, Queen's University, Belfast).

Jordan, Alison (1992), *Margaret Byers, Pioneer of Women's Education and Founder of Victoria College, Belfast*, Institute of Irish Studies, Queen's University, Belfast.

Jordan, Alison (1992), *Who Cared? Charity in Victorian and Edwardian Belfast*, Institute of Irish Studies, Queen's University, Belfast.

Luddy, Maria (1989), *Women and Philanthropy in Nineteenth Century Ireland*, (PhD thesis, University College, Cork).

McCafferty, W.H. (1953), *Belfast Domestic Mission: a Century of Social Service, 1853-1953*, Belfast.

McCarthy, Kathleen D. (1990), 'Parallel Power Structures: Women and the Voluntary Sphere' in McCarthy, K.D. (ed.), *Lady Bountiful Revisited: Women, Philanthropy and Power*, Rutgers University Press, New Brunswick, pp. 1-54.

McDowell, R.B. (1960), foreword to the first edition of *Mary Ann McCracken: a Belfast Panorama*, Allen Figgis & Co., Dublin.

McDowell, R.B. (1964), *The Irish Administration*, Routledge & Kegan Paul, London.

McNeill, M. (1971), *Vere Foster*, David and Charles, Newton Abbot.

178

McNeill, M. (1988), *Mary Ann McCracken: a Belfast Panorama*, Blackstaff Press, Belfast (first edition 1960, Allen Figgis & Co., Dublin).

Malcolm, A.G. (1848), *Cleanliness and the Advantage of the Bath*, (second edition), Belfast.

Malcolm, A.G. (1851), *The History of the General Hospital, Belfast, and the other Medical Institutions of the Town*, W. & G. Agnew, Belfast.

Malcolm, A.G. (1852), 'The sanitary state of Belfast with suggestions for its improvement', a paper read before the Statistical Section of the Belfast Social Inquiry Society, 7 September, published by Henry Greer for the Belfast Social Inquiry Society, Belfast.

Marshall, Robert and Kelly, Kathleen (1973), *The Story of the Ulster Hospital, 1873-1952* by Robert Marshall; *1952-1973* by Kathleen Kelly, Brough, Cox & Dunn, Belfast.

Mill, J.S. (1881), 'Limits of the Province of Government' in *Principles of Political Economy with some of their Applications to Social Philosophy*, Longmans, Green & Co., London, section 13, pp. 584-5.

Moore, Stephen C. (1986), 'The development of working class housing in Ireland, 1840-1912: a study of housing conditions, built form and policy' (unpublished DPhil dissertation, University of Ulster).

Murray, S. (1977), *The City Mission Story*, Belfast City Mission, Belfast.

Phelan, Denis (1835), *A Statistical Enquiry into the Present State of Medical Charities in Ireland, with suggestions ...*, Hodges & Smith, Dublin.

Report from the Select Committee on the Dublin Hospitals, pp. vi-viii, Evidence, p. 45, HC 1854 (338), xii.

Report of the First Annual General Meeting of the Nurses for the Sick Poor Society, Public Record Office for Northern Ireland, D 3480/21/1.

Robins, Joseph (1980), *The Lost Children: a Study of Charity Children in Ireland, 1700-1900*, Institute of Public Administration, Dublin.

Strain, R.W.M. (1953), 'The history and associations of the Belfast Charitable Society', *Ulster Medical Journal*, 22, pp. 31-60, May.

Strain, R.W.M. (1961), *Belfast and its Charitable Society: a Story of Urban Social Development*, Oxford University Press, London.

Tod, Isabella S.M. (1878), 'Boarding out pauper children', a paper read before the Economic Science and Statistics Section of the British Association for the Advancement of Science in Dublin, *Journal of the Statistical and Social Enquiry Society*, vii, pt. iv, August, pp. 293-99. See also her paper 'On a plan for the curative treatment of drunkards', read to the Society on Tuesday 15 December 1874, pp. 408-10 and her obituary in the *Englishwoman's Review*, (1897), January 15, pp. 58-63.

Verzin, J.A. (1987), 'The Mater Infirmorum Hospital', *Ulster Medical Journal*, vol. 56, August, pp. 565-71.

Williamson, A.P. (1970), 'The beginnings of state care for the mentally ill in Ireland', *Economic and Social Review*, pp. 281-90. See also 'Psychiatry, moral management and the origins of social policy for mentally ill people in Ireland', *Irish Journal of Medical Science*, vol. 161, No. 9, 1992, pp. 556-58.

Wollstonecraft, Mary (1992), *A Vindication of the Rights of Women*, Penguin, Harmondsworth; originally published in London by J. Johnston, 1792.

12   Government financial support for voluntary organizations: a preliminary analysis and discussion

John Simpson

Every government department in Northern Ireland has a relationship with parts of the voluntary sector. The wide-ranging nature of these contacts is well evidenced by the particular discussions highlighted in the different chapters. For a large number of voluntary agencies, particularly the larger 'service providing' agencies, there is a continuing and detailed contact with government and government agencies to provide a better understanding of their respective aims and objectives, co-ordinate their actions and, critically, to secure different forms of financial assistance from government towards the operation of the voluntary body and the provision of agreed services.

There is no convenient source of information which aggregates the total expenditure of the voluntary sector and assesses the proportion which is grant-aided for current or capital expenditure, or bought as a 'purchaser', by government. Part of the problem with a search for measures of total expenditure, and the scale of government support, lies in the diverse nature of the voluntary sector and the many different ways in which it is financed.

An official calculation of the grants paid to voluntary bodies in Northern Ireland by government departments gives one measure of the flow of funds. As will be illustrated in later paragraphs, even this calculation can be questioned in terms of adequacy of coverage and clarity of definition and purpose.

Table 1   Grants by government to voluntary organizations, 1987/88-1992/93

(£'m)

1987-88	101.1	1990-91	125.5
1988-89	119.2	1991-92	130.4
1989-90	127.2	1992-93	154.0

181

In a five year period the total increased by 52 per cent. This compares to inflation of 36 per cent over the same period. Superficially, this could be seen as a real increase of about 12 per cent. However, the range of grants changed significantly and such a calculation should only be regarded as illustrative of a continuing upward movement.

If a one-off grant of £17 million, in 1992-93, to registered housing associations to fund a special house purchase scheme is excluded, then the increase in money terms reduces to 36 per cent: just equivalent to the rate of price changes.

Information on the first two years in this series was collected and used in 1989 as part of a United Kingdom-wide efficiency scrutiny of government funding of the voluntary sector led by the Home Office (Home Office, 1990). Since then the Northern Ireland information has been up-dated annually. See the detailed listing published in reply to a House of Lords question by Lord Blease (House of Lords, *Hansard*, 6 July 1993, WA 52).

Departmental allocations

Table 2   Grants by government departments to voluntary bodies, 1992/93

	£'m
Agriculture	1.1
Economic Development	69.4
Education	4.2
Environment	67.3
Finance and Personnel	1.3
Health and Social Services	5.7
Northern Ireland Office (incl. CCRU)*	5.0
Total	**154.0**

* (CCRU: Central Community Relations Unit)

In total, over 600 groups received grants in 1992-93, ranging from £12.97 for Whiterock Senior Citizens' Group from the Department of the Environment, probably through a Belfast Action Team, to £49.9 million for voluntary bodies using the ACE (Action for Community Employment) scheme and £57.5 million to registered housing associations. The largest other grant to a single body may have been £1.8 million allocated to Derry Northside Development Trust.

182

The following paragraphs illustrate some of the main activities of each department by identifying only those groups who received more than £100,000 in that year together with the Department making the grant.

Department of Agriculture:
Rural Development Council and groups

Department of Economic Development:
247 groups using ACE; community workshops; community employment agencies; job clubs; Young Help; youth community projects; Disability Action; Northern Ireland Committee-ICTU; Thomas Doran Training Centre.

Department of Education:
Voluntary sports organizations; Workers Educational Association; youth clubs and organizations; NI Citizens Advice Bureaux; NI Council for Integrated Education; Linenhall Library; Forum for Community Work Education; Educational Guidance Service for Adults.

Department of the Environment:
Over 350 grants: many relatively small. Those over £100,000 were to: Belleek and District Development Association; Community Technical Aid; Derry Northside Development Trust; Disability Action; Dromore 2000 Ltd.; Extern; Keady and District Community Initiatives; Londonderry Inner City Trust; National Trust; North Belfast Resource Centre; registered housing associations £57.5 million, (including a special project for £17 million); St John's Parish Centre; Techno Tyrone; tenants' action projects; Tidy Northern Ireland group.

Department of Finance and Personnel:
Civil Service Sports Association; NI Economic Council; Public Service Training Centre; Chief Executives' Management Forum.

Department of Health and Social Services: (see qualifications outlined below)
a. for children and young people
   Catholic Family Care Society; Extern (for Making Belfast Work); NI Pre-School Playgroups Association
b. for general services
   Age Concern; Belfast Law Centre; Brownlow Community Trust; Disability Action; Joseph Rowntree Trust; Association for Mental Health; NI Council for Voluntary Action; NI Hospice; NI Voluntary Trust; Relate.

Northern Ireland Office, incl. Central Community Relations Unit:
Community Relations Council; Co-Operation North; Origin of Place Names; Extern; NIACRO; Presbyterian Church; Ulster Quakers Service Committee; Victim Support.

Identifying the groups which received the largest amounts gives an indication of the spread of organizations and services involved. Obviously, the size of grant is not a measure of the contribution of the organization or the value of the services. In some cases, organizations were awarded grants for specific services and not for their general activities but this is not necessarily clear from the published lists. For example, the Ulster Quakers Service Committee receives grant aid for welfare services at the prisons.

Each grant is made using particular pieces of enabling legislation. While voluntary organizations must qualify according to the purpose of their activities, in most cases the scale of grant aid, or proportion of expenditure grant-aided, is discretionary. As a result, government has considerable leverage over most of the aided voluntary organizations.

Conceptual distinctions

There are problems of definition to be solved if any detailed analysis is to be made of the links between government and the voluntary sector. What is government? The lists above include grants direct from what would normally be termed central government. Agencies and local government are not included.

What is a voluntary organization? The conventional image is a charitable body providing services to people in some kind of need. There are, however, many voluntary organizations which gain government grants which fall outside this narrow definition, such as the Northern Ireland Economic Council or the Civil Service Sports Association.

When does a payment from government funds constitute a 'grant to a voluntary organization'? For example, in the provision of nursing and residential care, government provides assistance for hospice care: not as much as the providing organizations might wish, but that is not an issue for this chapter. However, if the support from government takes the form, in part, of contributions from Income Support which are directly calculated on the entitlement of patients towards agreed charges, as well as contributions to the current operating costs and one-off grants towards capital expenditure costs, then the value of government support might be seen as the total of all these payments.

Arguably, such an approach would be misleading. Certainly, in analytical terms the funds earned by a hospice as a 'provider', whether financed by Income Support or Community Care budgets, are rather different from those paid directly to a hospice to help meet wider operational costs, or deficits, and encourage capital investment. If 'provider' charges are seen as support for the voluntary sector then a question must be asked about the line between the 'voluntary' (non-profit making) sector and the 'private' (profit, or loss, making) sector. In fact, logic points to the exclusion of all social security related payments to individuals from a working definition of grants to the voluntary sector, even when those entitlements transfer as payments to 'providers'. This is also consistent with the definition used in the recent official study, see below, of grant payments.

Government finance for the voluntary sector does, however, need to be analysed in ways which make a distinction in the different forms of support.

Home Office study

This was one of the important features highlighted in the *Efficiency Scrutiny of Government Funding of the Voluntary Sector*, published by the Home Office (1990).

The study compiled what may be the most up-to-date estimate of the expenditure by the United Kingdom Government, including departments in Northern Ireland, on grants to the voluntary sector. It identifies voluntary bodies (as defined in the study) in the United Kingdom which received £2,125 million in 1988-89.

Of the total grant aid paid in that year in the United Kingdom, £119 million was identified in Northern Ireland: 5.6 per cent of the total. Although later sections will express some doubts about the completeness and comparability of the coverage in this study, taken at face value, Northern Ireland departments and official agencies spend about double the amount which would be expected simply on a population basis. The details from the table of information from the Northern Ireland Office for 1987-88 and 1988-89 are set out in Annex 1 to this chapter.

A large part of the relative difference stems from the higher per capita spending in Northern Ireland on employment and training schemes such as ACE and the Youth Training Programme.

The largest single component in the Northern Ireland total was a commitment in 1988-89 of £45 million for housing associations. Similar, proportionately large, sums for housing associations were identified in Great Britain.

Analytical breakdown

In the analysis by the Home Office, government grant schemes were classified under one of the following headings:

185

- core
- service
- project
- multi-purpose

Even these classifications do not always provide readily understood and useful distinctions.

Core funding is defined as the provision of assistance for part of the costs of the central administration and management of voluntary organizations. Often this is critical to the ability of organizations to marshall the efforts of large numbers of volunteers who provide the client services usually without personal remuneration. In Northern Ireland, the Home Office report classified as examples of 'core' assistance the grant aid to:

- Industry Matters
- Community Relations agencies
- NIACRO, (The Northern Ireland Council for the Care and Resettlement of Offenders)
- Extern
- Northern Ireland Council on Disability

The distinction between service and project finance is less clear cut. Both include voluntary organizations which directly provide client services but the nature of the contract with government in some cases is for a defined period, or project, with a predetermined end date (leading to either an end to financial support for the project, or a review and a new agreement) whereas for others, the contractual relationship is for the provision of specific services.

These distinctions led the Home Office to the following illustrative classifications in Northern Ireland.

Project funding:
National Trust
Sports clubs
Belfast Action Teams
Community Technical Aid

Service funding:
Action for Community Employment (ACE)
Youth Training Programme
Registered Housing Associations

Another group of grants were deemed to be multi-purpose and examples were:

- Northern Ireland Co-operative Development Agency
- Sports Council for Northern Ireland

186

- Department of Health and Social Services (DHSS) grants using Children and Young Persons' legislation
- DHSS General Scheme

The DHSS grants seem to have been classified as multi-purpose simply because a more detailed breakdown was not used by the Home Office study. The more detailed breakdown shows that most of the grants, for example, aid to Northern Ireland Council for Voluntary Action, the Northern Ireland Hospice and Age Concern, might be classified as core funding.

Coverage

Although the Home Office report purports to be comprehensive, there is one area of activity in Northern Ireland which might be added to the assessment of the impact of central government on the voluntary sector. This is the activity of the Health and Social Service Boards which are, legally and effectively, agents of central government. This means that many social service activities, which in Great Britain would be the responsibility of local authorities and excluded from the Home Office study, are, in Northern Ireland, more closely linked to central government. The Home Office study makes a comparison based on the distinction between central and local government that applies in Great Britain.

Another exclusion is that no grants are identified for voluntary bodies which are involved in education, such as voluntary or church maintained schools, presumably because this was seen as a different relationship to that of normal voluntary bodies.

Health and social services

In a specially prepared analysis, the support from the DHSS and area boards has been calculated for the five years 1988-89 to 1992-93. The figures do not tie in completely with those reported by the Home Office but it is clear that the main difference is that the Home Office did not include grants made by the area boards.

Table 3   Reporting of grants made to voluntary bodies in Northern Ireland for the provision of health and social services, 1988-89

(£ thousand)

	Home Office	DHSS figures
From DHSS:		
General schemes	3,120	3,120
Children & Young Persons	763	774
Sub-total	**3,883**	**3,894**
From Boards	not included	6,352
Total grants paid	not included	**£10,246**

Sources: **Home Office, 1990 and special DHSS exercise.**

Whilst there is a small difference in the figures, which should be comparable, the main conclusion is that the Home Office did not include Northern Ireland's grants to voluntary bodies by excluding the effect of decisions made by area boards. These funds would, of course, be heavily concentrated on projects and services, rather than core funding.

The special DHSS compilation shows the trend in the last five years. Perhaps the most striking features are, first, that the grants from the four boards have been increasing rapidly, and more rapidly than those from the DHSS, and, second, the very different rates of increase from one board to another. Grants from the Southern and Western Boards have quadrupled, from the Northern Board have tripled, and from the Eastern Board have not quite doubled. The totals are set out in Table 4. Another feature is the degree of variation from year to year in the level of funds allocated to voluntary organizations. At a superficial level this lends support to the frequently expressed complaint from voluntary organizations that their funding is often decided at an uncomfortably late date and is too unstable or uncertain to allow sensible planning.

A second feature which is conspicuous in an examination of the allocations from each of the boards is the presence of large allocations, by each board, to the same organizations. This is a reflection of the contractual relationship for the provision of services or projects in different localities. However, whilst such delegation is desirable, one of the consequential issues is the degree to which the boards and the DHSS co-ordinate a consistent policy on the use of these voluntary organizations on a province-wide basis. This raises questions about the need to ensure that the principles, methods and amounts of grant aid are applied consistently.

Table 4   Grants to voluntary bodies in Northern Ireland for health and social services

(£ thousand)

	1988-1989	1989-1990	1990-1991	1991-1992	1992-1993
DHSS under:					
General Schemes	3,120	3,693	3,254	3,582	4,733
Children & Young Persons	774	1,362	880	891	963
sub-total	**3,894**	**5,055**	**4,134**	**4,473**	**5,696**
Boards:					
Northern	514	394	1,480	1,423	1,611
Eastern	4,782	4,980	6,920	5,520	7,988
Western	521	1,082	1,085	1,198	2,074
Southern	534	962	1,702	1,764	2,322
sub-total	**6,351**	**7,418**	**11,187**	**9,904**	**13,995**
Grand Total	**10,245**	**12,473**	**15,321**	**14,377**	**19,691**

Source: Special return from DHSS. (Totals may not reflect individual components as figures have been rounded to the nearest £1,000).

If the grants paid by the area boards are added to the total in the Home Office report, the total grant aid in 1988-89 becomes nearly £126 million. If a working estimate is made that area board grants are 50 per cent for projects and 50 per cent for services then spending was:

Table 5   Distribution of grant assistance in Northern Ireland, 1988-89

	£'m	%
Core funding	5.8	4.6
Project funding	9.4	7.5
Service funding		
Employment and training	60.3	47.9
Housing associations	45.3	36.0
Other	3.4	2.7
Sub-total (Service funding)	**124.2**	**86.6**
Multi-purpose	1.7	1.4
Total	**125.9**	**100.0**

Source: Home Office plus information on area boards.

This distribution of funds is not very different from the overall United Kingdom pattern, except that the amount spent on employment and training is much higher, proportionately, than is found in Great Britain.

One assumption is made in Table 5 which conflicts with the analysis undertaken by the Home Office. All of the DHSS general schemes of assistance, with the exclusion of the Joseph Rowntree Trust, the Community Volunteering Scheme and the EC Programme to Combat Poverty, have been classified as core funding, not as multi-purpose. This seems appropriate after the earlier examination of the individual allocations made by DHSS.

Policy questions

A number of issues which may justify further analysis and research emerge from this attempt to quantify the financial relations between government and the voluntary sector.

(a) Leverage

Although an estimate of government financial assistance of over £125 million per annum can be made, no detailed work is available to suggest how effective this expenditure is either in terms of the delivery of services and benefit to clients, or in terms of the leverage effect of this large sum.

Even where core funding is assisted up to 75 per cent or 80 per cent, many organizations find it difficult to raise the remaining funds from their own resources. Many an organization will argue that the financial value of the labour efforts of volunteers should be seen as an appropriate way of balancing official assistance. For obvious reasons, government is not easily persuaded by this argument.

The measurement of leverage effects is, therefore, ambiguous. Should it be a simple financial measurement relating official funding to funding raised from other sources, or does the value added by volunteers count in the assessment?

The Home Office report (1990) accepted the suggestion that private sector support was perhaps harder to raise in Northern Ireland because of the small size of the private sector and the exercise by central government of functions that, in England, would fall to local government.

(b) Contractual relationships

Many of the financial relationships linked to grant assistance for voluntary organizations have developed gradually over a number of years. There will always be a need to review the relationships to ensure that resources continue to be directed to areas of highest priority. The Home Office study found evidence that some bodies were being funded on a long-term basis without question about the optimum use of government resources. This question is just as applicable in Northern Ireland as elsewhere.

The classification used by the Home Office lends itself to a more critical method of reviewing government, and official, actions. Voluntary organizations who offer definable 'services' might be tested by the contracting process of provider to purchaser. Purchasing service from Crossroads or the Northern Ireland Association for Mental Health in given localities (using these as indicative examples) lends itself to the new shape of the social services and, in principle, for continuing services, these voluntary organizations do not need to be treated any differently from private sector providers. These voluntary organizations should be in a position to build up rolling contracts, sometimes based on competitive tendering, which fully fund the services which they provide.

Innovative projects would still command a discretionary element of funding assistance. The problem for government and voluntary organizations is that, inevitably, not all innovative projects will gain support. Some which do gain support will go on to become established, but others, at varying dates, must expect to lose official support.

Financial assistance for the initial stage of a project, on the implicit or explicit assumption that it will become self-financing, or based on over-optimistic aspirations by the agency taking the lead, is one of the most difficult problems for government. Inevitably, the originators will continue to seek support but government must have a framework which makes an end to support possible.

The most difficult decisions may lie in the area of core funding. DHSS provide, at varying rates, core funding for a very large number of organizations. Some, like the Northern Ireland Council for Voluntary Action are big intermediate bodies which receive over £300,000 per annum. Others, such as the British Fluoridation Society, receive very small amounts. All of these need to function with a finite commitment from government. A process of review, assessment, evaluation and priority identification means that every year some should cease to be officially supported.

The mechanisms to do this need to be clear. The Home Office recommend that continuing funding should not be for periods of more than three years without a review process. Not every voluntary organization will close down if it does not receive grant aid. Many will continue as pressure groups for specific causes.

The difficulty for government is that, whilst diversity and competing objectives are commonplace in the voluntary sector, government cannot be expected to support, even partially, those organizations whose aims are contrary to government policy. Equally, government cannot be expected to support politically motivated campaigning organizations.

191

Wherever the lines are drawn, the important improvement which must follow is that there should be greater clarity in government policy for the provision of financial support for voluntary bodies. Departments need to move to the position where, rather than being seen to refuse a renewal of assistance, the presumption of continuity is not made and a proposition must be assessed from first principles.

(c) Funding decisions

Although the history of assistance for voluntary organizations reveals a somewhat haphazard approach, even into the late 1980s, the creation of the Voluntary Activity Unit, in DHSS, in 1993 now offers a mechanism to encourage codification, clarification and consistency.

In a statement of support for the voluntary sector and community development, the principles are set out. Government departments will, *inter alia*:

- provide financial support to voluntary organizations whose activities help to achieve the overall policies of departments, which can achieve a practical effect, which uphold accepted ethical standards and which are efficiently and properly managed;
- introduce arrangements for the monitoring and evaluation of the financial support provided;
- support, where appropriate, the voluntary sector infrastructure;
- acknowledge the value of voluntary activity by promoting the effective involvement of volunteers;
- ensure that voluntary organizations have an opportunity to contribute to appropriate policy areas.

Principles of good practice will be directed to ensure, *inter alia*, that:

- for all grants or schemes, there are clear policy objectives, information requirements and criteria for the selection of applicants;
- in each offer of grant, there is a clear indication of the purpose for which the grant is given, the conditions which are attached ... and the arrangements which will be made for monitoring and evaluation;
- where it is consistent with the criteria applying to individual schemes, core funding is provided on a three yearly basis, subject to parliamentary approval of the relevant expenditure;
- there is no unnecessary duplication of activity by voluntary organizations in receipt of government funding, by encouraging such organizations to come together to provide the service, or by tendering for the service required.

Conclusion

The voluntary sector in Northern Ireland is large and multifaceted. It receives substantial financial support from government and its agents. The policy of government is directed to encourage the useful expansion of an efficient and effective vountary sector as an additional provider of services and an alternative to direct statutory provision in some cases.

Given the scale of government assistance, which now exceeds £150 million per annum, the services provided by the voluntary sector, in market terms, might be valued at over £200 million. This is the equivalent of nearly 2 per cent of the GDP and may involve over 10,000 people in various roles and capacities.

A sector using resources on this scale merits both appreciation and closer examination so that the benefits to those being served are maximised.

References

Department of Health and Social Services (1993), *Strategy for the Support of the Voluntary Sector and Community Development*, HMSO, Belfast.
Home Office (1990), *Efficiency Scrutiny of Government Funding of the Voluntary Sector: Profiting from Partnership*, HMSO, London.
House of Lords, *Hansard*, 6 July 1993.

ANNEX 1

List of government grant schemes from returns provided by departments

Grant Scheme	1987/88 (£000)	1988/89 (£000)	Grant Type
Young Farmers Clubs of Ulster	44	47	Service
Grants to Show Societies	2	3	Project
National Trust	127	100	Project
NI Cooperative Development Agency	95	130	
Industry Matters (NI)	50	77	Core
Youth Training Programme			
(a) Young Help	750	758	Service
(b) Community Workshops	16,180	17,152	Service
(c) Youth and Community Projects	758	786	Service
Action for Community Employment	28,829	41,554	Service
Community Volunteering Scheme	645	799	Project
Thomas Doran Training Centre	209	126	Service
Adult & Continuing Education	272	280	Core
Arts, Libraries & Museums	100	67	Core
Children's Community Relations and Holiday Scheme	119	140	Service
Community Relations	321	442	Core
Community Services	220	240	Core
District Councils: Centres for Voluntary Organizations	NK	33	Project
District Councils: Voluntary Groups	465	366	Project
Voluntary Sports Clubs	291	179	Project
Sports Council for NI	431	392	Multi-purpose
Voluntary Youth Organizations			
(a) Recurrent Grants	1,140	1,199	Core
(b) Capital Grants	337	501	Project
(c) Junior Sports	32	33	Project
(d) Gas Conversion	19	70	Project
(e) Youth Committee	33	94	Core
(f) Facelift Scheme	208	0	
Belfast Action Teams Initiative	542	2,666	Project
Environmental Improvement Scheme	191	0	
Conservation Wildlife, Countryside	163	186	Project
Housing Division	92	127	Multi-purpose
Registered Housing Associations	43,259	45,300	Service
Ulster Historical Foundation	25	72	Core
Road Safety Council & Royal Society for Prevention of Accidents	127	90	Core
NI Housing Executive	56	60	Multi-purpose
General Scheme	1,715	2,805	Multi-purpose

194

Grant Scheme	1987/88 (£000)	1988/89 (£000)	Grant Type
Children & Young Persons	452	763	Multi-purpose
Joseph Rowntree Trust	209	239	Project
2nd EC Programme to Combat Poverty	97	76	Project
EC Food Relief	57	0	
Additional Flood Relief	78	0	
Crime & Offenders (Northern Ireland Office):	249	401	Core
(a) NIACRO			
(b) EXTERN			
(c) NI Intermediate Treatment Association			
NI Federation of Victim Support Schemes	8	33	Core
Crime & Offenders (Probation Board)	800	905	Project
NI Council on Disability	104	55	Core
Community Technical Aid	57	52	Project

Home Office (1990), *Efficiency Scrutiny of Government Funding of the Voluntary Sector: Profiting from Partnership,* **HMSO, London. pp. 38-39.**

Index

201